Hands-On BASIC
FOR THE IBM PC*jr*

ABOUT THE AUTHORS

Arthur Luehrmann and Herbert Peckham are pioneers in computer education. They have worked at all levels to develop methods and materials for teaching about computers. They are the authors of many books and articles on programming and computers. Each was trained as a physicist and has taught physics. Together with Martha Ramírez, they formed the partnership Computer Literacy to develop educational materials for use with computers.

Arthur Luehrmann did his undergraduate and graduate work at the University of Chicago. While teaching at Dartmouth College in 1972, Dr. Luehrmann coined the phrase "computer literacy," and he has worked to promote the concept of computer literacy. Formerly, he was associate director of the Lawrence Hall of Science at the University of California, Berkeley. He now devotes full time to writing and speaking about computer literacy.

Herbert Peckham was graduated from the United States Military Academy. He received a master's degree in physics from the Naval Postgraduate School and did additional graduate work in physics at the University of California, Berkeley. He has taught physics, computer science, and mathematics at Gavilan College. He is a widely published author of instructional materials for use with computers.

A Computer Literacy BOOK

Editorial, design, and production supervision by
Ronald G. Kirchem, Director
INTERFACE Design Associates, Inc.

Hands-On BASIC
FOR THE IBM PC*jr*

by

Arthur Luehrmann

Herbert Peckham

Published by

International Business Machines Corporation

P. O. Box 1328-W
Boca Raton, FL 33432

and by

McGraw-Hill Book Company

Library of Congress Preassigned Catalog Number 83-43006

4 5 6 7 8 9 10 KPKP 92 91 90 89 88 87 86 85 84

ISBN 0-07-049169-0

AUTHORS' ACKNOWLEDGMENTS

We wish to thank the many people who made this book possible and gave us their valuable help. We thank our editor, Charles Stewart, for bringing our previous work to the attention of the PC*jr* group at IBM. Within that group, E. W. (Butch) Graves coordinated the legal aspects of the project; Carol Kemerer conducted the evaluation referred to below, giving us many important suggestions for improvement; Stephen Mendonca provided useful suggestions on format and style; and Dotty Robbins supervised the production of the character art.

Managing all the editorial, design, and production steps in this project has been a monumental task of coordinating the work of teams in Florida, California, New York, and Pennsylvania, keeping us all on schedule, and maintaining a high standard of quality from everyone. Responsibility for all these things fell to Ronald Kirchem. We were fortunate in having his unstinting, very professional services for the duration of the project.

The authors are grateful to the people at Function Thru Form Inc., who designed the book in an extraordinarily short time. These people included Mary Ann Mulhauser, Director, assisted by Teresa Harmon, Marcia Dalby, and Charles Yuen.

The authors particularly wish to thank the team of managers and technical people at York Graphic Services, Inc., who worked literally night and day to put together the finished book. This team included Jeff Eisenhart, Lacinda Kerstetter, Wilbur Forry, Keith E. Crone, Robert Gregory, Yvonne Leiphart, Martin H. Sowers, Jr., and Lowell Wirt.

We especially thank the many unnamed people who helped us evaluate this material as we wrote it. They were corralled into a small room in Boca Raton for many hours a day. Patiently, they went from cover to cover, reporting anything they did not understand or were confused by. Without their sharp eyes, critical minds, and enthusiastic assistance, numerous errors and ambiguities would remain in the published book. Those that do remain are the entire responsibility of the authors.

Finally, we thank our families for their cheerful tolerance of our 80-hour work weeks for the duration of the project.

A. L.
H. P.

CONTENTS

INTRODUCING THIS BOOK

T *he purpose of this book is to put* **you** *in control of your PCjr. You may never have touched the keyboard of a computer before now. You may neither have read books about computers nor studied them in school. But if you spend several evenings doing the first half-dozen sessions in this book, you will soon be in charge.*

What to Do First

If you have just opened the package containing your computer, read and follow the list of steps below. It will guide you in setting up the PCjr and getting ready to use it.

Step 1. Follow the directions that came with the computer for unpacking the parts.

Step 2. Read Section 1 of the *Guide to Operations.* Follow the steps there in setting up the computer and connecting the parts. You will need only two parts to do the first sessions of this book. These are the keyboard and the TV display. If you have a cassette recorder or printer, you don't have to connect them right away if you don't want to. You can do that later when you are more familiar with your computer.

Step 3. (Optional) Use Sections 2 and 3 of the *Guide to Operations* to get acquainted with your keyboard. Do not feel that you must remember the purpose of every key, though. In this book, whenever you need to use a new key, we will show you how the key works. If you already know about the key, the review won't hurt.

Step 4. Return to this book and continue reading.

Who Should Read This Book?

Part One is for everyone. Computers are showing up everywhere: in offices, factories, schools, and homes. If you do all the activities in Part One, you will learn all the "survival skills" you need to know to use the PCjr. Indeed, these same skills will help you use any computer. You will learn how to turn on the computer and load programs from a diskette or a cassette tape. You will learn how to write simple programs of your own and save them. You will use the color-graphics and sound features of your PCjr. Just as important as all these things, you will know how a computer works: You will know what a computer is doing when it is running a program. You will know what the computer's input, output, and memory units are and how they work together. At the end of Part One, you will have gained a high degree of **computer literacy**.

If you will be using the PCjr mainly to run programs other people have written, Part One may give you all you want or need to know. For example, to turn your PCjr into a word-processing system, you need to know only three things: These are how to load the word-processing program into the computer, how to use the PCjr keyboard, and how to use the program. You will find all this information in Part One plus the manual that comes with the word-processing program. In the same way, you will be able to use other programs to make your PCjr into a video-game player, a spread-sheet calculator, or a data-storage system.

But suppose you want to use your PCjr to do something new, something you don't have a program for. In that case, you will need to know more than what is in Part One. To make a computer do what you want it to, you must tell it what you want. You must write your instructions in a form the computer understands. This form is a computer program. And so you will need to learn more about writing your own programs.

Parts Two through Six will introduce you to all the main ideas and methods you will need to be able to write programs of your own.

- In Part Two, you will learn how to plan and organize your programs. You will also learn how to break complicated programming jobs into simple pieces.
- Part Three will show you what a variable is. Variables can make your programs more interesting and versatile.
- Part Four will give you a tool for telling the computer to do something again and again.
- Part Five adds a tool for telling the computer to do either one thing or another. (The tools introduced in Parts Four and Five are the only ones you will need to handle all problems in program logic.)
- Part Six shows you how to handle lists of words and numbers.

The Goals of This Book

Your PC*jr* comes with the BASIC language built in. This book teaches you a lot about BASIC. However, we have not tried to cover every last little detail of the BASIC language. The version of BASIC on your PC*jr* is a very large, complex language. It is designed both for beginners and for advanced programmers. So we have limited this book to two main areas of BASIC: First, you will learn about the dozen or so statements you will need to be able to do any programming at all. You will also learn about a half-dozen other statements that tell the computer to do exciting things such as playing music and drawing pictures.

Suppose that, when you finish this book, you are interested in learning more about PC*jr* BASIC. In that case, you should get a copy of the *BASIC* reference book for your IBM PC*jr*. That book explains all the features of the version of BASIC built into your PC*jr*. It also describes extra features available in Cartridge BASIC.

This book does not just teach you about BASIC. The big ideas of computing are the same, no matter what language you use. In that way, computer languages are just like ordinary languages: Both kinds of language give you a way to think about things and express ideas. People in the United States learn English. People in France learn French. But the important thing is that we all learn how to speak, read, and write, whatever our language.

Our main goal is to teach you the important ideas about computers and programming. In the future, you may decide to explore a different language on your PC*jr* or another computer. We have designed this book to make that step an easy one for you. The main topics you learn about here will apply to any computer language you may learn in the future.

How to Use This Book

This book is divided into six main parts. The parts are divided into chapters, called "sessions." There are 32 sessions in all. It is a good idea to set aside enough time to go through several sessions in a row. When you see a series of questions in the book, take a few moments to answer them. Check yourself against the answers in the back of the book. At the end of some sessions, there are programming projects for you to do. They give you a chance to practice what you have learned or to do some exploring on your own. Take time to work on the projects before going ahead to the next session.

This is *not* a book just for reading, browsing, or skipping around. Almost every session guides you through activities you must carry out at the keyboard of your PC*jr*. Some of what you learn will come from the book. However, most will come from your discoveries at the keyboard. If you do not actually do those activities, the book will seem incomplete and confusing to you.

Each session of this book builds on what has come before and adds to it. If you skip a few sessions and jump ahead, there is a good chance that you will miss an important idea needed later. It is much better to do all the sessions in order. However, remember that you can siop at the end of Part One if you want to.

Finally, take your time and enjoy yourself. There's no need to rush ahead. There's no final exam. No one is watching over you. If you get interested in some topic you have just learned about, stop and explore it a bit. Don't worry about doing something wrong and breaking the computer. There's nothing you can type on the keyboard that can harm your computer. If you ever get into a situation you don't know how to deal with, remember that you're in charge: As a last resort, you can turn off the power switch and start over.

TAKING CONTROL

PART ONE

When you finish the last session in this part, you will be well on your way toward computer literacy. You will know two very important things: First, you will know what a computer can do. Second, you will know how to tell your computer to do what you want it to do.

Along the way, you will learn the things you need to know to be able to use your PCjr—or any other computer. You will be able to turn the computer on. You will know how to load programs into the computer from a diskette or cassette tape, and run them. You will also learn how to write simple programs of your own. You will be able to save them on a diskette or cassette tape. In short, you will be doing some of the things that people who work with computers do every day.

The most important fact that you will discover in Part One is this: The only thing that any computer can do by itself is follow instructions. When you see a computer doing things that look clever, exciting, or beautiful (or stupid, boring, or ugly), you will know that the computer can do those things for only one reason: Some person wrote a program telling the computer exactly what to do and how to do it. There is no good or evil in the machine itself, only in the programs we humans put there.

As you learn how to write programs, you will be able to tell the computer to do many different things. Your PCjr can play music, do arithmetic, print words and numbers, and draw pictures in color. All it takes to do these things is a program you write telling the computer exactly what to do.

GETTING
STARTED

SESSION 1

Session Goals

- Turn the computer on and adjust the TV display.
- Become familiar with the keyboard.
- Learn how to correct typing errors.

Before Starting the Computer

All the parts of a computer are called a **system**. Before doing anything, take a close look at your PCjr computer system. There are three necessary parts: the **main unit**, the **keyboard**, and a **TV display**. The main unit contains the computer itself. The TV display is connected to the main unit. The keyboard can be used away from the main unit and need not be connected to it with wires.

Your system may also have a **diskette drive**. If your computer has a diskette drive, it will already be installed in the main unit. Look at the front of the main unit. On the right, you will see two small slots. Those are for plugging in cartridges. If you have a diskette drive, there will be a small handle and a long, thin slot above the cartridge slots. That is the front of your diskette drive—the place where you will later insert a diskette.

If you do not have a diskette drive, you may have a **cassette tape recorder**. Session 5 tells you how to connect a cassette tape recorder to the main unit.

Follow the instructions in Section 1 of the *Guide to Operations* for setting up the keyboard and connecting a TV display. Be sure that you have completed all the connections before going on.

The next two sections give instructions for starting the computer and adjusting the TV display for the best picture. These two sections will guide you, one step at a time, through one of two different ways to start the PCjr. You will use the first method if your computer does *not* have a diskette drive and the second if it does. For each section, first read the instructions for each step, and then carry them out. Take your time.

Starting the Computer without a Diskette Drive

> **NOTE** *Use the following steps if you do not have a diskette drive. If you do have a diskette drive, skip this section and go on to the next section, "Starting the Computer with a Diskette Drive."*

This section tells you how to start the computer without a diskette drive. You should also get the BASIC cartridge out if you have one. Then go on to the steps below. If, at any point, the computer does not seem to be doing the right thing, turn off the power. Then start over again.

Step 1. **Turn your computer off.** You do this by moving the power switch on the back of the main unit to the OFF position. You should be able to reach the power switch with your left hand. If the computer is already off, leave it off for now.

Step 2. **Be sure the TV display is turned on. If there is a volume control, turn it down.**

Step 3. **Remove any cartridges from the cartridge slots in the main unit. If you have the BASIC cartridge, insert it into either of the cartridge slots.** The cartridge label should be on the top. The open end goes into the slot.

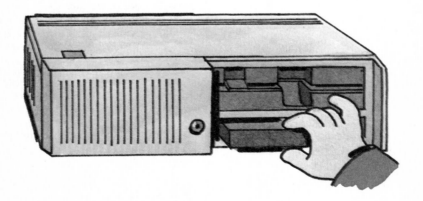

Step 4. **Move the power switch on the back of the main unit to the ON position. Don't type anything on the keyboard yet.** You should immediately see the initials "IBM" in large, striped letters on a blue background. At the bottom of the screen, you should see 16 colored bars and the phrase 004 KB.

In about 5 seconds, the number in the phrase should change. In a few more seconds, the screen should go blank. (If you see the message ERROR B on the screen, press the (Enter ⏎) key and proceed. If you don't see the message below after that, see Section 6 of the *Guide to Operations*. Your keyboard may not be working.)

About 10 seconds later, you should see some words at the bottom of the screen. There will also be a message similar to the one below at the top of the screen. **Adjust the brightness and contrast controls on your TV display if necessary.**

```
The IBM Personal Computer Basic
Version C1.20 Copyright IBM Corp 1981
62940 Bytes free
Ok
```

If the second line on your screen begins with the phrase Version C, your computer is using a version of the BASIC language called **Cassette BASIC**. If you inserted the BASIC cartridge in Step 3, however, you should see the phrase Version J at the beginning of the second line. This message tells you that your computer is using **Cartridge BASIC**. Cartridge BASIC contains all the features of cassette BASIC, plus a few extra ones. In this book, you will need only Cassette BASIC in most sessions.

Step 5. **Press the (Caps Lock) key, which is just to the right of the spacebar.** In this book, when we tell you to press a key, we mean that you should press the key and then release it. If we want you to hold it down without releasing it, we will say so. You will see nothing happen on the screen when you press the (Caps Lock) key. However, the words you type from now on will appear on the screen in capital letters.

Step 6. **Hold down the (Alt) key, which is just to the left of the spacebar. At the same time, hold down the (Ctrl) key, which is on the left edge of the keyboard. While holding both keys down, press and release the (→) key a few times. Be sure to watch the TV screen while you are doing this.** The (→) key is near the lower right-hand corner of the keyboard. **Next, repeat these steps with the (←) key. Again, be sure to watch the screen.** These keys allow you to move the whole TV picture left or right. **By using (Alt | Ctrl | →) and (Alt | Ctrl | ←), move the picture so that you can just see all the words on the screen.**

Step 7. **Type KEY OFF. Then, while looking at the screen, press and release the (Enter ⏎) key.** That is the large key on the right side of the keyboard. (If you make a typing error, press the (Enter ⏎) key and retype the words. Then press (Enter ⏎) again.) You should see the line of words at the bottom of the screen disappear.

At this point, you have turned the computer on and have adjusted the picture. Take a moment to review the seven steps you used and answer the questions below.

1. What message on the screen tells you whether you are using Cassette BASIC or Cartridge BASIC?
2. How do you move the TV picture to the right?

Starting the Computer with a Diskette Drive

NOTE *If you do not have a diskette drive, you should have used the steps in the previous section, "Starting the Computer without a Diskette Drive," to start your computer. If you do have a diskette drive, use the following steps to start your computer. You must also have the BASIC cartridge to use the diskette drive. If you do not have the cartridge, leave the diskette drive empty and follow the steps in the previous section.*

This section tells you how to start the computer *with* a diskette drive. You will also need the BASIC cartridge and the diskette labeled "DOS." A **diskette** is a small plastic disk like a phonograph record; information is stored on it magnetically. **DOS** stands for "disk operating system." Now, go on to the steps below. If the computer does not seem to be doing the right thing, turn off the power. Then start over again.

Step 1. **Turn your computer off. You do this by moving the power switch on the back of the main unit to the OFF position. You should be able to reach the power switch with your left hand. If the computer is already off, leave it off for now.**

Step 2. **Be sure the TV display is turned on. If there is a volume control, turn it down.**

Step 3. **Now it is time for you to put the DOS diskette into your diskette drive. Turn the latch on the diskette drive to the horizontal position. If there is already a diskette in the drive, take it out. Put the diskette labeled "DOS" into the drive.** The label on the diskette should be on top and on the edge of the diskette nearest you. **Turn the latch to the vertical position after you have inserted the diskette.**

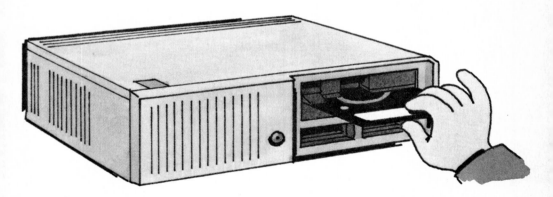

Step 4. **Remove any cartridges from the cartridge slots in the main unit. Insert your BASIC cartridge into either of the cartridge slots.** The cartridge label should be on the top. The open end goes into the slot.

Step 5. **Move the power switch on the back of the main unit to the ON position.** You should immediately see the initials "IBM" in large, striped letters on a blue background. At the bottom of the screen, you should see 16 colored bars and the phrase 004 KB.

In about 5 seconds, the number in the phrase should
change. In a few more seconds, the screen should go blank.
(If you see the message ERROR B on the screen, press the
(Enter ⏎) key and proceed. If you don't see the message
below after that, see Section 6 of the *Guide to Operations*.
Your keyboard may not be working.)

Next, you will hear a beep. Then the red light on the
diskette drive will come on. In a few more seconds, you
should see a message similar to the one below at the top of
the screen. **Don't type anything on the keyboard yet.**

```
Current date is Tue 1-01-1980
Enter new date:
```

Step 6. **Press and release the (Enter ⏎) key.** The (Enter ⏎) key is the
large key to the right of the letter keys. (You could have
entered today's date here, but it is not necessary to do so.)
In this book, when we tell you to press a key, we mean
that you should press the key and then release it. If we
want you to hold it down without releasing it, we will say
so. Next, you should see two new lines similar to the ones
below on the screen. **Once again, don't type anything on
the keyboard yet.**

```
Current time is 0:00:47.89
Enter new time:
```

Press and release the (Enter ⏎) key once more. (You could
also have entered the correct time, but it is not necessary to
do so.) You should see new lines similar to the ones on the
next page on the screen. **As before, don't type anything
yet.**

```
The IBM Personal Computer DOS
Version 2.00 (C)Copyright IBM Corp 1981,
 1982, 1983

A>
```

Adjust the brightness and contrast controls on your TV display if necessary.

Step 7. **Press and release the (Caps Lock) key, which is just to the right of the spacebar.** You will see nothing happen on the screen at this point. However, the words you type from now on will appear on the screen in capital letters.

Step 8. **Type BASIC. Then press the (Enter ⏎) key and release it.** (If you make a typing mistake, press the (Enter ⏎) key and retype the words. Then press (Enter ⏎) again.) You should see some words at the bottom of the screen. There will also be a message similar to the one below at the top of the screen. **Don't type anything on the keyboard at this point.**

```
The IBM PC jr Basic
Version J1.00
Copyright IBM Corp. 1981,1982,1983

59694 Bytes free

Ok
```

If the second line on your screen begins with the phrase Version C, your computer is using a version of the BASIC language called **Cassette BASIC.** If you inserted the BASIC cartridge in Step 4, however, you should see the phrase Version J at the beginning of the second line. This message tells you that your computer is using **Cartridge BASIC.** Cartridge BASIC contains all the features of Cassette BASIC, plus a few extra ones. In this book, you will need only Cassette BASIC in most sessions. However, to save BASIC programs on diskettes, you *must* have Cartridge BASIC.

Step 9. **Hold down the (Alt) key, which is just to the left of the spacebar. At the same time, hold down the (Ctrl) key, which is on the left edge of the keyboard. While holding both keys down, press and release the (⟶) key a few times. Be sure to watch the TV screen while you are doing this.** The (⟶) key is near the lower right-hand corner of the keyboard. **Next, repeat these steps with the (⟵) key.** Again, be sure to watch the screen. These keys let you

move the whole TV picture left or right. **By using**
(Alt│Ctrl│→) and (Alt│Ctrl│←), **move the picture so that you
can just see all the words on the screen.**

Step 10. **Type KEY OFF. Then, while looking at the screen, press
and release the** (Enter⏎) **key.** You should see the line of
words at the bottom of the screen disappear.

At this point, you have turned the computer on and have adjusted
the picture. Take a moment to review the 10 steps you used and answer
the questions below.

3. What message on the screen tells you whether you are using
Cassette BASIC or Cartridge BASIC?
4. How do you move the TV picture to the right?

Keyboard Experiments

Your PC*jr* keyboard is like the cockpit of an airplane. You use the keyboard to control nearly everything the computer does. Now is a good
time to explore some of the features of the PC*jr* keyboard. (If you began
with the keyboard activities in Sections 2 and 3 of the *Guide to Operations*,
you already know a lot about the keyboard. However, the following
review will remind you of the keys important for writing programs.)

The keyboard is usually used some distance away from the main
unit. It is not connected to the main unit with wires. Instead, it uses
invisible light waves to send information to the main unit. Since no
wires are needed, you can sit in a comfortable chair and watch the TV
display from across the room if you want to.

The most important keys are the ones in the **symbol group**. These
keys have letters, numbers, and punctuation marks printed above them.
If you have used an ordinary typewriter, the layout of keys will be familiar to you. Let's start by exploring these keys.

Type your name on the keyboard. Look at the screen. Did the letters come out in capitals or in lowercase? **Press and release the spacebar (the long bar at the bottom of the keyboard). Now press the** (Caps Lock) **key (just to the right of the spacebar). Type your name again.** Look at the screen once more. How did the letters come out this time? **Press the spacebar and** (Caps Lock) **again and retype your name.** How do the letters on the screen look now? **Now erase the whole line from the screen by pressing and releasing the** (Esc) **key (at the upper left-hand corner of the keyboard).**

The (Caps Lock) key is like the shift lock on a typewriter, except that it affects only the 26 letter keys. In the rest of this book, you will be using only capital letters. **Whenever you turn on the computer, be sure to put the** (Caps Lock) **key in the setting for capital letters. Type a few letters and look at the screen to be sure they are capitals. Then press and release** (Esc) **to erase the line from the screen.** "Esc" is short for **escape**. This key allows you to "escape" from typing errors by erasing the whole line.

Some keys in the symbol group have two symbols printed above them. For example, one of the keys in the top row has a white 4 and a black $ printed above it. Let's see how to type both the 4 and the $. **Press the key with these symbols a few times. Look at the characters on the screen. Find a key with the word "Shift" printed above it in black letters.** There is a (Shift ↑) key at each end of the bottom row of letter keys in the symbol group. **Hold down either** (Shift ↑) **key. While it is down, press and release the** (4) **key a few times.** Look again at the characters on the screen. Your computer's (Shift ↑) keys are like the shift keys on a typewriter. You may use either one to type the symbol printed in black above any key in the symbol group.

In the top row of the symbol group, you will find the 10 **number keys.** Some typists are in the habit of using the letter L for the number 1. They may also use the letter O for the number zero. **Type the** (1) **key a few times. Then type the** (L) **key a few times.** Look at the screen and notice the difference. **Next, type the zero key in the top row and the ⒪ key just below it.** Notice the slash through the zero on the screen. *It is very important to use only the number keys for numbers in your computer work.*

All people who work at keyboards make typing mistakes. Let's see how to fix mistakes. **Press and release (Esc) to erase the line on the screen. Now type MISTEAK.** That isn't the right way to spell "mistake." Here is how to fix the error without retyping the whole word: **Find the (Backspace) key, which is near the upper right-hand corner of the keyboard. Watch the screen as you press the (Backspace) key.** This key is like the backspace key on a typewriter, except that it actually erases letters on the screen as you go back over them. **Press (Backspace) until only the letters MIST are on the screen. Then release it. Now type AKE.** You can see that your typing error is fixed.

Now you will discover an interesting feature of your PC*jr* keyboard. It is useful, but it can also be surprising. **Press and release (Esc) to erase MISTAKE from the screen. Type your name again. But this time, hold the key down when you type the last letter in your name.** Notice the string of letters that appears on the screen. Nearly all the keys on the PC*jr* keyboard have this built-in **repeat action. Take your finger off the key. Press (Esc) to erase the whole line from the screen.**

Sometimes, you may hold a key down by misteak...oops...mistake and not notice the string of letters on the screen. There is a way to have the computer let you know that this is happening. **Hold down the (Alt) and (Ctrl) keys, which are at the left end of the keyboard. While they are both down, press the (Caps Lock) key. Then take your hands off the keyboard. Now hold any key down and listen. Turn the volume up on your TV display while holding the key down.** Look at the screen. You should hear a click each time a symbol is printed there. Some people like to hear a click as well as see a symbol on the screen when they type. The (Alt | Ctrl | Caps Lock) combination lets you turn the click on. If you do not want to hear the click, type another (Alt | Ctrl | Caps Lock) to turn the click off.

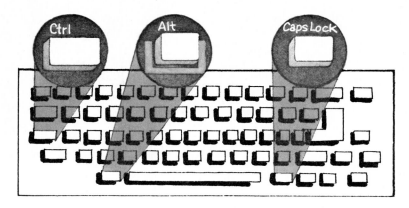

Before giving any instructions to your PC*jr*, you need to know about only one more key: the (Enter ⏎) key. **Type your name. Press and release the (Enter ⏎) key.** Look at the screen. Just below your name, you should see the phrase S y n t a x e r r o r on one line and O k on the next.

S y n t a x e r r o r is the computer's way of saying ''What?'' or ''Pardon me, I didn't understand what you said.'' Here is what happened: By pressing the (Enter ⏎) key, you told the computer that you wanted to give it some information. The computer then looked at the letters you typed before you pressed the (Enter ⏎) key. These letters spelled your name. The computer recognizes quite a few words. However, your name is probably not one of them. So the computer said S y n t a x e r r o r to let you know there was a problem. The computer then said O k to tell you that it was ready for you to type something else.

There are many other keys on your PC*jr* keyboard. However, the keys that you have learned about in this session are the ones you will use nearly all the time in your computer work.

 5. How do you erase characters from the line you are typing?
6. How do you erase the whole line you have typed?
7. How do you tell the computer you are through typing?

SUMMARY

In this session, you learned how to turn your PCjr on. You learned how to get it ready for Cassette BASIC or Cartridge BASIC. You then took a look at some important keys on the keyboard. The table below reviews these keys. You should read it carefully to make sure you know what each key does. If anything is still unclear to you, go back and read the appropriate parts of this session again.

Name of Key	Purpose
Symbol keys	To type letters, numbers, and symbols.
(Backspace)	To erase the previous character.
(Esc)	To erase an entire line.
(Shift ↑)	To type capital letters and symbols printed in black above the keys.
(Caps Lock)	To make the letter keys type capital letters.
(Enter ⏎)	To enter words and symbols into the computer.
(Alt | Ctrl | Caps Lock)	To switch the keyboard click on and off.
(Alt | Ctrl | →)	To move the TV picture to the right.
(Alt | Ctrl | ←)	To move the TV picture to the left.

NOTE *If you are not going on to the next session now, turn off the TV. You may leave the computer on, however. It uses little electric power and will wait patiently for you to return where you left off.*

TELLING THE COMPUTER TO DO THINGS

SESSION 2

Session Goals

- Restart the computer when the power is already on.
- Make sounds on the computer.
- Control color on the screen.
- Put words on the screen.
- Do arithmetic with the computer.

Restarting the Computer

If you turned off the TV display at the end of the last session, turn it on now. Your computer should already be on. If not, start it as shown in Session 1. If you need to turn your computer on and do not have a diskette drive, turn to page 16 and follow the steps that begin there. If you do have a diskette drive, follow the steps that begin on page 19.

In Session 1, you learned how to start the computer with the power off. This is called a **cold start**. You can also *restart* the computer when the power is already on. This is known as a **warm start**.

Sooner or later, you will get into situations where strange things are happening. The computer may seem to be out of control. At times like these, it is often best to just restart the computer. You can do this either with the power switch (a cold start) or from the keyboard (a warm start). However, if you choose to restart the computer, you will lose whatever program you have entered.

You already know how to do a cold start. Here is how to do a warm start: **With the power on, use two fingers to hold down the (Alt) and (Ctrl) keys, which are on the left side of the keyboard. While holding these keys down, press and release the (Del) key.** That key is near the lower right-hand corner of the keyboard. This has a similar effect to turning the power switch off and then on. However, unlike a cold start, a warm start is faster and causes no wear on the power switch. **Now complete the start-up steps as explained in the last session beginning with Step 5 on page 18 (without a diskette drive) or with Step 6 on page 20 (with a diskette drive).**

Using This Book with the Computer

The sessions in this book will guide you in learning how to use the IBM PC*jr*. You will not need any additional help, but you will have to read carefully. Open the book and put it on a table or in your lap. You should be able to read it easily while you are typing on the keyboard. You should also place the keyboard either on a table or in your lap where it is comfortable to use.

Here is some strong advice: Do not rush through the activities in this book. The temptation to keep doing things on the computer will be great. You should resist that temptation. Instead of plunging ahead, stop and think about what you have done. Read the paragraphs that explain how things work. Answer the questions at the ends of the sections. Check your answers against the ones at the back of the book. If there are projects at the end of a session, take time to do them.

In many places in this book, you will see words and numbers printed on the left side of the page. Just below each such group of words and numbers, you will see a heavy line. It will lead to a comment on the right side of the page. When you see a page like this, here is what you should do:

Hands-On Computer Activities

1. Always read the words and numbers at the left and the comment at the right before you do anything else.
2. Type exactly what you see in the left column above the line.
3. Look at the screen and press the (Enter ⏎) key after you have finished typing each line (unless you are told not to do so).
4. Look carefully at what happens on the screen.
5. Read the comment at the right again.

Messages to the Computer

All right, let's get started. Look at the TV display. You should see a flashing symbol on the screen. The flashing symbol is called the **cursor**. Every time you see it, it means the computer is waiting for you to type something. **Type these letters:**

CLA
_____

Look at the screen and press the (Enter ⏎) **key.** You got the Syntax error message. It means the computer didn't understand CLA.

CLB
_____

Look at the screen and press the (Enter ⏎) **key.** You got the Syntax error message again. The computer didn't understand CLB either.

CLS _____

Look at the screen and press the (Enter ◁) **key.** At last, the computer understood what you typed. CLS told it to "clear the screen." The computer did so and said OK.

1. What does CLS tell the computer to do?
2. What key should you press when you have finished typing a message to the computer?
3. What happens if you press the (Esc) key while typing a message to the computer?
4. How can you tell if the computer is waiting for you to type something?
5. How can you fix any errors you make while entering information?

Making Sounds

Let's move on to a new subject. Did you know you can tell your computer to make sounds? There are several words you can type to tell the computer to make sounds. You will learn about two of these next. **First, turn up the volume control on the TV display. Adjust the volume to a comfortable level as you go through the steps below.**

BEEP _____

Remember to watch the screen, press the (Enter ◁) key, and release it. What happened?

BEEP _____

If you pressed the (Enter ◁) key, you heard the tone again.

SOUND 440 , 10 _____

Be sure to use the number keys for 1 and 0. Remember to press the (Enter ◁) key.

SOUND440 ,10 _____

Whoops! Look at the screen. Without the spaces, the computer does not know what this means.

If everything went as planned, you heard the same note after each BEEP statement and a different note after the SOUND statement. BEEP always produces the same musical note with the same length. SOUND is more flexible, as you will soon see. You also found out that spaces count: Be careful about spaces when typing messages to the computer.

SOUND 440, 10

You did that before. Did you remember to press the (Enter ◄┘) key?

SOUND 494, 10

When 440 was changed to 494, what happened to the note you heard?

SOUND 523, 10

What happened this time?

SOUND 523, 20

What does the second number after SOUND appear to control?

SOUND 523, 40

What happened this time?

You will learn more about SOUND later in this book. This is enough detail for now.

6. What does BEEP tell the computer to do?
7. What does the first number after SOUND do?
8. What does the second number after SOUND do?

Switching Screens and Controlling Color

So far, the computer has printed white letters on a black screen. This is called the **text mode** of the PCjr. In this section, you will learn how to change to **graphics mode** and change the **background** color. (We will actually be using the medium-resolution graphics mode. There are other graphics modes, but we will only touch on them briefly.)

SCREEN 1

Look at the screen as you press the (Enter ◄┘) key. This changes the screen to graphics mode. Note that the cursor is now a solid square.

SCREEN 0

This changes back to the text mode. Notice that the cursor is flashing again.

SCREEN 2

This is high-resolution graphics mode. Notice the tall cursor and skinny OK.

SCREEN 0 _____ Whoops! You are back in text mode, but the letters on the screen are still skinny. You may have to use (Alt | Ctrl | →) to see all the letters.

WIDTH 40 _____ This gets the text screen back to 40-column mode.

SCREEN 1 _____ Now the computer is back in medium-resolution graphics mode.

COLOR 1 _____ You changed the background color from black to blue.

COLOR 2 _____ Now the screen is green.

COLOR 3 _____ This color is cyan.

COLOR 4 _____ A red screen.

COLOR 5 _____ Magenta.

COLOR 15 _____ Whoops!

You have a problem. Color 15 is white, so the computer prints white characters on a white screen. The characters are there, but you can't see them. Now, let's get back to the text screen. **Type SCREEN 0 and press the (Enter ↵) key.** You should see a black screen with a white OK at the top.

So far, you have seen nothing but text on the graphics screen. In Session 7, you will begin learning how to draw lines and plot points on the graphics screen.

9. How can you tell whether the computer is in text mode, medium-resolution graphics mode, or high-resolution graphics mode?
10. What does SCREEN 1 tell the computer to do?
11. In graphics mode 1, what does COLOR 4 tell the computer to do?

Putting Words on the Screen

You have seen how to tell the PC*jr* to make sounds, switch to graphics mode, and change background colors. Now let's see how to make the computer print words on the screen. **In the line below, be sure to type the BASIC word PRINT as well as "PCJR".**

PRINT "PCJR"

Then press the (Enter ⏎) key and look at the screen. You should see the letters PCJR on the line below the message you just typed.

PRINT "PCJR IS A COMPUTER"

Another message.

PRINT "PCJR IS A SMALL BUT POWERFUL PERSONAL COMPUTER"

This sentence was too long to fit on a single line, so the computer printed it on two lines.

PRINT "2 + 3"

This message had numbers in it.

PRINT 2 + 3

When the message lacks quotation marks, the computer does the arithmetic and prints the result.

PRINT 2+3

Some spaces don't matter.

PRINT2+3

Look at the screen as you press (Enter ⏎). The Syntax error message shows that some spaces do matter.

PRINT _____ This told the computer to print a blank line.

PRINT 8 - 5 _____ This time the computer did subtraction.

PRINT 6 * 5 _____ Multiplication.

PRINT 5280 / 3 _____ Division.

? 5280 / 3 _____ The question mark is an abbreviation for PRINT.

? "ABC" _____ The abbreviation also works for groups of characters in quotation marks.

 12. What does PRINT "HELLO" tell the computer to do?
13. In arithmetic, what does the slash symbol (/) tell the computer to do?

Table of Background Colors

(Set by COLOR _n_ in medium-resolution graphics. The actual colors you see on your TV display may look different.)

0		Black	8		Gray
1		Blue	9		Light Blue
2		Green	10		Light Green
3		Cyan	11		Light Cyan
4		Red	12		Light Red
5		Magenta	13		Light Magenta
6		Brown	14		Yellow
7		White	15		Bright White

SUMMARY You have begun to explore some of the color-graphics and sound features of your PC*jr*. The new words you used are listed in the table below. Read the table carefully and make sure you understand the new features fully. Go back and look at the session again if you don't. Remember our advice. Take your time. Don't hurry on to the next session if there are things you don't understand about this session.

Feature	Description
Sound modes	The PC*jr* can make musical sounds of controlled pitch (frequency) and length (duration).
BEEP	Sounds the speaker with a frequency of 800 Hz (cycles per second) and a duration of 1/4 second.
SOUND f, d	Sounds the speaker at f cycles per second for d clock ticks. The letter f stands for frequency, a number between 37 and 32767. The letter d stands for duration, a number between 0.0015 and 65535. One clock tick equals 1/18.2 seconds.
Display modes	The PC*jr* has a text mode and several graphics modes.
CLS	Clears the screen in any display mode.
SCREEN 0	Sets text mode with white letters on a black background. In this mode, the cursor is a flashing underline symbol.
SCREEN 1	Sets medium-resolution graphics mode. The cursor is a solid square.
SCREEN 2	Sets high-resolution graphics mode. The cursor is a tall rectangle.
WIDTH n	Sets the number of characters on a line to n, which may be either 40 or 80.
COLOR n	In medium-resolution graphics, sets the background color to n. The letter n stands for any number from 0 through 15. See the table on the previous page for the color equivalents of the numbers.
PRINT "HELLO"	Prints HELLO on the text screen or the graphics screen.
PRINT 8 + 7	Computes the sum of two numbers and prints the result.
PRINT	Prints a blank line on the screen.

WRITING AND EDITING SIMPLE PROGRAMS

SESSION 3

Session Goals

- Review the start-up steps for the computer.
- Write and run a simple program.
- Use line-number editing to make changes in the program.
- Learn how to run the program, list it on the screen, and erase it from memory.
- Learn how to renumber the lines of a program.

Review

In Session 1, you learned how to turn the computer on and adjust the display on the TV screen. Now is a good time for you to review the start-up steps. These are summarized below. If you need more details about anything, go back to pages 16–18 if you do *not* have a diskette drive and pages 19–22 if you *do*.

Starting without a Diskette Drive

Step 1. Turn the computer off.

Step 2. Turn on the TV set. Lower the volume.

Step 3. Remove any cartridges from the slots. Insert the BASIC cartridge if you have one.

Step 4. Turn the computer power on. If it is already on, hold the (Alt) and (Ctrl) keys down while you press and release the (Del) key. (By the way, if you insert or remove the BASIC cartridge with the power on, this happens by itself.)

Step 5. Wait 20 seconds for a message at the top of the screen. Press the (Caps Lock) key.

Step 6. If necessary, use (Alt│Ctrl│→) and (Alt│Ctrl│←) to adjust the picture.

Step 7. Type KEY OFF and press the (Enter ↵) key.

Starting with a Diskette Drive

Step 1. Turn the computer off.

Step 2. Turn on the TV set. Lower the volume.

Step 3. Insert the DOS diskette in the drive and close the latch.

Step 4. Remove any cartridges from the slots. Insert your BASIC cartridge.

Step 5. Turn the computer power on. If it is already on, hold the (Alt) and (Ctrl) keys down while you press and release the (Del) key. (By the way, if you insert or remove the BASIC cartridge with the power on, this happens by itself.)

Step 6. Wait for the date question. Press the (Enter ↵) key twice.

Step 7. Press the (Caps Lock) key.

Step 8. Type BASIC and press the (Enter ↵) key.

Step 9. If necessary, use (Alt│Ctrl│→) and (Alt│Ctrl│←) to adjust the picture.

Step 10. Type KEY OFF and press the (Enter ↵) key.

Writing a Program

In this section, you will write your first **program** for the computer. A program is a list of instructions for the computer to carry out, one step at a time.

Until now, the computer has carried out each of your instructions as soon as you pressed the (Enter ↵) key. However, you may not always want it to do things this way. Suppose, for example, that your instructions are long and complicated. In that case, it is better to write them all out, read them over, and fix any mistakes you find. Only then would you tell the computer to carry out the instructions. In this session, you will learn how to do this. **Adjust the volume on your TV as you do the steps below. Be sure to type exactly what you read at the left. Computers are very fussy about spelling and punctuation.**

BOP

Look at the screen as you press (Enter ↵). The Syntax error message means that the computer does not know how to BOP.

BEEP

But it can BEEP.

PRINT "BEEP BEEP"

And it can print BEEP BEEP.

25 BEEP

Look at the screen. Nothing happened: no beep or error message.

32 PRINT "BEEP BEEP"

Again, nothing happened.

RUN _____ Now BEEP and
PRINT "BEEP BEEP" worked.
(If you got a Syntax error,
press (Enter ◡) and retype the line.)
Let's try it again.

RUN _____ It worked again.

LIST _____ Look at the screen. There are the
lines you entered earlier.

Putting a number before BEEP or PRINT changes the way the computer does things. Without a number at the beginning of a line, the computer acts immediately: It sounds a note or prints letters on the screen. With a number, nothing happens when you enter a line: But the computer does remember your lines.

You have just written your first program for the PC*jr*. Your program has these two lines:

```
25 BEEP
32 PRINT "BEEP BEEP"
```

This program is written using a **computer language** called BASIC. (The letters of the name stand for Beginner's All-purpose Symbolic Instruction Code.) In the BASIC language, each program line starts with a **line number**. The line number is followed by a **statement**. In the first line of your program, the line number is 25. The statement is BEEP.

The computer does not, however, do what the statement tells it to do until you enter the word RUN. RUN is a **command**. It tells the computer to **perform** all the statements in your program. Commands are special words that tell the computer to do something with or to a program.

LIST is another command your computer understands. LIST tells the computer to print the lines of your program on the TV screen. Let's try these commands again. **Remember to look at the screen whenever you press the (Enter ◡) key.**

LIST _____ LIST tells the computer to show
the program.

RUN _____ RUN says to perform the
statements in the program.

CLS _____ That cleared the screen. Is the
program gone also?

LIST _____ No, the computer still remembers the program.

RUN _____ And the computer can perform the program again.

NEW _____ This is a another command. Let's see what it did.

LIST _____ Notice the screen. LIST does nothing now. The computer no longer remembers your program, even though you, yourself, can still see it on the screen!

RUN _____ RUN does nothing now.

The program you just wrote is very simple. It had only two lines, but you can learn a lot from it. Take a moment to think about the answers to the questions below:

1. What are the two parts of every program line?
2. What does the LIST command tell the computer to do?
3. What does the RUN command tell the computer to do?
4. What word tells the computer to erase the screen?
5. What does the NEW command tell the computer to do?

Line-Number Editing

The program you just wrote had only two lines. Most programs have dozens of lines. A computer program can be very complicated. You will spend most of your time at the computer entering and changing programs. One way to change programs is called **line-number editing**. You will learn how to do that next.

Be prepared for mistakes when you write programs. All programmers, no matter how experienced, make mistakes. **If you get a Syntax error message at any time, press (Enter ⏎) and retype the line. Be sure to spell and punctuate correctly.**

CLS _____ Clear the screen.

NEW _____ Erase any program in the computer.

```
10 BEEP
```

Be sure to use the number keys to enter the line number.

```
RUN
```

The computer performed your one-line program.

```
20 SOUND 659, 10
LIST
```

Watch the screen and press (Enter ⏎) **after each line.** Now your program has a second line.

```
RUN
```

Listen to the two tones.

```
30 SOUND 523, 40
LIST
RUN
```

Watch the screen and press (Enter ⏎) **after each line.** Now there are three lines.

Here is what your program should look like now:

```
10 BEEP
20 SOUND 659, 10
30 SOUND 523, 40
```

When you ran this program, you heard three tones. The first was produced by the BEEP statement in line 10. The next two tones were produced by the two SOUND statements. Note that the tone produced by line 30 lasts four times as long as the one produced by line 20. (Why?)

```
25 SOUND 587, 10
```

Where do you think this new line will go in the program? Let's see.

```
RUN
LIST
```

Look at the screen. Were you right?

The computer always keeps BASIC program lines in the same order as their line numbers. You used this fact to **insert** a new statement between line 20 and line 30. Now let's see how to **delete** a statement from your program. Here is how to get rid of the BEEP statement:

10 _____ Just type the number and press the (Enter ⏎) key.

RUN
LIST _____ Look at the screen. Line 10 is gone from the program.

You deleted line 10 by simply typing the number 10 and pressing the (Enter ⏎) key. This method works for any line in a program: Just type the number of the line and then press the (Enter ⏎) key. Next, let's see how to **change** a statement in a program. Suppose you want to change the duration of the tone in line 30 from 40 to 10. Here is how:

30 SOUND 523, 10
LIST _____ Look at line 30 now.

RUN _____ Listen to the new results.

You can change any line in a BASIC program by retyping the line using the same line number. Since you have made several changes, use the LIST command to make sure your program now looks like this:

```
20 SOUND 659, 10
25 SOUND 587, 10
30 SOUND 523, 10
```

You now know how to do line-number editing: inserting, deleting, and changing lines. If your program looks different, use these tools to fix it. Now let's add three more lines to your program:

22 PRINT "MA-"
27 PRINT "RY"
40 PRINT "HAD" _____ Press (Enter ⏎) after each line. Where will these new lines go?

LIST _____ Now you know.

RUN

The computer performs the lines in the same order it lists them. (If you get a Syntax error, press (Enter ⏎) and retype the line.)

10 PRINT
LIST

There is nothing after PRINT in line 10. What will line 10 cause the computer to do?

RUN

Look at the screen. Notice the blank line after the word RUN.

RENUM
LIST

The lines are now numbered differently.

RUN

But they tell the computer to do the same thing as before.

The RENUM command tells the computer to renumber the lines. This is useful when you need to make room to insert new lines in a program. You will be inserting lines next. After you have used the RENUM command, your program should look like this:

```
10 PRINT
20 SOUND 659, 10
30 PRINT "MA-"
40 SOUND 587, 10
50 PRINT "RY"
60 SOUND 523, 10
70 PRINT "HAD"
```

RENUM 100
LIST

Look at the new line numbers. Let's add more lines next.

95 SCREEN 1
115 COLOR 1
135 COLOR 14
155 COLOR 4

Press (Enter ⏎) after each line.

Writing and Editing Simple Programs **43**

```
LIST
```
What will this program do?

```
RUN
```
The program should work the same way. (Fix any errors you find.)

Now you have used printed messages, sound, and screen color together. Let's have the program clear the screen all by itself.

```
97 CLS
LIST
```
Check the program.

```
RENUM 100
LIST
RUN
RUN
```
Look at the screen as you press (Enter ↵) after each line. Now the program is getting classy!

The computer screen is still in the graphics mode. (Notice the shape of the cursor.) The program would be better if it told the computer to go back to text mode. Let's add this statement at the end:

```
300 SCREEN 0
```
This tells the computer to return to text mode.

```
RUN
```
We still have a problem: Before, the program ended with a red screen. This time, there was no red screen.

```
290 SOUND 32767, 1
RUN
```
That worked: The red screen is visible now.

```
RENUM 100
LIST
```
Here is the program.

The SOUND statement is a little tricky. Here is how it works: When the computer performs a SOUND statement, it turns a note on. It then keeps performing statements. If the computer reaches another SOUND statement *before* the first note is finished, it stops and waits. So your *fourth* SOUND statement kept the red screen visible until the *third* note was finished. But what does the frequency 32767 mean? Nothing, unless you are a bat! The pitch is too high for you to hear. So you get a "rest note." Finally, as soon as the computer begins the rest note, it goes on to the SCREEN Ø statement and sets text mode.

Here is how your program should look after you have made all the changes:

```
100 SCREEN 1
110 CLS
120 PRINT
130 SOUND 659, 10
140 COLOR 1
150 PRINT "MA-"
160 SOUND 587, 10
170 COLOR 14
180 PRINT "RY"
190 SOUND 523, 10
200 COLOR 4
210 PRINT "HAD"
220 SOUND 32767, 1
230 SCREEN Ø
```

Line-number editing gives you a way to add, delete, or change lines in a BASIC program. You will use line-number editing whenever you write a BASIC program. So it is a good idea to review how to do it. Take a moment to answer the questions below:

6. How would you insert a statement between lines 120 and 140 of a program?
7. How would you delete the statement in line 50 from a program?
8. If you enter a line that has the same line number as a line already in a program, what happens?
9. What does the command RENUM 500 tell the computer to do?

PROJECT

● When you were running the program now in your computer, you probably recognized the music as the first part of "Mary Had a Little Lamb." As a project, add the lines to the program that will play more notes of the song.

Don't spend too much time on this project. You don't yet know how to save programs, so your work will be lost when you are finished. In Sessions 5 and 6, you will learn how to save programs on cassette tape or diskette.

Remember that you can make each note longer or shorter by changing the second number in the SOUND statement. You will also need to know the frequencies for other notes in the scale. Here is a table of frequencies for some of the "white notes" on a piano:

Note	Frequency
C	523
D	587
E	659
F	698
G	784
A	880
B	988
C	1046

The first note in the table is middle C. The last note is the C that is an octave above middle C.

When you have finished working with the program, use the NEW command to clear it from the computer before you start another program.

SUMMARY

To make a computer do what you want it to, you must write programs that contain your instructions to the machine. In this session, you have written and edited your first programs for the PC*jr*. These programs were short and simple. But the ideas you have learned here are the main ones you will be using in the future. The new ideas and commands in this session are summarized in the tables below. Read them carefully and review the session as seems necessary. Again, take your time.

Line-Number Editing	*Description*
Changing a line	Retype the line, using the same line number.
Deleting a line	Type only the line number, and press the (Enter ↵) key.
Inserting a line	Choose a line number between those of the lines that will go before and after the new line.

Command	*Description*
LIST	Tells the computer to print the lines of the program on the TV screen.
NEW	Tells the computer to erase the program now in memory.
RENUM *n*	Tells the computer to renumber the program lines. The first program line number is changed to new line number *n*. Every line number after that is 10 bigger than the one before.
RUN	Tells the computer to perform all the statements of the program, starting with the first.

HOW THE COMPUTER WORKS

SESSION 4

Session Goals

- Learn the main parts of any computer.
- Learn how the parts work together to input, process, and output information.
- Use a simple picture to understand how the computer runs, lists, and erases programs.

The Information Machine

In the first three sessions of this book, you have learned to do the things that you will need to do most often in your work with the PC*jr*. You know how to start the computer. You know your way around the keyboard. You know how to correct typing errors. And you know how to enter programs, run them, change them, list them on the screen, and erase them from the computer. Along the way, you have learned the BASIC statements for making sounds, changing from text mode to graphics mode, setting the background color, printing letters on the screen, and clearing the screen. You will be using these skills again and again in the future.

To learn these things, you have had your fingers on the keyboard every few seconds. You have been constantly discovering new features of the PC*jr*. You have been frequently entering program lines or commands. At this point, you may feel awash in new information and new ideas, especially if you are new to computers. This is a good time for you to step back and take another look at what you have seen so far. It is time for you to begin learning what a computer is, what it does, and how it works.

That last phrase, "how it works," may alarm you. To use a computer happily and successfully, you do *not* have to understand electronics, silicon chips, bits, or bytes. Many people who deal with computers every day know little about how they work as electronic machines. But you will soon find that it becomes much easier to use the computer when you understand how it works as an **information machine**.

Whenever you use a computer, you enter information into it. The information goes somewhere inside the computer. It gets changed and moved around. Finally, the computer puts information back out for you to see. In this session, we will begin to develop a picture of the computer as a machine for doing things with information. You will see what goes on when you enter a program, run it, list it, and erase it.

The Parts of a Computer

Leave the computer. Go find a comfortable chair, take this book, and spend the next 15 minutes reading.

What are the main parts of your computer? There is the keyboard, which you use to put information into the computer. Thus, the keyboard is an **input unit**. The computer puts information out through the TV screen and the loudspeaker. Thus, these are **output units**. Inside the computer, information is stored in a part called the **memory unit**.

The drawing below shows a useful way of thinking about these three main parts of the computer. The mail slot on the top of the box stands for the input unit. Information enters the computer through the input slot. The scroll of paper on the left stands for the output unit. The computer writes information on the output scroll. If more space is needed, the computer turns the scroll up a little. The chalkboard on the right stands for the memory unit. The computer writes information on the memory chalkboard. The information on the memory chalkboard can also be erased.

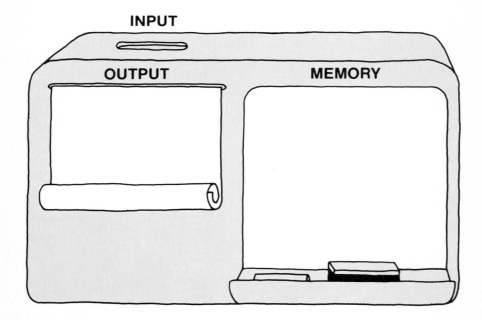

1. What is the purpose of the input unit?
2. What is the purpose of the output unit?
3. What is the purpose of the memory unit?

Putting the Picture to Work

Let's see how the parts work together when you use the computer. As an example, imagine that you are about to enter the eight lines below on your PC*jr* keyboard. Think for a moment about what your PC*jr* would actually do after you entered each line, one after the other.

```
PRINT "CAT"
20 PRINT "DOG"
10 PRINT "HOT"
CLS
RUN
CLS
LIST
NEW
```

Let's start with the first line. Imagine that you have just entered PRINT "CAT" through the input slot in our picture of the computer. The computer responds by printing PRINT "CAT" on one line of the output scroll, CAT on the next line, and OK on the third line. Here is how the output scroll and memory chalkboard look afterward:

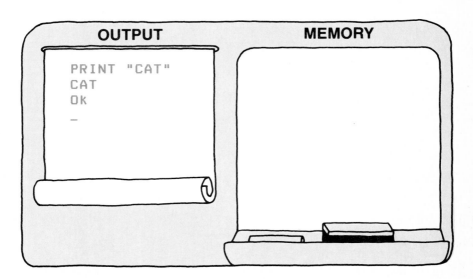

The next line entered is 20 PRINT "DOG". It has a line number. So the computer does not perform the PRINT statement right away. Instead, it writes the line on the memory chalkboard and output scroll.

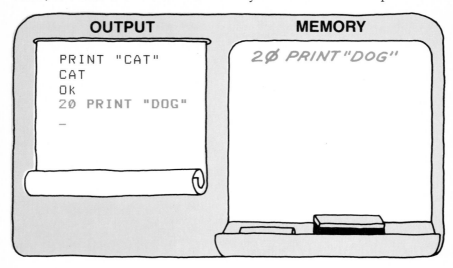

BASIC statements can be used in two ways. In the **program mode**, you type a line number followed by the statement. The computer then stores the statement in memory without performing it. In the **immediate** mode, you omit the line number. The computer then performs the statement at once, without storing it in memory.

The third line to be entered is 10 PRINT "HOT". This line also has a line number. Thus, the computer writes it on the memory chalkboard and on the output scroll. But notice *where* it goes on the chalkboard: The computer keeps the statements in line-number order in memory.

The fourth line to be entered is CLS. This line tells the computer to clear the output scroll. However, it does *not* tell the computer to clear the memory chalkboard.

4. How do you tell the computer to put a statement into its memory unit?
5. What determines the order in which statements are listed in the memory unit?

Running the Program in Memory

The fifth line to be entered is the RUN command. This line tells the computer to perform the statements of the program on the memory chalkboard. On your PC*jr*, this happens with lightning speed. It may seem to you that the whole program is performed in one step. But it actually is done in a series of steps. Let's now look at what happens more closely.

Our picture of the computer needs two new features: The first is a line pointer that tells which statement the computer is to perform next. The second is a control crank to move the line pointer to the next statement. When the RUN command is entered, the computer first prints RUN on the output scroll. It then puts the line pointer at the first line of the program on the memory chalkboard. Here is our new picture of the computer:

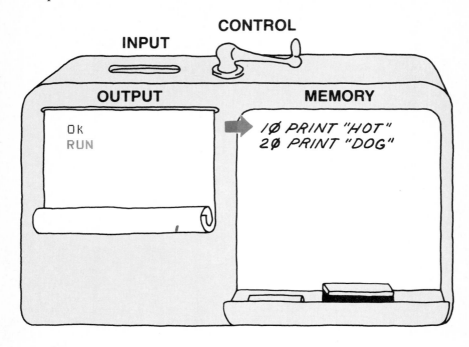

The cursor is missing because the computer is not ready for input now. The computer must always perform the **current line**—the one pointed at by the line pointer. Here is the picture after line 1∅ is performed:

The computer wrote HOT on the output scroll. The control crank then moves the line pointer to the next line.

Now the computer performs the *new* current line, line 20. It says to print DOG on the output scroll.

Finally, the control crank moves the line pointer down. There are no more statements on the chalkboard. Thus, the computer prints OK on the output scroll and turns the cursor back on. You can see the picture at the top of the next page. The computer has now finished running the program. No matter how fast it looks on your PCjr, running a program always means the same thing: The computer reads one statement at a time, performs it, and then goes on to the next statement.

 6. What is the purpose of the line pointer?
7. How can you tell whether the computer is waiting for input from the keyboard?

Listing and Erasing the Program in Memory

Only three more lines out of the original eight remain to be entered into the computer. They are CLS, LIST, and NEW. Here is the picture after CLS is entered:

The seventh line to be entered is LIST. In many ways, this command is like RUN. The computer puts the line pointer at the first program line on the memory chalkboard, reads the line, prints it on the output scroll, moves the line pointer down, and so on. Here is the picture afterward:

The last line to be entered is NEW. This command tells the computer to erase the memory chalkboard, but *not* the output scroll. Here is the final picture:

8. How can you find out if there is a BASIC program in the memory unit?
9. How are NEW and CLS alike? How are they different?

Commands and Built-in Programs

In this session, you have seen what the computer does when you enter commands such as RUN, LIST, and NEW. You may have guessed that your computer is specially built to recognize and carry out all the commands in BASIC. Fortunately, that is not true. If it were, you would need a different computer for every programming language.

The only reason your computer knows what to do when you enter the LIST command is that some person wrote a special program. It tells the computer all the steps needed to list the BASIC program in memory. This program, the LIST program, is contained in a special part of memory. This part of memory is not erased when you turn off the power. Without the LIST program, your PC*jr* would still be a computer. However, it would not know how to list BASIC programs.

Whenever you enter a BASIC command, the computer immediately begins performing one of these built-in programs in its memory. The cursor disappears until the program ends. Then the computer says OK and puts the cursor back. This tells you that the computer is ready for you to enter a command or a program line.

At first, it may seem to you that computers are very complex and very clever machines. In fact, they are simple and lack intelligence. The only thing any computer can do is follow instructions just as they are given. The cleverness is in the programs, which are written by people. Some clever programs are already built into your PC*jr*. You will be adding others yourself as you learn more about programming.

SUMMARY

In this session, you have begun to get a picture of what goes on inside your computer—and every other computer. You have learned the main parts of the computer and how they work together. These topics are summarized in the table below. If something is not clear to you, review that topic in the session.

Topic	Description
Input unit	The part of a computer used to enter information.
Output unit	The part of a computer used to give out information.
Memory unit	The part of a computer used to store information, including program statements.
Control unit	The part of a computer that steps through the statements in a program.
Immediate mode	Performing statements as soon as they are entered into the computer. In BASIC, statements without line numbers are performed in the immediate mode.
Program mode	Storing statements in memory as they are entered into the computer. In BASIC, the RUN command tells the computer to perform the statements in memory, beginning with the first.

CASSETTE SAVING AND LOADING

SESSION 5

Session Goals

- Write copies of programs on cassette tapes.
- Read programs from a cassette tape and write them into memory.
- Find what programs are written on a cassette tape.

Installing and Using the Cassette Unit

To save programs on a cassette tape, you must have a cassette tape recorder connected to your computer. There are many different brands and models of cassette tape recorders. Ask your computer dealer to show you models that work with the PC*jr*. The instructions that follow are correct for most recorders. If you have any problems, ask your computer dealer for help.

The IBM cassette cable has a single connector at one end and three plugs at the other end. **Plug the single connector into the matching cassette socket on the rear of the main unit of your PC*jr*.** The letter "C" is molded into the computer case next to the cassette socket.

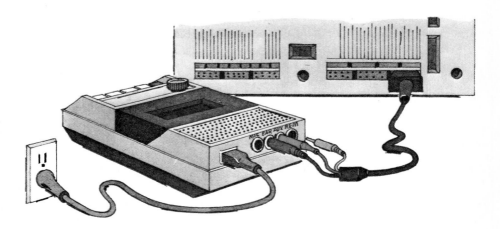

The other end of the cable has three plugs colored red, black, and gray. **Connect the black plug to the recorder socket labeled EAR or EARPHONE. Then connect the red plug to the socket labeled AUX or AUXILIARY. Leave the gray plug disconnected from the recorder.** The gray plug is needed for automatic operation of the cassette recorder. We will show you how to use the cassette recorder by a manual method that is easier to learn at first.

Next, you must apply electric power to your recorder. **Plug the power cable into the power socket on the recorder. Plug the other end into a standard wall socket. If there is a power switch on the recorder, turn it on.** Your recorder may also operate on batteries. If so, we recommend that you *not* use battery power when recording computer programs. When the batteries run down, the recorder motor turns more slowly. Later, with fresh batteries, the motor runs properly again. However, the computer may be unable to read programs recorded at the slower speed.

Now you are ready to test the recorder. **If there is a cassette tape in the recorder, take it out. Press the recorder's PLAY key.** You should see the right-hand tape-drive shaft start turning. If not, check the power cable and the power switch. Make certain the gray plug is not connected to the recorder. **Press the recorder's STOP key.** The right-hand shaft should stop turning. **Press the recorder's REWIND key.** The left-hand shaft should turn rapidly. **Press the STOP key again.** The shaft should stop turning.

Finally, you need to adjust the setting on the volume control. **If you have a prerecorded music cassette, put it in the recorder and press PLAY. Temporarily disconnect the black plug from the EAR socket. Adjust the volume until the music is fairly loud but does not sound distorted. Mark this setting on the volume control knob. Use this setting for your computer work. Reconnect the black plug to the EAR socket.** If you do not have a music cassette, just set the volume control to the middle of its range.

1. Which recorder-cable plug goes into the EAR socket? Which plug goes into the AUX socket?
2. What should you do with the gray plug on the IBM cassette cable?

Saving a Program

Your cassette tape recorder should be connected to the main unit and plugged into a wall socket, as described above. The volume control should be turned to the proper setting. **If necessary, start your computer as outlined in Session 3.**

You will now enter a short program into the computer's memory. After that, you will record a copy of the program on a cassette tape. You will need a blank tape, or a tape that you do not mind erasing.

```
NEW
CLS
```
Erase the memory and clear the screen.

```
10 PRINT "HELLO"
LIST
RUN
```
This is a short program.

Now, let's put a copy of your program on a cassette tape. Here are the steps:

Step 1. **Put a tape cassette into the recorder. Close the door. Press the REWIND key. After the shafts stop turning, press the STOP key.** The tape is ready to be used.

Step 2. **Type SAVE "GREETING" but do not press the** (Enter ⏎) **key yet.** (If you are using Cartridge BASIC and a diskette drive, type SAVE "CAS1:GREETING".)

Step 3. **Press the recorder's RECORD and PLAY keys at the same time. Both must stay down.**

Step 4. **Wait about 10 seconds. Then press the** (Enter ⏎) **key.** The cursor should disappear while the computer writes a copy of your program on the tape. Then you should see OK and the cursor on the screen.

Step 5. **Press the STOP key on the recorder.**

Did you notice the 10-second delay in Step 4? Every tape has a non-recording strip at the beginning called a **tape leader**. You have to skip past the tape leader before you can begin recording on the tape.

If all went well, you have now written a copy of your program on the cassette tape. (If you had any problems, check all cable connections carefully.)

3. What recorder keys must be down when you are saving a program on a cassette tape?
4. What BASIC command tells the computer to write a copy of your program on tape?

Loading a Program

You have written a copy of your one-line program on a cassette tape. Let's see whether the original version is still in the computer.

LIST ——————————————— It looks OK.

RUN ——————————————— It still works.

NEW
LIST ——————————————— Now it's gone from memory.

Next, let's see how to put a copy of the program on the tape back into the computer. **Be sure the volume control on the recorder is set properly.**

Step 1. **Make sure the tape cassette is in the recorder and the door is closed. Press the REWIND key. After the shaft stops turning, press the STOP key.** The tape is now in the correct position.

Step 2. **Type LOAD "GREETING". Then press the (Enter⏎) key.** The cursor should disappear. (If you are using Cartridge BASIC and a diskette drive, type LOAD "CAS1:GREETING".)

Step 3. **Without waiting, press the PLAY key on the recorder.** After about 15 seconds, you should see the message GREETING.B Found. In a few more seconds, you should see OK and the cursor on the screen. (If you see nothing after a minute, go on to Step 4.)

Step 4. **Press the STOP key on the cassette tape recorder.**

Step 5. **Enter the LIST command. Check to see that the program is back in memory.**

If all went well, you moved a copy of the program on the tape into the computer's memory. (If you had any problems, check your cables carefully. Make sure the black plug is in the EAR socket. Then start over with Step 1. If you still have problems, the volume setting may have been too low when you saved the program. Try setting the volume higher. Then go back to the previous section, "Saving a Program," and repeat the steps there.)

5. What BASIC command tells the computer to bring into memory a copy of a program on cassette tape?
6. What recorder key must be pressed to allow the computer to carry out the command in question 5?

Names of Files

When you used the SAVE command, you followed it by the name GREETING inside quotation marks. Information is stored on magnetic tapes or diskettes in units called **files**. Each file has a name. Your SAVE command told the computer to put a copy of your one-line program into a file with the name GREETING.B. The computer added .B to remind you that the file contains a BASIC program.

File names may be from one to eight characters long, not counting the .B part. It is a good idea to use only letters and numbers in file names.

There is a simple way to find the names of all files on a tape: Tell the computer to load a file that is not on the tape. **Using the file name "ZZZ", go through the first four steps in the previous section.**

If all went well, you should have seen the message GREETING.B Skipped during Step 3. After a minute or so, you should have seen the message Device timeout just before the Ok message and the cursor returned. Suppose your tape had several files on it. In that case, the computer would have printed the name of each one along with the message Skipped.

You can record several programs on one tape. But it is not a very good idea to do so. Finding the program you want on the tape can be tricky and take a lot of time. Adding a new program is risky: You may erase part of an old one. We recommend that you buy a number of very short tapes (C5 or C10 would be good). Then put one program on each tape. Another good idea is to record the same program twice—once on each side of the tape.

7. What are some examples of legal file names?
8. How can you find the names of all the files on a cassette tape?

SUMMARY In this session, you have learned how to move copies of programs back and forth between memory and a cassette tape. The commands you used are summarized in the table below. Read the table carefully and make sure you understand the commands. Review the session as necessary.

Command	Description
SAVE "*name*"	Tells the computer to put a copy of the program in memory on the cassette tape under the name you choose. The computer adds the suffix ,B to the name. Any other information on that part of the tape is erased as the program is recorded.
LOAD "*name*"	Tells the computer to erase the program now in memory and then to move a copy of the program named from the cassette tape into memory.

DISKETTE SAVING AND LOADING

SESSION 6

Session Goals

- Format a diskette.
- Move programs from the computer onto a diskette.
- Move programs from a diskette into memory.
- List a directory of programs on a diskette.
- Remove programs from a diskette.

Formatting Diskettes

You will need a diskette drive and a BASIC cartridge in your computer to do this session. If you have a cassette tape recorder, read Session 5 instead. It tells you how to save programs on, and recall them from, tape cassettes.

Diskettes must be **formatted** before the computer can either write information on them or read it from them. A formatted diskette has special magnetic marks recorded on it. These guide the computer when it writes or reads programs on the diskette. Once you have formatted a diskette, you do not have to do it again. The magnetic marks stay on the diskette.

You will need to have at least one formatted diskette. However, it is a good idea to format several diskettes at the same time. You can buy diskettes at your neighborhood computer store. Be sure to ask for diskettes for the IBM PC*jr*.

Follow the steps below to format diskettes. **If you already have a formatted diskette, skip all these steps.**

Step 1. **Turn off your computer if it is on. Then follow the steps outlined at the beginning of Session 3. Use Steps 1 through 10 under the heading "Starting with a Diskette Drive" at the bottom of page 37. Leave your BASIC cartridge in the cartridge slot.** Make sure you see O k at the bottom of the screen before you go on.

Step 2. **Type SYSTEM and press the** (Enter ◁┘) **key.** This takes the computer out of BASIC and back to the **system level**. At the system level, you see A > instead of O k. (You saw A > during the start-up steps.) **Before going further, be sure that A > is on the screen.**

Step 3. **Type FORMAT and press the** (Enter ◁┘) **key.** You should see the following new lines on your screen:

```
Insert new diskette for drive A:
and strike any key when ready
```

Step 4. **Remove the DOS diskette from the diskette drive. Place a new diskette (or one that contains information you don't mind losing) into the diskette drive. Close the latch.** The diskette label should be up and on the edge of the diskette closest to you.

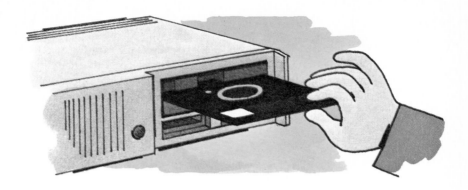

Step 5. **Press the (Enter⏎) key.** You will see the message

    Formatting...

on the screen while the computer formats the diskette. When the formatting is complete, you should see a message on the screen similar to the one below:

    Formatting...Format complete

      362496 bytes total disk space
      362496 bytes available on disk

    Format another (Y/N)?

Step 6. **Remove the formatted diskette.** (If you have several diskettes, you should format them all at this time. Place another diskette in the drive. Press the (Y) key and go back to Step 5.)

Step 7. **When your last diskette has been formatted, press the (N) key.** At this point, you should once more see A> on the screen. This means the computer is back at the system level.

Step 8. **Take the last formatted diskette out of the drive. Put the diskette labeled "DOS" back into the drive and close the latch. Now do Steps 8 through 10 of the normal start-up process summarized at the bottom of page 37.**

When you finish these steps, your computer is back in BASIC. You should now see the Ok prompt on the screen.

1. Why do you have to format a diskette?
2. How can you tell whether your computer is at the system level or in BASIC?

Saving and Loading Programs

Take the DOS diskette out of the drive in your computer. Put one of your formatted diskettes into the drive and close the latch. You will now enter two short programs. You will then write copies of them on the diskette.

> **NOTE** *Spaces sometimes make no difference in BASIC statements. But spaces always matter when they are written between quotation marks. The string constant* `"BYEBYE"` *is different from* `"BYE BYE"`. *Be careful about spaces as you enter the lines below.*

```
NEW
CLS
```
Erase the memory and clear the screen.

```
10 PRINT "HELLO"
LIST
RUN
```
This is a one-line program.

```
SAVE "GREETING"
```
The red light on the diskette drive should come on. After a few moments, the computer should print OK on the screen.

```
FILES
```
You should see the red light come on again. You should also see GREETING.BAS on the screen.

Programs are stored in **files** on the diskette. The FILES command tells the computer to print on the output screen the names of all files on the diskette in your diskette drive. Your diskette now has only one file. Its full name is GREETING.BAS. The characters .BAS were put there by the computer. They mean that the information stored on the diskette is a BASIC program.

```
NEW
LIST
```
That erased the program from memory.

```
FILES
```
But it is still on the diskette.

```
10 PRINT "SO LONG"
LIST
RUN
```
Now you have a new program in memory.

```
SAVE "BYEBYE"
```
This moves a copy of the new program to the diskette. Its file name is BYEBYE.BAS.

```
NEW
```
Now it is gone from memory.

```
FILES
```
But it is on the diskette along with program GREETING.

```
LOAD "BYEBYE"
```
The LOAD command tells the computer to move a copy of a program from the diskette into memory.

```
LIST
```
Check that BYEBYE was loaded into memory.

```
FILES
```
Notice that BYEBYE is still on the diskette.

```
KILL "BYEBYE.BAS"
FILES
```
BYEBYE is no longer on the diskette.

```
LIST
```
But it is still in memory.

```
LOAD "GREETING"
LIST
```
When GREETING was loaded, it took the place of BYEBYE in memory.

```
KILL "GREETING.BAS"
FILES
```

The File not found message
means that there are no files left
on the diskette.

```
NEW
LIST
```

GREETING is gone from memory.

3. What does the FILES command tell the computer to do?
4. How would you move a program named RECORD from memory onto a diskette?
5. How would you move a program named RECORD from a diskette into memory?
6. How would you erase a program named RECORD from a diskette?

SUMMARY

Information on a diskette is divided into units called **files**. Your command SAVE "GREETING" told the computer to do two things: First, create a file named GREETING.BAS. Second, put into the file an exact copy of the BASIC program in memory. LOAD "GREETING" also told the computer to do two things: First, find on the diskette a file named GREETING.BAS. Second, put an exact copy of it into memory, erasing whatever was already in memory.

File names must begin with a letter of the alphabet. They can contain only letters and numbers. Not counting the .BAS part, the name can be up to *eight* characters long.

The table below summarizes the diskette commands you have learned in this session. Read the table carefully and make sure you understand the commands. Review the session if you need to.

Command	Description
SYSTEM	A BASIC command that tells the computer to leave BASIC and go to the system level.
FORMAT	Tells the computer to record magnetic marks on a diskette. The computer uses these marks when reading or writing information. This is a DOS command, so you must enter the SYSTEM command first.
SAVE "*name*"	Tells the computer to move a copy of the program in memory into the diskette file and store it under the name you select. The computer adds the suffix .BAS to the name. Whatever is already in the file is erased.
LOAD "*name*"	Tells the computer to erase the program now in memory and then to move a copy of the program from the diskette file named into memory.
KILL "*name*.BAS"	Tells the computer to erase the file named from the diskette. The suffix .BAS must be added after the name of the program.
FILES	Tells the computer to show on the screen the names of the files on the diskette.

INTRODUCTION TO GRAPHICS

SESSION 7

Session Goals

- Learn how to draw and erase points on the graphics screen.
- Learn how to draw lines and boxes on the graphics screen.
- Learn how to draw solid boxes in different colors.
- Learn a new way to make changes in program lines.

Exploring Graphics

There are really two important topics in this session. The first is **graphics**: using BASIC statements to draw points, lines, and solids. The second is **cursor editing**: using the cursor arrow keys and special editing keys to change a program line without retyping the whole line. We begin with graphics.

In Session 4, you learned that you can give the computer instructions in either the *immediate mode* or the *program mode*. In the immediate mode, the computer carries out the instructions as soon as you press the (Enter ⏎) key. In the program mode, nothing happens until you type RUN and press the (Enter ⏎) key.

Using the immediate mode is a good way to learn about new features of BASIC. That way, you can see what each new feature does as soon as you press the (Enter ⏎) key. In this session, you will work with graphics statements using the immediate mode. You will see how these statements tell the computer to plot points and draw lines on the screen.

Graphics Statements in Immediate Mode

Turn the computer on as outlined in Session 3. If you do not have a diskette drive, use Steps 1 through 7 at the top of page 37. If you have a diskette drive, use Steps 1 through 10 at the bottom of page 37. Then go on to the activities below. Use the (Shift ↑) key with the (9) and (0) keys to type the parentheses. If you get a Syntax error message, retype the line. Remember, spelling and punctuation matter.

PSET (100, 0)
_____

Illegal function call is a new error message. PSET is illegal on the text screen.

SCREEN 1
PSET (100, 0)
_____

There was no error message this time. PSET works on the graphics screen.

Look closely at the top of the screen. There should be a small dot about one-third of the way across the screen. PSET is one of the graphics statements on your PCjr.

COLOR 1
_____

Now you have a blue background.

```
PSET (200, 0)
PSET (300, 0)
```

Now you should see three dots across the top of the screen.

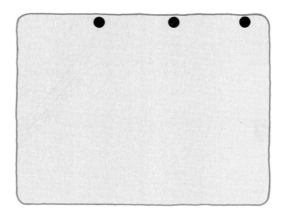

The first number after PSET tells the computer how far *across* the screen to place the dot. Zero is at the left edge of the screen and 319 is at the right edge. Let's see what the second number does.

```
CLS
PSET (160, 0)
PSET (160, 100)
PSET (160, 199)
```

Now you should see three dots down the center of the screen.

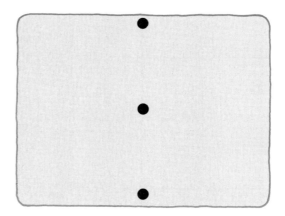

The second number after PSET tells the computer how far *down* the screen to place the dot. Zero is at the top of the screen and 199 is at the bottom.

The statement PSET (160, 100) tells the computer to draw this point:

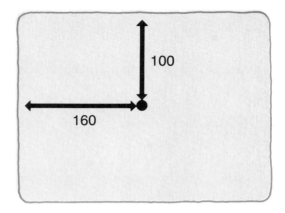

The four PSET statements below draw dots at the four corners of the screen. You might need to use (Alt│Ctrl│→) and (Alt│Ctrl│←) to see all the dots.

```
SCREEN 1
PSET (0, 0)
PSET (319, 0)
PSET (0, 199)
PSET (319, 199)
```

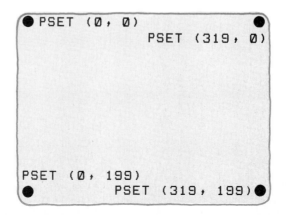

Now let's see how to erase a point on the screen. Here is the statement for that job:

PRESET (160, 100) _____

Don't press the (Enter ◁─┘) key yet. Look at the dot at the center of the screen. Now press the (Enter ◁─┘) key. What happened?

 1. What does PSET tell the computer to do?
2. How would you tell the computer to plot a point at the upper right-hand corner of the screen?
3. What numbers stand for the center of the screen?
4. What statement tells the computer to erase points from the screen?

Graphics Statements in Program Mode

You have seen how to use two graphics statements (PSET and PRESET) in the immediate mode. Let's shift to the program mode for the next experiments.

**NEW
CLS** _____

Erase the memory and clear the screen.

**10 CLS
20 PSET (200, 100)
30 PSET (280, 180)
LIST** _____

Check the program. Think about where the dots will appear when you run the program.

RUN _____

You should see two dots in the lower right-hand part of the screen.

**40 LINE (200, 100) - (280, 180)
LIST** _____

You have added a new line to the program. Notice that the two sets of numbers after LINE are the same as the numbers after the two PSET statements.

RUN
_____ The LINE statement draws a line.

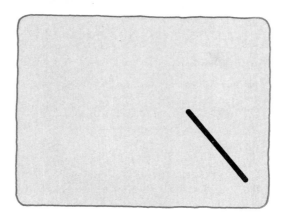

LIST
_____ Do you think it is necessary to
have the two PSET statements to
mark the ends of the line? Let's
find out.

20
30
LIST
_____ Now the program has only lines
10 and 40.

RUN
LIST
_____ Now you know.

 5. What is the purpose of the LINE statement?
6. What do the numbers in the LINE statement tell the computer to
do?

Cursor Editing

You have learned the main facts about the first topic in this session:
drawing points and lines. Now we turn to the second topic: a new way
to edit a program.

Look at the lower right-hand corner of the keyboard. You will see a
group of four keys with arrows printed next to them. You will be using
these keys along with the (Fn) key in this section.

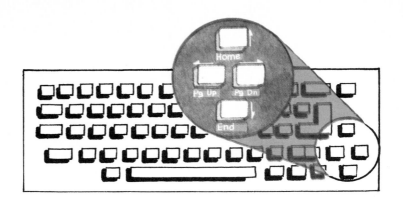

Press the ⬜➡️ **key several times and watch the screen.** The cursor should move to the right. **Press the** ⬅️⬜ **key a few times and watch what happens.** The cursor should move to the left.

You already know how to use line-number editing to remove, replace, or insert whole lines. You will next learn how to do **cursor editing**. You will find out how to make changes in a program line without retyping it. To do cursor editing, you will use the ⬅️⬜ and ⬜➡️ keys to move the cursor back and forth.

The following program should still be in memory:

```
10 CLS
40 LINE (200, 100) - (280, 180)
```

If it is not, enter it now. Then type the commands below:

RUN _____ You have seen this before.

EDIT 40 _____ Line 40 is printed on the screen.

EDIT 40 tells the computer that you want to edit line number 40. The computer prints the line on the screen. It places the cursor at the left end of the line and waits for you to do something. (If the computer finds a syntax error in a running program, it prints the bad line exactly as if you had typed the EDIT command.)

Use the ⬜➡️ **key to move the cursor to the 2 in 200. Press the number key** ①**and then the** (Enter ↵) **key.**

LIST _____ Look carefully at line 40.

Your new line 40 should look like this:

```
40 LINE (100, 100) - (280, 180)
```

You changed one character in line 4Ø without having to retype the whole line. Now let's find out what line this tells the computer to draw.

RUN ————————————————— The computer drew a new line.

EDIT 4Ø ————————————————— Let's edit line 4Ø again.

    Move the cursor over to the 2 in 28Ø. This is a good time to use the repeat-action of your keyboard: Just hold the ⟨→⟩ key down until the cursor is where you want it. **Press the number key ⟨1⟩ and then the ⟨Enter ↵⟩ key.**

LIST
RUN ————————————————— Still another line on the screen.

EDIT 4Ø ————————————————— Now for a new wrinkle.

    Look at the ⟨↓⟩ key. Notice the word "End" printed on a green stripe below the key. Also find the ⟨Fn⟩ key at the upper right-hand corner of the keyboard. It has a green border around three sides. The ⟨Fn⟩ key is called the "function" key. The ⟨Fn⟩ key is like a limited shift key. It gives different meanings to all the keys on the keyboard that have green stripes below them.

    Here is how to use the function key to move the cursor to the end of the line: **Press the ⟨Fn⟩ key and release it. Now press the ⟨↓⟩ key.** You should see the cursor move to the end of line 4Ø.

    In the future, instead of telling you to press these two keys, we will say to use the ⟨End⟩ function. You must remember to press the ⟨Fn⟩ key first. The colored stripes will help you remember to do that.

With the cursor at the end of line **40**, type **, ,** **B** and press the **(Enter ⏎)** key. You have added something to line **40**. The new line looks like this:

```
40 LINE (100, 100) - (180, 180),, B
```

Now run the program.

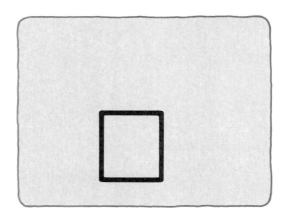

Before, the computer drew a line between the two points. Now, with the two commas and B at the end of the L I NE statement, the computer drew a box with the two points as opposite corners. B is an abbreviation for *box*.

Use the ED I T command and the (End) function again to change line **40** to look like this:

```
40 LINE (100, 100) - (180, 180),, BF
```

List the program and check it. Now run it. The symbol BF says to draw a box that is filled with a color. In the next section, you will see how to choose the color of the box.

7. How would you tell the computer you want to edit line 340?
8. What is the purpose of the (End) function?
9. How do you tell the computer you want the (End) function?
10. How do you tell the computer you are finished editing a line?

Controlling Screen Colors

You have just used the LINE statement to draw lines on the screen. When you add a B at the end of the statement, the computer draws boxes. When you add BF instead, the computer draws filled boxes. The next step is to learn how to control the "fill" color. You will also learn more about cursor editing.

In this section, you will use the (Ins) key to insert characters into a line. You will use the (Del) key to delete characters from a line.

The program below should still be in memory. **If it is not, enter it now.**

```
10 CLS
40 LINE (100, 100) - (180, 180),, BF
```

Next, you will use the EDIT command.

EDIT 40 _____ Look at the screen.

You should see line 40 with the cursor at the left end. Now let's see how (Del) works.

Use the (⟶) key to move the cursor to the L in LINE. Now, watch the screen and press the (Del) key once. The L should disappear. The rest of the line should move left one space. **Press (Del) three more times.** Now all of LINE is gone. **Press (Enter ⤶) now. Then list the program and look at line 40.**

"Del" stands for *delete*. The (Del) key tells the computer to delete a character from the line. The cursor position tells it which character to delete.

Now let's put LINE back into line 40. **Type EDIT 40 again. Use the (⟶) key to put the cursor at the second space after the line number. Press and release the (Ins) key.** Notice the shape of the cursor: It is now a short rectangle. This tells you that the computer is in **insert mode.**

Now press the ⓛ key. Notice that the letter L appeared at the cursor position. The cursor and the rest of the line moved one space to the right. **Finish typing INE. Then press one of the arrow keys.** Look at the cursor: The computer is no longer in insert mode. **Finally, press** (Enter ⏎) **and list your program. It should look like this again:**

```
10 CLS
40 LINE (100, 100) - (180, 180),, BF
```

The (Ins) key tells the computer to enter insert mode. Characters you type after that are inserted into the line at the position of the cursor. Touching a cursor key ends insert mode. As always, you must press (Enter ⏎) when you finish all editing of a line.

Now let's get back to graphics. You have probably been wondering about the two commas at the end of line 40. It may seem strange to have two commas together separating nothing. You can put a number between the commas to select a fill color. Cursor editing is the easiest way to do this job.

EDIT 40

Call up line 40 for editing.

Move the cursor to the comma just before the BF. Press the (Ins) **key.** Notice that the computer is now in *insert mode*. **Type a space and a 1.** Notice that you have inserted two new characters into the line. **Press the** (Enter ⏎) **key.** The big cursor is back. This tells you that the computer is no longer in insert mode.

List the program. Here is what it should look like:

```
10 CLS
40 LINE (100, 100) - (180, 180), 1, BF
```

Now run the program. Notice the new color of the box.

Use the EDIT command and cursor editing to change the 1 before BF to a 2. Run the program again. Did the fill color change? **Now change the 2 to a 3 and run the program again.** The box should be white once more.

Call up line 40 again for editing. Move the cursor to the space before the 3. Now press the (Del) **key.** Notice that the space disappeared. **Press the** (Del) **key again.** Now the 3 is gone. **Press** (Enter ⏎) **to finish the editing. Then list and run the program.** As you see, leaving out the fill-color number has the same effect as using 3 for the color.

11. What fill colors correspond to numbers 1, 2, and 3?
12. How can you insert new characters into a program line?
13. How can you delete a character from a program line?

Duplicating Program lines

Often when you are writing a program, many lines are almost the same. In that case, you can use the EDIT feature of the PC*jr* to save a lot of typing. **Call up line 40 for editing.** The cursor should be over the 4 in the line number. **Type 5 and press the (Enter ⏎) key. List the program.** What has happened?

Here is what took place: When you changed the 4 to a 5, the line number on the screen became 50. Then when you pressed the (Enter ⏎) key, the computer copied the whole line from the screen, just as if you had typed it on the keyboard. The line has 50 as its line number. So your program has a new line 50 as well as the old line 40. Both lines contain the same statement. This is a handy way to make a copy of a line without retyping it.

Use the method you have just learned again. Make a new line 60 with the same statement as in lines 40 and 50. Here is what your program should look like now:

```
10 CLS
40 LINE (100, 100) - (180, 180),, BF
50 LINE (100, 100) - (180, 180),, BF
60 LINE (100, 100) - (180, 180),, BF
```

Now edit lines 40, 50, and 60 so the fill colors look like this:

```
10 CLS
40 LINE (100, 100) - (180, 180),1, BF
50 LINE (100, 100) - (180, 180),2, BF
60 LINE (100, 100) - (180, 180),3, BF
```

Run the program a few times. You can see the three colors, but they change rapidly. Let's improve the picture.

In line **50**, change the upper left-hand corner numbers from (**100 , 100**) to (**120 , 120**). Then in line **60**, change the upper left-hand corner numbers from (**100 , 100**) to (**140 , 140**). Now **list the program and check it out.** It should look like this now:

```
10 CLS
40 LINE (100, 100) - (180, 180),1, BF
50 LINE (120, 120) - (180, 180),2, BF
60 LINE (140, 140) - (180, 180),3, BF
```

Then run the program. You should see three overlapping boxes, each with a different color.

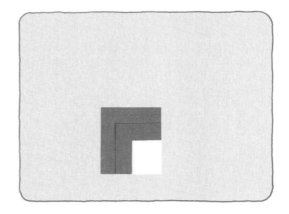

Let's make one more box. You will need another L I NE statement. **First, make a copy of line 60, changing the line number to 70. Then change the first pair of numbers in line 70 to (160 , 160). Finally, change the color number to 0.** The new line should look like this:

```
70 LINE (160, 160) - (180, 180), 0, BF
```

LIST
RUN

Now there are four filled boxes on the screen. The smallest one has the same color as the background.

COLOR 2

That changed the background color.

<u>**COLOR 3**</u>

So did that. The big square is still there. However, its color is the same as the background.

<u>**COLOR 4**</u>

The background is red now.

> **Type SCREEN 0 and press the `Enter ⏎` key to switch back to the text screen. List the program. Run it.** The program lists as usual, but it won't run. The `Illegal function call in 40` error message shows up again. It appears for the same reason it did at the beginning of this session: Like `PSET`, `LINE` works only on the graphics screen. You can avoid problems like this by putting a `SCREEN 1` statement in any program that uses the graphics screen.

```
5 SCREEN 1
6 COLOR 1
LIST
RUN
```

There should be no error message this time.

14. In your own words, explain how to make a copy of line `50` in which the only difference is that the new line number is `60`.
15. What happens if you ask the computer to perform a `PSET`, `PRESET`, or `LINE` statement while on the text screen?

PROJECT

● At the end of this project, you will want to save your program on cassette tape or diskette. Refer to Sessions 5 and 6 if you have forgotten how to save a program.

The figure below shows the positions of five points on the graphics screen. If you connect them one way, you will draw a pentagon. If you connect them another way, you will draw a star. Write a program using five LINE statements to draw the pentagon. Add five more statements to draw the star. Remember to include statements at the beginning of the program to switch to the graphics screen, clear the screen, and select a screen color.

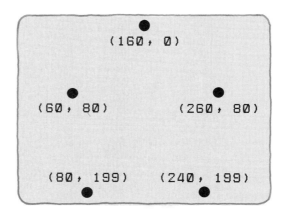

When you have finished the program, save it on a diskette or tape cassette under the name DESIGN. You may want to show your program to friends and explain to them how it works.

SUMMARY
In this session, you learned three new graphics statements. You also learned how to use cursor editing to change program lines without retyping them. These topics are summarized in the tables on the next two pages. Take a moment to review each topic. If you are not sure you understand a topic, turn back to the section where it is discussed and read about it again. Don't move ahead in this book until you feel confident that you are learning things well.

Cursor Editing	Description
EDIT *n*	Command that writes the line with line number *n* on the screen and puts the cursor at the beginning of the line. After all changes are made, the new line is put in memory when the (Enter ◄┘) key is pressed.
(⟶)	Right-arrow key; moves the cursor right in the edit line.
(⟵)	Left-arrow key; moves the cursor left in the edit line.
(Fn)	Function key; gives another meaning to a key with a green stripe below it, which is pressed next.
(End) function	(Fn) key plus the (L) key; moves the cursor to the end of the edit line.
(Ins)	Insert key; opens the line being edited at the position of the cursor. Characters typed after that are inserted into the line. Insert mode ends when the (Enter ◄┘), (⟵), or (⟶) key is pressed.
(Del)	Delete key; removes the character at the cursor position. All characters to the right are shifted left one space.

Screen Coordinate	Description
X-coordinate	Locates a point measured horizontally to the right from the left edge of the screen. In medium-resolution graphics, 0 is at the left edge of the screen and 319 is at the right edge.
Y-coordinate	Locates a point measured vertically down from the top of the screen. In medium-resolution graphics, 0 is at the top of the screen and 199 is at the bottom.

Statement	Description
PSET (x, y)	Pronounced "point set." Tells the computer to draw a point at screen coordinates x and y. In medium-resolution graphics, the letter x stands for a horizontal-coordinate number between 0 to 319. The letter y stands for a vertical-coordinate number from 0 to 199.
PRESET (x, y)	Pronounced "point reset." Tells the computer to erase a point at screen coordinates x and y. The letters x and y have the same meanings as above.
LINE (x1, y1) - (x2, y2)	Tells the computer to draw a straight line from screen coordinates x1 and y1 to screen coordinates x2 and y2. In medium-resolution graphics, x1, y1, x2, and y2 stand for coordinate numbers as above. The phrases , , B or , n, BF can be added to the end of the LINE statement. , , B tells the computer to draw a box using the points in the LINE statement as diagonal corners. , n, BF tells the computer to fill in the box with fill color n. The letter n stands for a number between 0 and 3. (See below.)

Table of Foreground Colors

Fill Number	Color
0	Background
1	Cyan
2	Magenta
3	White

INTRODUCTION TO MUSIC

SESSION 8

Session Goals

- Learn to use the music sublanguage in Cartridge BASIC.
- Learn to read standard music scores in terms of the music sublanguage.
- Transcribe a simple tune into the music sublanguage.

The PLAY Statement

You don't have to do this session if you don't want to. However, it can be a lot of fun. You can do this session only if you have Cartridge BASIC on your PCjr. In this session, you will learn how to tell your computer to play music. You will tell it to do so using a special language similar to the ordinary way music is written. Even if you have never had music lessons, you should be able to do most of the things in this session.

Start the computer with Cartridge BASIC in the usual way. Turn up the volume on your TV set, if you are using one. Then go on to the activities below.

```
CLS
SOUND 1046, 9.1
```
You have used the SOUND statement before. On the piano, the C above middle C has a frequency of 1046 Hz. A duration of 9.1 equals 1/2 second.

```
PLAY "C"
```
That produced the same note. In Cartridge BASIC, PLAY can be used as well as SOUND for music.

```
PLAY C
```
Oops! The letters after PLAY must be inside quotation marks.

```
PLAY "Q"
```
Oops again! You can play C but not Q. Q is not a note on the musical scale.

```
PLAY "C D E"
```
You can play several notes in a row.

```
PLAY "CDE"
```
It's OK to leave out the spaces between the note letters. However, spaces make the musical phrase easier to read.

```
CLS
NEW
10 PLAY "C D E F G A B C"
```
You can use PLAY in program mode.

Now you have a simple one-line program. It tells the computer to play a scale corresponding to the white notes on the piano. Notice that the last C in the scale sounded the same as the first. Let's make the last C an octave higher. **Use the EDIT 10 command and the (Ins) key to change line 10 to look like this:**

```
10 PLAY "C D E F G A B > C"
```

Run the program and listen carefully to the scale. This time, the C after the > symbol should be an octave higher than the first C.

Run the program again. Now insert another > symbol after the first quotation mark. Line 10 should look like this:

```
10 PLAY "> C D E F G A B > C"
```

Run the new version. This time the whole scale should sound an octave higher than it did the first time. The second C should be *two* octaves higher.

Now use the EDIT command to change the first > symbol in line 10 to a < symbol. Run the program once more. This time, the scale should sound an octave lower than it did the first time you heard it.

Use EDIT again to insert another < symbol after the first quotation mark in line 10. It should now look like this:

```
10 PLAY "< < C D E F G A B > C"
```

Run this version. You moved the scale down another octave.

You should think of > and < as "octave-shift" symbols. Each one changes the octave in which the notes are to be played. The > symbol moves the notes one octave higher. The < symbol moves the notes one octave lower.

There is another way to tell the computer what octave to use. **Replace the two < symbols by O2 in line 10. Be sure to use the letter O, not the number 0.** The line should now look like this:

```
10 PLAY "O2 C D E F G A B > C"
```

Run the program. Notice that the scale sounded the same as it did the last time. The symbol O2 tells the computer to begin playing the scale in octave number 2. If you do not tell the computer what octave to use, it uses octave 4. So two < symbols will lower the pitch to octave 2. That is why the two scales you just played sounded the same.

You have seen how to play all the "white key" notes of the piano scale. Now let's see how to play the "black key" notes. Enter this line:

```
20 PLAY "O2 C C+ D E- E F F+ G A- A B- B > C"
LIST
```

Check the new program line carefully. It will appear on two screen lines.

```
RUN
```

Now the program plays two scales.

The musical phrase in line 10 tells the computer to play the white notes beginning at C in octave 2 and ending at C in octave 3. The musical phrase in line 20 tells the computer to play the white *and* black notes in the same range. A plus sign after a letter stands for a *sharp* note. A minus sign stands for a *flat* note.

Line 20 is very long. So let's break it into two lines and see what happens. **First, use the EDIT command to make a copy of line 20 with the line number changed to 30. Then list the program. Make sure you have the same statement twice.**

Second, edit line 20 by deleting all notes after F+.

Third, edit line 30 by deleting O2 and all the notes through F+. Then list the program. It should now look like this:

```
10 PLAY "O2 C D E F G A B > C"
20 PLAY "O2 C C+ D E- E F F+"
30 PLAY "G A- A B- B > C"
```

Run this version of the program. There should be no change in the sound from the last time. Notice that the G in line 30 was played in the same octave (octave 2) as the F+ in line 20. *Once you set an octave, it stays in effect until you tell the computer to change it.*

1. How would you write "F sharp" in the music sublanguage?
2. If you type PLAY "H", why will the computer print an error message on the screen?
3. If you do not give an octave in the PLAY statement, which octave will the computer use?
4. The computer is playing notes in octave 3. What are two ways to tell it to change to octave 4 before playing the next note?

Note Lengths and Pauses

The music sublanguage in Cartridge BASIC gives you a way to play every note in the scale in any of seven octaves. The notes are named A through G. You may add + for sharps and – for flats. You tell the computer which octave to use by putting in an O followed by a number. The lowest octave is numbered 0. The highest is 6. You saw that if you do not tell the computer which octave to use, it picks octave 4. The seven-octave range lets you play any of the notes on the piano.

Of course, there is more to music than playing different notes. Notes usually have different lengths. Often, there are also pauses of different lengths in the music. The tempo at which music is played changes from piece to piece or even within a piece. You will learn how to tell the computer about these things next.

You should have the program below in your computer. **If not, enter it now.**

```
10 PLAY "O2 C D E F G A B > C"
20 PLAY "O2 C C+ D E- E F F+"
30 PLAY "G A- A B- B > C"
```

Remember that line 10 tells the computer to play the white-note scale on the piano. Lines 20 and 30 tell the computer to play a scale with both white and black notes.

15 PLAY "P4"
LIST
RUN

Now there is a pause between the two scales.

There is no note named P in the scale. Instead, a P in a musical phrase tells the computer to make no sound. This is exactly the same as a **rest note**. P1 produces a *whole-note* rest. P2 produces a *half-note* rest, P4 a *quarter-note* rest, P8 an *eighth-note* rest, and so on.

We used P4 for the pause, since the notes you have been playing are also quarter notes. Unless you tell the computer otherwise, it always plays quarter notes. Let's see next how to change the length of a note.

Edit line 10 so that it looks like this:

```
10 PLAY "O2 C8 D E8 F G8 A B8 > C"
```

Run the program a few times. Listen carefully to the lengths of the notes.

In the scale, you heard D, F, A, and C as quarter notes. (Remember that if you don't specify a length, the computer will play quarter notes.) C, E, G, and B were eighth notes, caused by the 8 after each of these notes. If a 1, 2, 4, 8, 16, 32, or 64 follows a note in a musical phrase, that note is played as a whole, half, quarter, eighth, sixteenth, thirty-second, or sixty-fourth note. In music notation, these notes and the equivalent rests look like this:

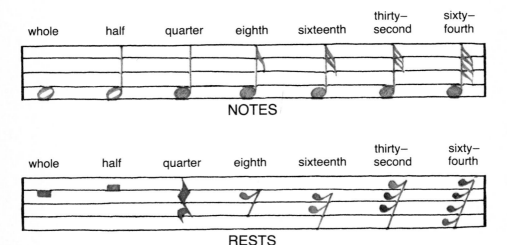

5. What characters would you put into the musical phrase after PLAY if you wanted an eighth-note rest?
6. Explain in your own words what the musical phrase O3 C1 D2 E4 F8 in a PLAY statement would tell the computer to do.
7. Write a musical phrase for a PLAY statement that tells the computer to do the following: Play a complete scale using the white keys only, in octave 2, with all sixteenth notes.

Controlling Tempo and Style

You have learned a lot about playing music on your computer. You can now tell the computer to play any note in any of seven octaves. Moreover, you can also control the lengths of the notes and rests. But there are still some elements of good music that you haven't studied yet.

If you watch an orchestra play, you can easily see that the beat is set by the conductor. If the conductor moves the baton faster, the **tempo** (or beat) is higher. The slower the conductor moves the baton, the slower the tempo. In addition, the player controls the style in which the music is played. Music can be played with no silence between notes (*legato*) or with noticeable silence between notes (*staccato*).

Erase any program you may have in your PC*jr*. Enter the program below. The statements are all the same. Thus, you may want to use the EDIT command to copy the first line you type.

```
NEW
100 PLAY "O3 C C E E G G E2 P1"
110 PLAY "O3 C C E E G G E2 P1"
120 PLAY "O3 C C E E G G E2 P1"
LIST
```
———————————————————— Check the program for errors.

```
RUN
```
———————————————————— You should hear the same phrase three times.

Now let's add three more lines to your program and find out what they do. (Don't type NEW now, since you are adding lines to the old program.)

```
95 PLAY "T60"
105 PLAY "T120"
115 PLAY "T240"
LIST
RUN
```
———————————————————— That should have made a big difference.

You can control the tempo at which the computer plays a musical phrase by putting a T (which stands for *tempo*) into a PLAY statement. The number following T tells the computer how many quarter notes to play per minute. T60 tells the computer to play 60 quarter notes per minute. This is a very slow, or *largo*, tempo. T240 is very fast, or *prestissimo*. If you do not tell the computer anything about tempo, it will use a value of 120, which is the *moderato* tempo.

Now let's explore the "connections" between notes. **Enter the following lines:**

```
NEW
```
———————————————————— Erase the old program in memory.

```
100 PLAY "T240"
110 PLAY "A A A A A A A P4"
120 PLAY "A A A A A A A P4"
130 PLAY "A A A A A A A P4"
RUN
```
———————————————————— That is pretty long.

```
105 PLAY "ML"
115 PLAY "MN"
125 PLAY "MS"
LIST
```
——————————————————— Check the program for errors.

```
RUN
```
——————————————————— Listen carefully to the three sets of notes.

```
RUN
```
——————————————————— Listen again.

In line 105, ML stands for **music legato**. Each of the notes is played for its full length. The notes run together with no break between them. In line 115, MN stands for **music normal**. Each of the notes is played for seven-eighths of its full length. You can just barely hear a short break between the notes. If you don't have an M in a musical phrase, the computer assumes MN, or music normal. Finally, in line 125, MS stands for **music staccato**. Each of the notes is played for three-fourths of its full length. There is a noticeable break between the notes. You can use these features to control the "smoothness" of the music.

8. What statement would tell the computer to play music in a *legato* style with a tempo of 80?
9. If the phrase MS T180 O2 is used in a PLAY statement, what does this tell the computer to do?

Standard Music Notation

This section will help you read standard music and write it for the computer. The drawing below shows part of a piano keyboard with each of the keys labeled.

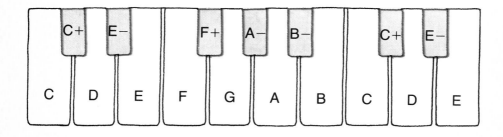

Music is written on a *staff* with five lines and four spaces. The drawing below shows the staff in the *treble clef* with the lines and spaces labeled.

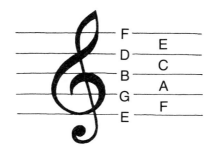

There is a memory trick you can use to remember the names of the lines and spaces. The lines are the same as the first letter in each word of the phrase "Every Good Boy Deserves Fudge." The spaces form the word FACE.

PROJECTS

● The music score below is the complete melody of "Mary Had a Little Lamb." Use the tools you have learned about in this session to play this music on the PCjr. If you want to save your program and have forgotten how, see Sessions 5 and 6.

Mary Had a Little Lamb

● The PLAY statement is a good deal richer than we have shown here. Now is a good time to learn to use other sources of information about your PCjr. If you have the IBM PCjr BASIC reference book, turn to Chapter 4. Look up the PLAY statement there. You will find a description of the complete form of the statement. There is also a general discussion of how it works. Finally, there is a full description of all the symbols you can use in the statement. Take a few minutes to read the pages that tell about the PLAY statement.

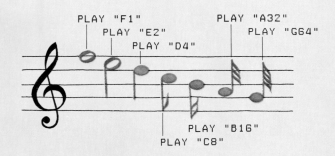

SUMMARY

In this session, you learned how to use the PLAY statement to tell the computer to play music. You saw that PLAY is always followed by a musical phrase in quotation marks. You learned that there are two main kinds of musical statements: One tells the computer *what* notes or rests to play. The other tells the computer *how* to play the notes. The table on the next page summarizes this information. Look at it carefully. If there is something you still don't understand, go back and read about it in the session.

PLAY *Statement Symbols*	*Description*
A to G	Tells the computer to play the note named. If the note corresponds to a black key on the piano, the letter may be followed by a + (sharp) or by a - (flat). Also, each letter may be followed by *n*, a number that tells how long to play that single note. Examples of the meaning of *n* are shown in the table below:

n	*Length*
1	Whole note
2	Half note
4	Quarter note
8	Eighth note
16	Sixteenth note
32	Thirty-second note
64	Sixty-fourth note

P *n*	Produces a rest. The length of the rest is determined by *n* as shown in the table above.
O *n*	Sets one of seven octaves. The lowest octave is numbered 0, the highest 6. If this symbol is not included, the computer uses octave 4. Middle C is the C in octave 3.
>	Changes the octave to the next higher octave. If the octave is already octave 6, no change takes place.
<	Changes the octave to the next lower octave. If the octave is already octave 0, no change takes place.
T *n*	Sets the tempo to *n* quarter notes per minute. If this clause is omitted, 120 quarter notes per minute is used.
ML	Stands for *music legato*. Each note is played its full duration and connects without a break to the next note.
MN	Stands for *music normal*. Each note is played seven-eighths of its full duration. If no M symbol is present, the computer uses this mode.
MS	Stands for *music staccato*. Each note is played three-quarters of its full duration. There is a noticeable break between notes.

SOFTWARE TOOLS

PART TWO

*B*efore you go on, now is a good time to take stock of all the things you've done and learned so far. You know how to turn the computer on. You can write and edit simple programs. You can save and load programs on a cassette or a diskette. You can list programs on the screen. You can tell the computer to play music and draw pictures in color.

Just as important, you know a lot about what computers can do. You know the main parts of a computer. You know how the parts work together to carry out commands and to run programs. With all this new knowledge and these new skills, you have a right to feel very accomplished—and maybe just a bit bushed.

This is a good time to decide what you want to do next with your PCjr. Perhaps you want to use it to help with writing and typing. Or perhaps you want the PCjr to help you keep track of your record collection or the entries in your address book. Or else you may want your computer to play a game. For these uses, all you need now are the right programs. Your computer dealer will be happy to show you dozens of programs to do these jobs.

But what if—now or in a few weeks—you want your computer to do something for which there is no program? If you know how, you can write the program you need yourself. The rest of this book will give you the tools you need to write your own programs. Part Two begins with the most important tool of all: That is a systematic way to break complex problems into simple pieces. All your programming in the future will depend on this tool.

We can't overemphasize the importance of the material in Part Two. If you master each of the sessions, you will be able to move easily through the rest of the book. On the other hand, lack of understanding of the key points in Part Two will return to plague you through the rest of the book. Our advice is to take your time and review whenever necessary.

INTRODUCTION
TO SUBROUTINES

SESSION 9

Session Goals

- Group blocks of statements into subroutines.
- Learn how to organize programs using subroutines.
- Learn to use an advanced method of screen editing.

Review

In Part One, you have learned to take control of your PC*jr*. By now, you are familiar with the keyboard. You know how to edit program lines. You have used a few BASIC statements in programs. You have explored sound and color. Most important, you have started building a mental picture of how the computer carries out your commands.

So far, your programs have been fairly short. Mainly, you have been exploring individual commands and statements to see how they work. As you learn more, your programs will become longer and more complex. As that happens, you will pay less attention to how each individual statement works. You will care more about how to organize the statements into meaningful units.

Most beginners try to solve a large programming problem by just writing one statement after another. Seldom do they do any planning or organizing. This approach is sure to lead to failure and frustration. The writer gets lost in the details. Programs written this way are known as "plates of spaghetti." They are tangled collections of statements. They are hard to read and understand. Changes made in one part of such programs often cause unexpected results in other parts.

There is a well-organized way to write programs. It avoids most of these problems. People use the terms **structured programming** and **top-down organization** to describe this method. In this session, you will learn how to use the **subroutine**. Subroutines are a key part of this better kind of programming.

Packages of Statements

In Session 3, you wrote a program that played the first few notes of "Mary Had a Little Lamb." As the computer played each note, it changed the screen color and wrote messages on the screen. Your program was fairly long. If you completed the project and finished the song, your program began like this:

```
100 SCREEN 1
110 CLS
120 PRINT
130 SOUND 659, 10
140 COLOR 1
150 PRINT "MA-"
160 SOUND 587, 10
170 COLOR 14
180 PRINT "RY"
190 SOUND 523, 10
200 COLOR 4
210 PRINT "HAD"
220 SOUND 587, 10
230 COLOR 14
240 PRINT "A"
250 SOUND 659, 10
260 COLOR 1
270 PRINT "LIT-"
280 SOUND 659, 10
290 COLOR 1
300 PRINT "TLE"
310 SOUND 659, 10
320 COLOR 1
330 PRINT "LAMB"
```

You can see that a lot of lines are repeated in the program. For example, the SOUND and COLOR statements in lines 130–140 are the same as in lines 250–260, 280–290, and 310–320.

Your program would be simpler if you could take out the repetition. It would be nice to tell the computer certain things only once. These include how to play a note, what color to use with that note, and what message to print on the screen. You might do so by deciding on a group of statements you want to use over and over. Then, whenever you wanted to use those statements, you might simply ask the computer to perform the whole group.

BASIC, like all other programming languages, gives you a way to do this. First, you must package the group of statements together into a **subroutine**. Next, you must use a new statement to tell the computer to perform the whole package.

Let's begin by building the package. Our first package will tell the computer to do these three things: First, sound the note middle C. Second, set the background color to blue. Third, print the word DO (as in "do, re, mi …"). **Start the computer in the usual way. If it is already on, enter the NEW command. Remember to read the comments on the right before entering the characters on the left. Now do the things below:**

SCREEN 1 —————————— Set graphics mode.

```
100 SOUND 523, 10
110 COLOR 1
120 PRINT "DO"
```
LIST —————————— Check for errors.

RUN —————————— Watch and listen.

If everything went as planned, you first heard middle C (which has a frequency of 523 Hz). Next, the screen turned blue. Then, the word DO was written on the screen. It took three statements to do these things. You can perform this three-statement package by typing RUN. But there is another way to do the same things. Let's take a look at it next.

130 RETURN —————————— That's a new statement.

LIST
RUN —————————— The program ran, but there was an error message about a missing GOSUB.

GOSUB 100 —————————— This time the three-statement package was performed with no problems.

CLS
LIST —————————— Read the complete program.

A block of statements that ends with a RETURN statement is called a **subroutine**. You tell the computer to perform a subroutine with a GOSUB statement. The word GOSUB must be followed by the line number of the first line of the subroutine. You used GOSUB in the immediate mode. You can also use it in the program mode.

The subroutine you've been writing plays middle C, sets the background color to blue, and prints the word DO. Here is all of this subroutine:

```
100 SOUND 523, 10
110 COLOR 1
120 PRINT "DO"
130 RETURN
```

1. What statement must go at the end of a subroutine?
2. Describe two ways you can tell the computer to perform a package of statements.

Labeling Your Subroutine

The computer accepted the subroutine you have just written with no complaint. Computers pay no attention to matters of style. However, style *is* important to people who work with programs. How easy is it for *you* to read the subroutine? How easy is it for you to read any other part of a program? From now on, we will stress style and organization in programs. A clear style of writing will make it easy to read, understand, and change your programs. Let's begin by adding a remark at the beginning of the subroutine. It will serve to remind you of what the subroutine does.

90 REM SUB DO ——————— REM is a new statement.

CLS
LIST ——————— This is your subroutine.

GOSUB 90 ——————— The computer should perform the subroutine as before.

90 'SUB DO ——————— The apostrophe key is just to the left of the (Enter ⏎) key.

```
CLS
LIST
```
Read the program. Now line 90 is different.

```
GOSUB 90
```
Again, the computer performed the subroutine correctly.

Both versions of line 90 are **remark** statements. A remark statement begins with the letters REM or an apostrophe. When the computer sees REM or an apostrophe after the line number, it ignores the rest of the line. The remark statement allows you to put any words you want into a program. Such remarks make the program easier to read and understand. On your PC*jr*, you can use an apostrophe as an abbreviation for REM. We will do so from now on.

You should always begin each subroutine with a remark statement that tells the purpose of the subroutine. Since this subroutine plays DO, we have said so in the remark statement. The word SUB in the remark statement reminds you that the package of statements is a subroutine. (Later on, you will write other kinds of program blocks. Thus, it is wise to get in the habit of labeling them.)

Next, let's renumber the subroutine lines. This moves them out of the way of other lines you will add to the program later. **Enter the command RENUM 1000.** Your program should now look like this:

```
1000  'SUB DO
1010  SOUND 523, 10
1020  COLOR 1
1030  PRINT "DO"
1040  RETURN
```

3. With what kind of statement should a subroutine begin?
4. What does an apostrophe stand for?

The statement GOSUB 1000 tells the computer to perform the three-statement package in lines 1010–1040. You could see these three statements more easily if they were indented like this:

```
1000 'SUB DO
1010    SOUND 523, 10
1020    COLOR 1
1030    PRINT "DO"
1040 RETURN
```

There is a blank space after each line number. If the statement is a remark, an apostrophe goes in the next space. Otherwise, another blank space goes there. The subroutine begins in line 1000 with a remark statement. It tells the purpose of the subroutine. The subroutine ends with the RETURN statement in line 1040. The lines in between are indented two extra spaces. This shows clearly that they are the main part of the subroutine. This is called the **body** of the subroutine.

Now let's add these spaces to the subroutine. You already know how to use the EDIT command to make changes in program lines. However, there is an easier way to do a job like this:

Step 1. **Clear the screen and list the program.**
Step 2. **Press the ⬆ cursor key, which is near the lower right-hand corner of the keyboard. Use this key to move the cursor up to line 1010.**
Step 3. **Use the ➡ key to move the cursor to the space after the line number.**
Step 4. **Press the (Ins) key and type three spaces.**
Step 5. **Press the (Enter ⏎) key.**
Step 6. **Repeat Steps 3, 4, and 5 for lines 1020 and 1030 of the subroutine.**
Step 7. **Repeat Step 3 for line 1040. Press the (Ins) key. Insert only one space this time. Then press the (Enter ⏎) key. Use the ⬇ key to move the cursor down out of the program.**
Step 8. **List the program and check for errors. It should look like this:**

```
1000 'SUB DO
1010    SOUND 523, 10
1020    COLOR 1
1030    PRINT "DO"
1040 RETURN
```

Here is how screen editing works: If you place the cursor in a program line on the screen and then press the (Enter ◄┘) key, the effect is the same as if you had typed the whole line on the keyboard. In the editing process on the previous page, you inserted spaces in each line. You then pressed the (Enter ◄┘) key each time. (You could also have deleted or retyped characters in the line before pressing the (Enter ◄┘) key.) The computer wrote each line into memory with the old line number but *with the new changes.*

Suppose you need to make several changes in a program. This method is much faster than calling up each line with the EDIT command. If the cursor is at a line that needs no changes, simply press the (↓) key to skip that line. *When you are finished, be sure to use the (↓) key to move the cursor below the program.*

Let's explore screen editing a bit more. **Use the arrow keys to put the cursor on the word OK, which is just below the program listing. Press the (Enter◄┘) key.** You got the Syntax error message because you entered the word OK, which is not a BASIC command or statement. Remember, any time you press the (Enter ◄┘) key, you are entering a line into the computer.

Move the cursor to line 1040. Use the (End) function: Press the (Fn) key first and the (↓) key second. The (End) function works the same way in screen editing as with the EDIT command. This is also true of the other editing keys.

Use the (◄─) key (not the backspace key) to move the cursor to the R in RETURN. Hold down the (Ctrl) key. While the (Ctrl) key is down, press the (Fn) key and then the (↓) key. (We will call this the (Ctrl|End) function in the future.) The (Ctrl|End) function is a quick way to delete the end of a line. It chops the line off from the cursor position to the last character.

Next, press (Esc). It is on the upper left-hand corner of the keyboard. The (Esc) key erases the whole line from the screen. **Use (Esc) to erase the other four program lines.**

Your program listing is no longer on the screen. However, it is still in memory. (Thus, you did not change the version in memory. You did not press the (Enter ◄┘) key while editing.) Here is an easy way to get a new listing: **Move the cursor to the word LIST and press the (Enter◄┘) key.** This has exactly the same effect as typing LIST and pressing the (Enter ◄┘) key.

Finally, let's explore the (Home) function. **Press the (Fn) key and release it. Then press the (↑) key.** (In the future, we will refer to this key combination as the (Home) function.) Notice where the cursor is now. This is called the "home" position. **Hold down (Ctrl). While it is down, use the (Home) function again.** This clears the screen and sends the cursor home. **Enter the LIST command.** Notice that the (Ctrl|Home) function erased the screen but not the memory.

We've now taken a look at all the editing keys. In case you're wondering, the (PgUp) and (PgDn) functions have no effect in BASIC. The other editing keys may be used with the EDIT command. They can also be used to edit any line on the screen. The changes you make in a line take effect only when you press the (Enter ◄┘) key. When you do that, the whole line is entered into the computer. The effect is the same as if you had typed the line on the keyboard. Suppose you make a change and forget to press (Enter ◄┘). In that case, the change exists on the screen only.

5. What are two ways to clear the screen on your PC*jr*?
6. What are the different effects of the (End) function and the (Ctrl | End) function?
7. A friend says, "Look at line 320. I just edited it. You can see the changes at the top of the screen. I listed the program and you can see that line 320 wasn't changed. Why?" What did your friend probably forget to do?

SUMMARY

In this session, you wrote your first subroutine. You used the GOSUB statement to tell the computer to perform the subroutine. Finally, you used screen editing to indent the body of the subroutine. The table below summarizes these new ideas. Read the table carefully. If you find anything you don't understand, review the session.

Statement	Description
GOSUB n	A statement telling the computer to perform the subroutine beginning at line n. The letter n stands for the line number.
RETURN	A statement telling the computer to stop performing the statements in a subroutine.
REM	A statement that allows you to put any remark you want into a program without affecting the way the program works. (In this version of BASIC, you may use an apostrophe to stand for REM.)

Editing Feature	Description
(↑) (↓)	Up-arrow and down-arrow keys move the cursor from line to line on the screen.
(Ctrl | End) function	Deletes all characters to the end of the current program line, beginning with the character at the cursor position.
(Home) function	Moves the cursor to the upper left-hand corner of the screen.
(Ctrl | Home) function	Clears the screen and puts the cursor at the upper left-hand corner.

WRITING A PROGRAM WITH SUBROUTINES

SESSION 10

Session Goals

- Learn two modes of playing music.
- Add two subroutines to the one you wrote in the last session.
- List a specific block of program lines.
- Write a main routine to control the subroutine.
- Start building a subroutine "toolkit."

The SOUND Statement in Cartridge BASIC

In Session 3, we told you that the SOUND statement works differently in Cassette BASIC and Cartridge BASIC. Now is the time to learn the difference. *You will need to know about this difference whether you are using Cassette BASIC or Cartridge BASIC.*

In Session 3, you found that the first SOUND statement in a program tells the computer to *start* playing a note. Before the note is finished, the computer goes on to the next statement in the program. It keeps performing statements until it reaches another SOUND statement. What happens next will depend on whether you are using Cassette BASIC or Cartridge BASIC.

In Cassette BASIC, the computer always halts until the previous note has finished playing. Then the new SOUND statement starts a new note, and the computer goes on performing statements until it reaches another SOUND statement. This way of playing music is called the **foreground music mode**.

This mode is also available in Cartridge BASIC. However, in addition, Cartridge BASIC has another mode called **background music mode**. In background mode, the computer does not halt when it reaches each new SOUND statement. Instead, the computer puts each new note value in a special place in memory called the **music buffer**. Then the computer goes on to the next statement in the program.

The music buffer in Cartridge BASIC can hold data for 32 notes. Thus, the computer can perform 32 SOUND statements in a row without halting. (After that, the next SOUND statement will cause a halt until there is room in the buffer.) While there are any notes in the buffer, the computer will play them, one after the other.

Background mode has some interesting uses in advanced programming applications. But it can be very confusing at first. After all, the big idea in programming is that the computer does one step at a time, in order. Background mode seems to break the rule: The computer is both playing music and performing statements at the same time.

Actually, there is no real mystery about background mode. Your PC*jr* has two separate processor chips. One processor plays music notes, one at a time. The other processor performs statements, one at a time. Each processor works by itself. Thus, both can be doing something at the same time.

The main problem with using background mode in a program is that there is no easy way to keep your SOUND statements in step with PRINT or other statements. The computer just keeps going ahead, performing all the statements in your program. Usually, that is not what you want to happen. So, even if you have Cartridge BASIC, you will usually want to avoid background mode.

That sounds easy. Unfortunately, it is not as easy as it sounds. *Cartridge BASIC automatically sets background mode whenever you enter the* RUN *command*.

That means *you* must add a statement to your Cartridge BASIC programs to tell the computer to set foreground mode. The statement is this:

```
PLAY "MF"
```

The symbol MF stands for "music foreground." (You can also use MB in the PLAY statement. It returns the computer to background mode.)

From now on in this book, we will begin adding PLAY "MF" statements to all programs that use SOUND statements. This addition will make Cartridge BASIC programs work correctly. *Unfortunately, it will also cause an error message if used in Cassette BASIC programs.*

Warning to Cassette BASIC Users!

In the rest of this book, ignore all program lines that contain a PLAY "MF" statement. Do not use this statement in your programs!

You do not need this statement: The foreground mode is the only one available in Cassette BASIC. In addition, the PLAY statement does not exist in Cassette BASIC. Using PLAY will lead to a Syntax error message.

---

1. What statement must be added to a Cartridge BASIC program to make SOUND statements work the same way as in Cassette BASIC?
2. If you add the statement referred to in question 1 to a program, what will happen when you run the program in Cassette BASIC?

Writing New Subroutines

Now, let's return to the topic of subroutines. If you just finished Session 9, the subroutine listed at the top of the next page should be in memory. **If not, start your computer and enter the subroutine now. Be sure to indent the body of the subroutine properly.**

```
1000 'SUB DO
1010    SOUND 523, 10
1020    COLOR 1
1030    PRINT "DO"
1040 RETURN
```

If you are using Cartridge BASIC, add the line below. If you are using Cassette BASIC, leave the line out!

```
1005 PLAY "MF"
```

In this session, you will develop a series of subroutines, or blocks of statements. Each of these subroutines plays a note, sets the screen color, and writes the name of the note on the screen. The subroutine above does that for middle C. That note is *do* in the *do, re, mi* scale.

Now, let's write a similar subroutine for D, or *re*. Here is what it should look like in the Cartridge BASIC version:

```
1100 'SUB RE
1105    PLAY "MF"
1110    SOUND 587, 10
1120    COLOR 2
1130    PRINT "RE"
1140 RETURN
```

Notice that subroutine RE and subroutine DO are not very different. *Whenever you see two blocks of statements that are almost alike, you can usually save time by editing the old block to produce the new one.* You can use screen editing to change the line number of a line and then press the (Enter ⏎) key. The computer then copies the *new* line, but it keeps a copy of the old one too. You did this before while using the EDIT command. You can do the same thing in screen editing. **List subroutine DO. Then use the new editing method you have just learned in Session 9 to make a new subroutine.**

It is a good idea to use blank lines to separate subroutines from one another. This makes them easier to read. Unfortunately, there is no way to enter a completely blank line. Every line needs a line number. Suppose you enter just a line number and press the (Enter ⏎) key. If you do so, you are telling the computer to delete that line from the program. So that method won't work.

The way out is to enter a remark statement. Just use the apostrophe abbreviation, but don't put anything after the apostrophe. **Add the blank remark at line 1090.** When you are finished, your Cartridge BASIC program should look like this:

```
1000 'SUB DO
1005    PLAY "MF"
1010    SOUND 523, 10
1020    COLOR 1
1030    PRINT "DO"
1040  RETURN
1090 '
1100 'SUB RE
1105    PLAY "MF"
1110    SOUND 587, 10
1120    COLOR 2
1130    PRINT "RE"
1140  RETURN
```

Now let's try running each of the subroutines. We will use the GOSUB statement in the immediate mode.

SCREEN 1 _____ Switch to graphics mode.

GOSUB 1000 _____ That produced a blue screen and the note DO.

GOSUB 1100 _____ That produced a green screen and the note RE.

SCREEN 0 _____ Switch back to text mode.

3. What lines contain the body of subroutine RE?
4. Why should the body of a subroutine be indented?
5. What is the purpose of a ''blank'' line between subroutines?

Adding More Subroutines

Now you should have two subroutines in memory. Each subroutine packages the statements for a single job. Next, let's add two more. Below is the third subroutine in the Cartridge BASIC version. (If you are using Cassette BASIC, leave out the PLAY statement.)

```
1190 '
1200 'SUB MI
1205     PLAY "MF"
1210     SOUND 659, 10
1220     COLOR 3
1230     PRINT "MI"
1240 RETURN
```

And here is the Cartridge BASIC version of the fourth subroutine:

```
1290 '
1300 'SUB FA
1305     PLAY "MF"
1310     SOUND 698, 10
1320     COLOR 4
1330     PRINT "FA"
1340 RETURN
```

You can enter these new subroutines in one of two ways: Type each on the keyboard. Or use screen editing to make the new subroutines from the previous one. When you have finished, use the LIST command to print all four subroutines on the screen.

You have a new problem. The program is getting too long to fit on the screen. You will now learn how to list parts of programs. That way, you can take a look at any part of a long program.

LIST -1090 ————————————— There is the first subroutine.

LIST -1190 ————————————— There are the first two.

LIST -1290 ————————————— There won't be room for all four subroutines on the screen.

LIST 1300- _____ There is the last subroutine.

LIST 1200- _____ There are the last two subroutines.

As you have seen, LIST tells the computer to print on the screen the lines specified by the line numbers that follow. If you put a dash before the line number, the computer lists all the lines from the beginning of the program up through that line number. If you put a dash after the line number, it lists all the lines from that line number through the end of the program.

More often, you will want to list a particular block of lines within a program. You may have already guessed how to do that.

LIST 1100-1180 _____ There is the subroutine for RE.

LIST 1200-1280 _____ There is the subroutine for MI.

LIST 1005-1030 _____ And there is the body of the subroutine for DO.

LIST 1030-1005 _____ Nothing happens if you try to list a block in reverse order.

You can list any part of a program by putting a **line-number range** after LIST. The computer will print all statements that have line numbers in that range. For example, LIST 200-350 tells the computer to list all the lines from 200 through 350.

Suppose you can't remember the line-number range of the block of statements you want to see. One way to solve the difficulty is to list the entire program. Then stop the listing process when the part you are interested in scrolls by on the screen. You can do this by pressing and releasing the (Fn) key and then pressing and releasing the (Q) key. (Notice the word "Pause" under the (Q) key: In the future, we'll call (Fn) followed by (Q) the (Pause) function). To restart the listing of the program, press any key in the symbol group.

Practice using the (Pause) function: Enter the LIST command, and quickly tap the (Fn) key and then the (Q) key. Now press any symbol key. Use the (Pause) function again. Press another symbol key.

6. What command tells the computer to list all statements in a program up through line 375?
7. What command tells the computer to list all statements in a program from line 440 to the end?
8. How would you tell the computer to list all statements in the line-number range 240 through 425?

Putting GOSUB Statements in a Program

You now have four subroutines in memory. You can use a GOSUB statement to tell the computer to perform any of the subroutines. So far, you have used the GOSUB statement only in the immediate mode. Now it's time to learn how to use the GOSUB statement in the program mode. **Enter these lines:**

```
SCREEN 0
```
Return to text mode.

```
100  'PROGRAM NOTES
110     SCREEN 1
120     GOSUB 1200
200  END
999  '
LIST -1200
```
This is the first part of the program. What will it do?

```
RUN
```
Were you right?

```
130     GOSUB 1100
140     GOSUB 1000
```
Put four spaces after each line number.

```
LIST -200
```
Make certain line 200 is still there. What will the program do now?

```
RUN
```
Were you right?

```
120
130
140
CLS
LIST -200
```
What will happen now?

```
RUN                                    Did that surprise you?

120     GOSUB 1000     'DO
130     GOSUB 1100     'RE
140     GOSUB 1200     'MI
150     GOSUB 1300     'FA        Be sure to put an apostrophe
                                  before DO, RE, MI, and so on.

CLS
LIST -200                         What will this do?

RUN                               Right?
```

The last version of program NOTES should have played a four-note scale. The program began like this:

```
    100   'PROGRAM NOTES
·   110       SCREEN 1
    120       GOSUB 1000     'DO
    130       GOSUB 1100     'RE
    140       GOSUB 1200     'MI
    150       GOSUB 1300     'FA
    200   END
```

When you entered the RUN command, the computer began at the first statement. It was a remark statement, so the computer skipped it. The next statement told the computer to set graphics mode. Then GOSUB 1000 told the computer to perform the subroutine beginning at line 1000. In the same way, GOSUB 1100, GOSUB 1200, and GOSUB 1300 told the computer to perform subroutines beginning at lines 1100, 1200, and 1300. Finally, the END statement in line 200 told the computer to stop performing statements and turn the cursor back on.

This block of statements is called the **main routine**. A main routine should always begin with a remark statement. You use it to tell the purpose of the program. In this case, the purpose is to play notes. The main routine *must* end with an END statement. The statements in between form the **body** of the main routine. Usually, most of the statements in the body of the main routine are GOSUB statements. They tell the computer which subroutines to perform and in what order. You found that when there were no GOSUB statements, the computer did not perform any of the subroutines. Each GOSUB statement in a main routine should be followed by a **trailing remark**. This is an apostrophe and a word or phrase that tells the purpose of the GOSUB.

The main routine is always at the top of the program. That is so because the computer begins performing statements from the top. The main routine is like a directory of what is happening in the program. In this case, the directory is quite simple. It describes the order in which the notes are to be played.

9. What is meant by the "body" of the main routine?
10. What kind of statement should go at the beginning of a main routine?
11. What kind of statement must go at the end of a main routine?

PROJECTS

- You have completed subroutines for the first four notes in the scale beginning at middle C. Write the four subroutines needed to complete the eight-note scale. Use the table below to get the correct frequencies for the SOUND statement. Change the main routine to play the whole scale.

Note	Name	Frequency
C	do	523
D	re	587
E	mi	659
F	fa	698
G	sol	784
A	la	880
B	ti	988
C	do	1046

- Musical notes sound better if there is a short pause after each note is played. The statement

  ```
  SOUND 32767, 1
  ```

  will cause such a short pause. Add this statement just before the RETURN statement in each subroutine. It should go after the PRINT statement in each subroutine. Run the program and listen for the pause after each note.

● Most music needs "rest notes." A rest causes a fixed amount of silence. You can get 10 clock ticks of silence (about half a second) by using this statement:

```
SOUND 32767, 10
```

Create a new subroutine, beginning at line 1800, that tells the computer to "rest" for 10 clock ticks.

When you have finished, delete your main routine. (You can do this by entering the command DELETE 100-200.) Then save the set of nine subroutines on either cassette tape or diskette under the name TOOLKIT. See Sessions 5 and 6 for a reminder about saving programs.

● (Optional) Use the new subroutines to play "Mary Had a Little Lamb." Write a new main routine that contains a GOSUB statement for *each* of the notes shown below. (You may want to save the program when you finish.)

mi, re, do, re, mi, mi, mi, rest
re, re, re, rest, mi, mi, mi, rest
mi, re, do, re, mi, mi, mi, rest
mi, re, re, mi, re, do

● (Optional) Rewrite the main routine to play "Twinkle, Twinkle Little Star." The notes are given below. (You may want to save the program when you finish.)

do, do, sol, sol, la, la, sol, rest
fa, fa, mi, mi, re, re, do, rest
sol, sol, fa, fa, mi, mi, re, rest
sol, sol, fa, fa, mi, mi, re, rest
do, do, sol, sol, la, la, sol, rest
fa, fa, mi, mi, re, re, do, rest

SUMMARY

In this session, you learned how to group blocks of statements into subroutines. You told the computer to perform a subroutine with the GOSUB statement in the main routine. The new statements and commands are summarized in the table below. Read the table carefully. If anything is still unclear to you, go back and review the session as needed.

Topic	Description
Background music mode	Music notes in SOUND and PLAY statements are not played immediately. Instead the note values are placed in memory, and the computer continues performing statements in the program.
Foreground music mode	Music notes are played immediately unless a previous note is still sounding. If the note cannot be played, the computer halts and waits for the previous note to finish.
PLAY "MB"	A Cartridge BASIC statement that sets music mode to background.
PLAY "MF"	A Cartridge BASIC statement that sets music mode to foreground.
(Pause) function	The (Fn) key followed by the (Q) key. It tells the computer to pause while listing or running a program. The pause ends whenever you press any symbol key.
LIST m-n	A command that tells the computer to print on the screen the lines of the program with line numbers in the range m through n.
LIST -n	A command that tells the computer to print on the screen the lines of the program from the beginning through line number n.
LIST n-	A command that tells the computer to print on the screen the lines of the program from line number n through the end.
END	A statement used to mark the end of a main routine. It tells the computer to stop performing the program.

TOP-DOWN PROGRAMMING

SESSION 11

Session Goals

- Review the way subroutines work.
- Review the form of main routines and subroutines.
- Use top-down design to plan a new program.

Review

Now is a good time to review what you have learned about subroutines and top-down programming. **Enter the NEW command. Then leave the computer. Spend the next 15 minutes or so reading this session.** When you have finished reading, you will have some programming projects to do.

In Sessions 9 and 10, you saw how you can build complicated programs from groups of statements called subroutines. Each subroutine used simple BASIC statements to define a complex action. You learned that the GOSUB statement tells the computer to perform a subroutine. You used the GOSUB statement in the immediate mode. You also used GOSUB inside the main routine of a program.

The important thing about subroutines is that they give you a way to define new actions for the computer to carry out. You learned in Session 9 that there is no single BASIC statement you can use to tell the computer to do a certain group of things. These things include setting music foreground mode, playing middle C, changing the background color of the screen to blue, and printing the word DO on the screen. But you can make the computer do these things by adding these statements to your program:

```
1000   'SUB DO
1005      PLAY "MF"
1010      SOUND 523, 10
1020      COLOR 1
1030      PRINT "DO"
1035      SOUND 32767, 1
1040   RETURN
```

Then, any time you want the computer to do this group of things, you need only put the line GOSUB 1000 in your program.

You put GOSUB statements in a program that played "Mary Had a Little Lamb." The order of the notes played was determined by the order of the GOSUB statements. GOSUB *is the statement that tells the computer to perform the action defined in the subroutine.* If there is no GOSUB statement in the main routine, the computer will not perform the subroutine. If the same GOSUB statement appears twice in the main routine, the computer will perform the subroutine twice.

1. What part of a program tells the computer how to carry out a new action?
2. What tells the computer to perform a subroutine?
3. Suppose that a program contains two subroutines. What determines the order in which the computer performs the subroutines?

The Structure of a Well-Written Program

A well-written computer program is like a well-written English composition. Both are easy to read.

The first few sentences of a composition should explain what the whole composition is about. Each major idea should be in a separate paragraph. Each paragraph should have a topic sentence. Paragraphs should be separated from one another by blank lines.

The routines of a well-written program are like the paragraphs of an English composition. The main routine should tell what the whole program is going to do. Each major action should be in a separate subroutine. Each subroutine should have a name that gives the reader an idea of what it will do. Subroutines should be separated from one another by blank remark lines.

When you are writing an English composition, you must check your spelling and punctuation. When you are writing a program, the computer checks your spelling and punctuation. When you are writing a composition, you must organize your ideas and write them clearly. Unfortunately, the computer does not help you organize your programs so they are clear and easy to read. The computer will run hard-to-read programs without complaint. So it is up to you to learn a few rules that will make your programs easy to write, read, and change.

The best way to start both an English composition and a computer program is with an outline. Here is a general outline that works for *all* programs:

    I. Main routine
   II. First subroutine
 III. Second subroutine
 IV. Third subroutine
      etc.

Every program that contains subroutines should begin with a main routine. It is usually short. It gives a complete picture of the whole program, but it leaves out the details. No matter what the program does, the structure of the main routine should be the same. Here is an outline:

```
___   'PROGRAM  name of program
___
___
___       body of main routine
___       (mostly GOSUB statements)
___
___
___   END
```

The blanks show where line numbers will go. The first statement in the main routine should be a remark statement giving the name of the program. The last statement *must* be an END statement. The remark statement opens the main routine. The END statement closes it. The body of the main routine tells which subroutines are to be performed and in what order.

The details of a program appear in the subroutines. All subroutines have the same form, no matter what they do. Here is an outline:

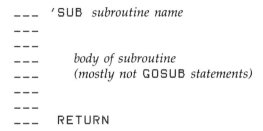

Every subroutine should begin with a remark statement that names the action the subroutine defines. Every subroutine *must* end with a RETURN statement. The remark statement opens the subroutine. The RETURN statement closes it. The body of the subroutine contains the statements that define the action of the subroutine. The body of a subroutine can contain a GOSUB statement to another subroutine. Each subroutine is a tool for doing a certain job. When a subroutine has a GOSUB to another subroutine, it is an example of one tool using another.

It is a good idea to indent the body of each routine. Indentations make it clear where the body begins and ends. Blank remark lines between routines make it clear where one routine ends and the next one begins.

Some of the rules given above are required by the computer: There *must* be an END statement between the main routine and the first subroutine. There *must* be a RETURN statement at the end of every subroutine. (In Session 12, you will see what happens if you break these rules.) Other rules given above are not required: The computer ignores remark statements, indentations, and blank lines. These things have only one purpose: to make it easy for you and others to read your programs.

4. What goes at the top of a main routine?
5. What goes at the bottom of a main routine?
6. Why must the body of the main routine contain GOSUB statements if the program has subroutines?
7. What is the purpose of the RETURN statement?
8. Why should the body of a routine be indented?
9. What is the purpose of blank remark lines in a program?

Top-Down Design of a Program

Let's use the outlines you have learned to help you design a new program. Suppose you have three friends named Ana, Nan, and Ann. All of them want to see their names in lights. You decide to write a program to do just that. You decide to make the letters in their names appear in a vertical line down the screen. The program will have a subroutine to print a big letter *N*. The program will have another subroutine to print a big letter *A*. With these two subroutines, the program can spell all three names.

You may be asking yourself these questions: How can I make the computer print a big *N*? A big *A*? It is easy to get bogged down in details like these when you are trying to solve a problem. It is almost always better to ignore such details at first. Start with the main routine. Figure out what it must tell the computer to do. There may be no BASIC statements that tell the computer to do what you want it to do. In that case, use a GOSUB statement instead.

Below is an outline of the main routine. It is written partly in English and partly in BASIC.

```
100  'PROGRAM NAMES
110     clear screen
120     print a big N
130     print a big A
140     print a big N
150  END
```

You can tell the computer to perform line 110 with a single BASIC statement. That statement is CLS. To perform line 120, the computer will need several PRINT statements. Together, they will make a letter like this one:

```
XXX   XX
XXXX  XX
XX XX XX
XX  XXXX
XX   XXX
```

You might also use one or more empty PRINT statements to put blank lines between the letters.

Let's not worry about the details of the PRINT statements now. Instead, we will "bury" them in a BIG N subroutine. We can write that subroutine after we finish the main routine. Here is the completed main routine, plus an outline of the subroutines:

```
100  'PROGRAM NAMES
110     CLS
120     GOSUB 400  'BIG N
130     GOSUB 600  'BIG A
140     GOSUB 400  'BIG N
150  END
390  '
400  'SUB BIG N
---
---      print big N
---
500  RETURN
590  '
600  'SUB BIG A
---
---      print big A
---
700  RETURN
```

From now on, you can fill in the program details. In the projects at the end of this session, you will finish the subroutine for big *N* and the subroutine for big *A*.

The method you have been using to solve this problem has a name. It is called *top-down* programming. Here are the steps you used:

The Rules of Top-Down Programming

Step 1. Write an English version of the body of the main routine.

Step 2. Convert into BASIC each English phrase that you can express by one or two BASIC statements.

Step 3. If you cannot convert the English phrase into one or two BASIC statements, convert it to a GOSUB statement.

Step 4. After you convert all the English phrases in the main routine, repeat this whole process for each subroutine named in Step 3.

Top-down programming has two good effects: First, it makes you think about what the whole program is supposed to do. Second, it keeps you from getting bogged down in details.

10. In your own words, what does top-down programming mean?
11. Why is top-down programming helpful?

PROJECTS

● Use the top-down method to complete the plan for program NAMES. Go to the computer and erase whatever program is in memory. Then enter all three routines. The computer should print the names vertically down the left side of the screen. Run the program and fix any errors.

● Change the main routine in program NAMES to print Ann's name. (The big letters will appear in a vertical line down the side of the screen.) Change the program again to print Ana's name. Change it again to print Nana's name.

● The statement SCREEN 0, 1 sets text mode. However, it also allows you to print the text in color on a color TV. Put this statement at the beginning of your main routine. Next, put a COLOR statement ahead of each GOSUB statement in your main routine. Experiment with different numbers in the COLOR statement. If you have Cartridge BASIC, change the SCREEN statement to SCREEN 3 and run the program.

SUMMARY

In this session, you have started learning how to organize programs into meaningful blocks of statements. The key ideas are summarized in the table below.

Topic	Description
Top-down programming	A method of writing programs. The important ideas all appear in the main routine. Details appear in subroutines.
Main routine	The first block of statements in a well-written program. The main routine should begin with a remark statement telling the name of the program. It must end with an END statement.
Subroutine	A block of statements ending with a RETURN statement. The first statement should be a remark telling the name of the subroutine.
SCREEN 0, 1	A BASIC statement that tells the computer to set text mode, but with color enabled. In this mode, the COLOR statement sets the color of the letters to be printed on the screen.

SUBROUTINE BUGS

SESSION 12

Session Goals

- Study the missing END statement bug.
- Study the missing RETURN statement bug.
- Study GOSUB bugs.

Optional Session

The goal of this session is to explore the problems that can arise when using subroutines. If you always begin and end subroutines correctly, then this session is optional. You can go on to the other sessions of the book. However, if you start to have trouble because of subroutines in your programs, you should take time out, return, and go through this session carefully. If you have time, we advise you to spend an hour or so now learning more detailed information about subroutines and how they work.

How Subroutines Work

There is a very simple way to think about how subroutines work. The GOSUB statement tells the computer to perform the *body* of a subroutine. You can imagine that the computer snips out the statements that make up the body of the subroutine. The computer then inserts them into the program in place of the GOSUB statement.

If subroutines are written correctly, this is a good way of looking at how they work. However, suppose there are errors in the program. Then, this idea of substituting statements for the GOSUB statement doesn't work as well.

If you always followed the proper rules for writing subroutines, there would be no need to worry about "buggy" programs. This is what programs with errors are called. But, sooner or later, you will forget to put an END statement at the end of the main routine. Or you will leave out the RETURN statement at the end of a subroutine. Mistakes like these sometimes produce error messages and sometimes not. Let's take a look at these often surprising situations.

The "Missing END" Bug

The purpose of the END *statement is to stop the computer at the end of the main routine.* One of the most common bugs in programs with subroutines happens when you leave out the END statement. We will use a short program to see what happens as a result of the "Missing END" bug.

Start the computer as usual. Then enter the lines at the top of the next page. (If the computer is already on, enter the NEW command.)

```
100  'PROGRAM BUGS
110     PRINT  "ONE"
120     GOSUB  200    'TWO
130     PRINT  "THREE"
140  END
190  '
200  'SUB TWO
210     PRINT  "TWO"
220  RETURN
```
_____ Enter the program.

```
CLS
LIST
RUN
```
_____ Check the program and the
output.

The program is working correctly if you see ONE, TWO, and THREE
down the left side of the screen. Correct any errors in your program
before going on.

```
CLS
LIST
```
_____ Here is your program.

```
TRON
```
_____ This is a new command, not a
movie title.

```
RUN
```
_____ Note the numbers in brackets.

TRON is short for "trace on." This command tells the computer to
print a line-by-line trace of every step of the program when you run it.
Here is what you should see on the screen now:

```
[100][110]ONE
[120][200][210]TWO
[220][130]THREE
[140]
```

This tells you that the computer began at line 100. It next performed
line 110. That line told it to print ONE on the screen. It then went on to
line 120, the GOSUB 200 statement. That is why the next bracketed
number after 120 is 200.

So, the computer performed line 200. It then went on to line 210. That line caused TWO to be printed. Next, the computer reached line 220, which is a RETURN statement. That statement told the computer to go back to the line *after* the GOSUB. That is why the next bracketed number after 220 is 130.

The computer then performed line 130, printing THREE. Finally, it came to line 140, which ended the program.

Now, let's turn the trace off and introduce the "Missing END" bug:

TROFF
RUN —————————————— The trace numbers should be gone now.

140 —————————————— Delete the END statement.

CLS
LIST —————————————— Make sure it's gone.

RUN —————————————— Run the program.

By removing the END statement, you put an error in the program. You see ONE, TWO, and THREE as before. But now there is an *extra* TWO. There is also a message that says RETURN without GOSUB in 220. Why do you think this happened?

TRON —————————————— Set trace on.

CLS
LIST
RUN —————————————— This is the traced program.

You should now see these six lines on your screen:

```
[100][110]ONE
[120][200][210]TWO
[220][130]THREE
[190][200][210]TWO
[220]
RETURN without GOSUB in 220
```

The first three lines of the trace are exactly the same as before. The problem happened after the computer performed line 130, printing THREE on the screen. This time there was no END statement. As a result, the computer just kept going. It performed lines 190, 200, and 210, printing TWO again. It then reached line 220. Line 220 contains a RETURN statement. But this time there was no GOSUB statement telling the computer to perform subroutine TWO. The computer just "fell" into the subroutine by accident. That is why the computer printed the message RETURN without GOSUB in 220. This message almost always means that you have left out the END statement in the main routine.

1. What is the purpose of the END statement?
2. If the END statement is missing from the main routine, what will happen?

The "Missing RETURN" Bug

Another common bug is forgetting to put a RETURN statement at the end of a subroutine. Let's look at this bug next.

Turn the trace off (TROFF). Put the END statement back at line 140. Run the program and check it. Then list it. You should see this listing on your screen:

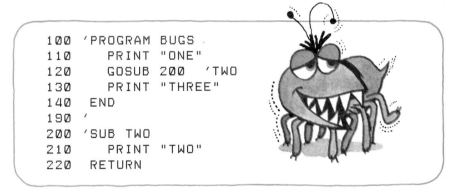

```
100 'PROGRAM BUGS
110     PRINT "ONE"
120     GOSUB 200    'TWO
130     PRINT "THREE"
140 END
190 '
200 'SUB TWO
210     PRINT "TWO"
220 RETURN
```

Now, let's put the "Missing RETURN" bug into the program.

220 ——————————————— Delete the RETURN statement.

RUN ——————————————— Look at the results.

This bug produced very interesting results. ONE and TWO are printed on the screen. But THREE is missing. What is most interesting, however, is that *there was no error message*. The program is not working properly. Yet you would get no clue to this if you simply ran the program and looked at the results! **Turn the trace on. Run the program again. Notice the last bracketed number.**

Without the RETURN statement in line 220, the last line in the program is line 210. When the computer was sent to the subroutine, it performed lines 200 and 210. Finding no more statements, it stopped. The missing RETURN statement is needed to tell the computer to go back to the statement *after* the GOSUB statement that sent it to the subroutine. If the RETURN statement is missing, there is no way for the computer to go back.

Another kind of missing RETURN bug can show up if there is more than one subroutine in a program. **Turn the trace off. Put the RETURN statement back in line 220. Then add the new lines shown here:**

```
100  'PROGRAM BUGS
110     PRINT "ONE"
120     GOSUB 200    'TWO
130     PRINT "THREE"
135     GOSUB 400    'FOUR
140  END
190  '
200  'SUB TWO
210     PRINT "TWO"
220  RETURN
390  '
400  'SUB FOUR
410     PRINT "FOUR"
420  RETURN
```

List your program. Read it carefully. Fix any errors before going on. Think about what this program tells the computer to print on the screen. Then run the program.

This program should have no bugs. It is correct if the computer printed ONE, TWO, THREE, and FOUR down the left side of the screen. Now let's put in a bug.

220 _____ Delete the RETURN statement in line 220.

CLS
LIST
RUN _____ See what happens.

This time, you got ONE, TWO, FOUR, THREE, and FOUR. But, *there was no error message.* Now the program certainly *is* buggy. What happened?

To the computer, the subroutine beginning at line 200 looks like this:

```
200  'SUB TWO
210     PRINT "TWO"
390  '
400  'SUB FOUR
410     PRINT "FOUR"
420   RETURN
```

The two remark statements in lines 390 and 400 are invisible as far as the computer is concerned. So, now the subroutine tells the computer to print TWO *and* FOUR. **Set the trace on. Clear the screen. List the program. Run it again.**

The trace numbers show you exactly what went wrong. The first two trace lines are the same as before. But after the computer printed TWO, it simply went on to the next statement. This time it was *not* a RETURN statement, but a remark statement. So the computer continued to line 410, printing the extra FOUR. It next reached line 420, which *was* a RETURN statement.

At that point, the computer finally returned to line 130, the line after the GOSUB 200 statement. It then printed THREE. The rest of the program worked correctly. You can see this by following the trace to the end.

The missing RETURN statement caused bizarre results. Yet there were no error messages. Remember this important idea: Just because information comes from a computer, that does *not* mean it must be correct. You should be on the lookout for strange things that can happen because of program bugs.

3. What is the purpose of the RETURN statement?
4. What happens if the computer performs a subroutine that has no RETURN statement at the end?
5. Will a missing RETURN statement always cause an error message?
6. What will the computer do if you accidentally put two RETURN statements at the end of a subroutine?

GOSUB Bugs

Missing GOSUB statements will cause bugs in programs. So will GOSUB statements with incorrect line numbers.

Set the trace off. Put the RETURN statement back at line 220. Run the program. Make sure that it works correctly again. Now remove the GOSUB statement at line 120. Run the program again. Then list it. This time you see ONE, THREE, and FOUR on the screen. You probably knew that would happen. TWO is missing because the GOSUB to the subroutine that prints TWO is missing. The computer will not perform a subroutine just because it is in the program. There *must* be a GOSUB to that subroutine.

See what happens if your program has a GOSUB to a line number that is not in the program.

7. What is the purpose of a GOSUB statement?
8. What happens if a GOSUB statement is missing?
9. Will a missing GOSUB statement cause an error message?

Bugs in Nested Subroutines

Now let's take a look at some other program bugs. These bugs can show up when a subroutine contains a GOSUB to yet another subroutine. We'll need a new program to study these bugs.

```
NEW
CLS
```
Erase the program and clear the screen.

```
100 'PROGRAM MORE BUGS
110    GOSUB 200    '1
120  END
190 '
200 'SUB 1
210    GOSUB 300    '2
220    PRINT "THERE"
230  RETURN
290 '
300 'SUB 2
310    PRINT "HI"
320  RETURN
```

Enter the new program.

```
CLS
LIST
RUN
```
———————————————— Check the results. You should see
HI and THERE.

```
TRON
CLS
LIST
RUN
```
———————————————— Look carefully at the line-number
trace.

Notice that SUB 1, the first subroutine, contains a GOSUB to SUB 2, the second subroutine. We say that SUB 2 is **nested** inside SUB 1. Now let's look at the same kinds of bugs you have already seen.

```
120
```
———————————————— Take out the END statement.

```
CLS
LIST
RUN
```
———————————————— Look at the line-number trace.

Here is what you should see on the screen:

```
[100][110][200][210][300][310]HI
[320][220]THERE
[230][190][200][210][300][310]HI
[320][220]THERE
[230]
RETURN without GOSUB in 230
```

Study this trace until you understand what happened.

```
120   END
```
———————————————— Put back the END statement.

```
230
```
———————————————— Take out the first RETURN
statement.

```
CLS
LIST
RUN
```
———————————————— Look at the trace.

This time, the screen shows HI, THERE, and HI, plus the trace. There was no error message. You should be able to explain all the trace numbers.

230 RETURN	Put the first RETURN statement back in.
320	Take out the second RETURN statement.
CLS **LIST** **RUN**	What happened?

The screen shows HI, but not THERE. There was no error message. Again, you should be able to explain the trace numbers. **Turn the trace off.**

These kinds of things can happen if you make mistakes while writing subroutines. Although the results seem strange at first, you should be able to figure out why and how they happened. The moral is this: Always write your main routine and subroutines according to the rules given in Session 11.

10. What is a nested subroutine?
11. What would happen if you put the subroutines at the top of a program and the main routine at the bottom?

A Subroutine with a GOSUB to Itself

The final bug you will see leads to a new kind of error. This one may seem very mysterious to you.

NEW **CLS**	Erase the old program and clear the screen.
100 'SUB AGAIN **110 PRINT "AGAIN AND"** **120 RETURN**	Enter the new program.
GOSUB 100	Perform the subroutine in the immediate mode.

So far, nothing new has happened. The PRINT statement inside the subroutine told the computer to print AGAIN AND on the screen. Now for something different:

```
115      GOSUB 100    'AGAIN
CLS
LIST
```
_____ Take a good look at the subroutine.

This new version of the subroutine raises an interesting question. Can a subroutine contain a GOSUB to *itself*? There is one way to find out.

```
GOSUB 100
```
_____ Again, perform the subroutine in the immediate mode.

```
TRON
GOSUB 100
TROFF
```
_____ Look at the trace.

```
LIST
```
_____ Here is the program.

The new GOSUB *inside* the subroutine completely changed things. Now, instead of a single AGAIN AND, you see a whole series of these phrases. They are followed by the message Out of memory in 110. This is probably the first time you have seen this error message.

The computer uses part of its memory to store the instructions that tell it how to return to the main routine from subroutines. Each time the computer performs a GOSUB statement, it needs one more location in this part of its memory to store the return instructions. Each time the computer performs a RETURN statement, it clears one location in memory. But in this case, the computer kept meeting GOSUB statements without meeting any RETURN statements. So, it kept adding instructions to its memory without taking any out.

On the PC*jr*, 34 locations are available in memory to store instructions relating to subroutines. (If you count the number of AGAIN AND messages on the screen, you will see that there are 34 of them.) Once those locations in memory are used up, the computer can't perform the next GOSUB. So it stops and prints the Out of memory message.

12. Does BASIC allow you to write a subroutine containing a GOSUB to the beginning of the same subroutine?
13. What happens when the computer performs the subroutine described in question 12?

Avoiding Subroutine Bugs

It is easy to avoid problems with subroutines if you keep these rules in mind when writing programs: You *must* end the main routine with an END statement. You *must* end each subroutine with a RETURN statement. You *should* begin each subroutine with a remark statement that explains its purpose. You *should* indent the body of subroutines. You *should* use blank lines between subroutines to make them easier to read.

It is wise to read a program from top to bottom, checking for these rules, before trying to run it. As you have seen, a program with bugs in it may run, give incorrect results, but produce no error messages.

SUMMARY In this session, you learned about program bugs in subroutines. You used the trace capability of the PC*jr* to find bugs in programs. The important ideas are summarized in the tables below.

Topic	Description
Bug	An accidental error in a program.
Debugging	Finding errors in programs and fixing them.
"Missing END" bug	Leaving out the END statement in the main routine.
"Missing RETURN" bug	Leaving out the RETURN statement in a subroutine.

Statement	Description
TRON	Tells the computer to "trace" each program line by printing its line number whenever the computer performs it.
TROFF	Tells the computer to stop tracing program lines.

A TOP-DOWN EXAMPLE

SESSION 13

Session Goals

- Use the top-down planning method to write a musical program.
- Use the TOOLKIT subroutines.
- Learn how to test subroutines.
- Add two new subroutines to the TOOLKIT.

Musical Forms

In the last four sessions, you have learned how to use END, GOSUB, and RETURN statements to divide a large program into smaller parts. In all but the simplest programs, it is a good method to put your big ideas in the main routine and hide the details in subroutines. When working on the main routine, you should be thinking about the overall form and shape of the whole program. Later, you can think about each part separately and make sure it does what needs to be done. These are the steps of the top-down method of solving problems.

Computer programmers are not the only ones who use the top-down method. People who write for newspapers use this approach. They try to get the main ideas of a news story into the first paragraph. After that, they fill in the details in later paragraphs. People who write music often solve their problems the same way. They begin with an idea of the overall form of the piece they want to write. Later, they work with the parts that will go together to make up the whole piece.

In Session 10, you wrote a program to play "Twinkle, Twinkle Little Star." The musical notes it played were as follows:

    do, do, sol, sol, la, la, sol, rest
    fa, fa, mi, mi, re, re, do, rest
    sol, sol, fa, fa, mi, mi, re, rest
    sol, sol, fa, fa, mi, mi, re, rest
    do, do, sol, sol, la, la, sol, rest
    fa, fa, mi, mi, re, re, do, rest

Look at the overall organization of these notes. Do you see any patterns? Are there parts at the beginning that appear again later?

If you are a musician, you have probably recognized that this piece, like many songs, has "A-B-A form." The song starts with the following "A-part":

    do, do, sol, sol, la, la, sol, rest
    fa, fa, mi, mi, re, re, do, rest

After that comes the "B-part" of the song:

    sol, sol, fa, fa, mi, mi, re, rest
    sol, sol, fa, fa, mi, mi, re, rest

Finally, the A-part is played again and the song ends.

1. Name two songs that have A-A-B-A form.
2. What is the form of "London Bridge is Falling Down"?

Top-Down "Twinkle, Twinkle"

You can write a main routine that tells the computer to play *any* song written in A-B-A form. You do this by thinking only about the *form* of the song. Later, in your subroutines, you can tell the computer what tune is the A-part and what tune is the B-part. The subroutines will have GOSUBs to the DO, RE, MI, etc., subroutines that tell exactly what musical frequencies to play.

You will need the music subroutines in the TOOLKIT file you saved at the end of Session 10. Start your PCjr as usual. Then load file TOOLKIT into the computer. List the file. Then delete all lines before line 990, if there are any.

In the top-down method, we always start with an outline of the main routine. The outline should be partly in English and partly in BASIC. Here is an example:

```
___    'PROGRAM SONG
___        set graphics screen
___        play A-part
___        play B-part
___        play A-part
___        set text screen
___    END
```

This main routine does five steps, one after the other. You can see that it correctly tells the computer to play *any* song written in A-B-A form. The next step is to convert the main routine to pure BASIC. Here is the finished routine:

```
100 'PROGRAM SONG
110    SCREEN 1
120    GOSUB 200    'A-PART
130    GOSUB 300    'B-PART
140    GOSUB 200    'A-PART
150    SCREEN 0
160 END
```

Enter the main routine into the computer now.

Now that we have finished the main routine, we must go to work on the subroutines. We will use the same method we used for the main routine: (1) Write an outline in a mixture of English and BASIC. (2) Convert the outline to pure BASIC, using GOSUBs to avoid bothersome details.

Since the two subroutines are similar, we can plan them both at the same time. Look again at the elements of the song. The song is made up of phrases with seven notes and a rest. Notice that the A-part of the song has two *different* phrases. The B-part also has two phrases, but they are exactly the *same*. Here are the subroutine outlines:

```
190  '
200  'SUB A-PART
___       play phrase A1
___       play phrase A2
___   RETURN
290  '
300  'SUB B-PART
___       play phrase B1
___       play phrase B1
___   RETURN
```

If you are using Cartridge BASIC, you could now convert from English directly to the PLAY statement. However, let's continue to use only the SOUND statement, which is already in your TOOLKIT subroutines. Here are the complete A-PART and B-PART routines:

```
190  '
200  'SUB A-PART
210      GOSUB 400     'PHRASE A1
220      GOSUB 500     'PHRASE A2
230   RETURN
290  '
300  'SUB B-PART
310      GOSUB 600     'PHRASE B1
320      GOSUB 600     'PHRASE B1
330   RETURN
```

Enter these two subroutines into the computer now.

3. Why are there two *identical* GOSUBs in the B-PART subroutine, but not in the A-PART subroutine?
4. Will your program now handle *any* song in A-B-A form?

Testing the Program

The program in your computer is getting big. You are probably beginning to want to test it and look for errors. It is true that you have not yet written the subroutines at lines 400, 500, and 600. Nonetheless, there is an easy way you can begin testing at this point. The trick is to write **skeleton subroutines** like these:

```
390 '
400 'SUB PHRASE A1
410    PRINT "PHRASE A1"
480  RETURN
490 '
500 'SUB PHRASE A2
510    PRINT "PHRASE A2"
580  RETURN
590 '
600 'SUB PHRASE B1
610    PRINT "PHRASE B1"
680  RETURN
```

Lines 410, 510, and 610 are examples of **debugging messages**. When you run the program, these messages show up on the screen. They will tell you which subroutines are being performed and in what order. **Enter these three skeleton subroutines into the computer now. Then, run the program.**

Well, that did not help, unless you got a Syntax error message. (If so, correct the error and rerun.) The debugging messages disappeared as soon as they were printed. This happened because line 150 told the computer to go back to the text screen. You can avoid this by using a new statement. **Add this line to your program while debugging:**

```
145    STOP
```

Now run the program. You should see these seven lines on the screen:

```
PHRASE A1
PHRASE A2
PHRASE B1
PHRASE B1
PHRASE A1
PHRASE A2
Break in 145
```

If you see a Syntax error message, edit the faulty line. If a debugging message is missing from the screen, check your GOSUB statements. If there are too many debugging messages, your program probably has a "Missing RETURN" bug somewhere.

Enter the TRON command and run the program again. Then use TROFF to turn the trace off. You should understand the order of the line numbers in the trace. **Now delete the STOP statement.** Your main routine and new subroutines should look like this:

```
100 'PROGRAM SONG
110    SCREEN 1
120    GOSUB 200    'A-PART
130    GOSUB 300    'B-PART
140    GOSUB 200    'A-PART
150    SCREEN 0
160 END
190 '
200 'SUB A-PART
210    GOSUB 400    'PHRASE A1
220    GOSUB 500    'PHRASE A2
230 RETURN
290 '
300 'SUB B-PART
310    GOSUB 600    'PHRASE B1
320    GOSUB 600    'PHRASE B1
330 RETURN
390 '
400 'SUB PHRASE A1
410    PRINT "PHRASE A1"
480 RETURN
490 '
500 'SUB PHRASE A2
510    PRINT "PHRASE A2"
580 RETURN
590 '
600 'SUB PHRASE B1
610    PRINT "PHRASE B1"
680 RETURN
```

Once you have fixed any errors, you have finished your skeleton program. You have only one thing left to do. You should replace the debugging statements by the actual notes of the three musical phrases. Here is how the PHRASE A1 subroutine should look:

```
390  '
400  'SUB PHRASE A1
410     GOSUB 1000    'DO
420     GOSUB 1000    'DO
430     GOSUB 1400    'SOL
440     GOSUB 1400    'SOL
450     GOSUB 1500    'LA
460     GOSUB 1500    'LA
470     GOSUB 1400    'SOL
475     GOSUB 1800    'REST
480  RETURN
```

Edit subroutine PHRASE A1 to look like this. Before going on, enter SCREEN 1 to get on the graphics screen. Then debug the phrase by entering GOSUB 400 in the immediate mode. You should hear the first phrase of "Twinkle, Twinkle Little Star." If not, list the new subroutine and fix any errors.

Edit subroutine PHRASE A2 to play these notes: fa, fa, mi, mi, re, re, do, rest. (The FA, MI, and RE subroutines are at lines 1300, 1200, and 1100.) If necessary, switch the computer to the graphics screen with SCREEN 1. Debug by entering GOSUB 500 in the immediate mode. You should hear the second phrase of the A-part. Now you can test subroutine A–PART: **In the immediate mode, enter GOSUB 200.** You should hear both phrases of the A-part now.

Edit subroutine PHRASE B1 to play these notes: sol, sol, fa, fa, mi, mi, re, rest. Debug it by entering GOSUB 600 in the immediate mode. When that subroutine works, you can test subroutine B–PART: **In the immediate mode, enter GOSUB 300.** You should hear all the B-part of the song.

5. How can you test a single subroutine on the computer without running the whole program?
6. Why is it better to test one subroutine at a time instead of just running the whole program?

Final Testing and Refining

Your whole program (not counting the TOOLKIT subroutines) should look like the one below. Take a moment to look carefully at the parts of the program and see how they work together. Which part gives the overall form of the song? Which parts tell the actual melodies to be played?

```
100 'PROGRAM SONG
110     SCREEN 1
120     GOSUB 200     'A-PART
130     GOSUB 300     'B-PART
140     GOSUB 200     'A-PART
150     SCREEN 0
160   END
190 '
200 'SUB A-PART
210     GOSUB 400     'PHRASE A1
220     GOSUB 500     'PHRASE A2
230   RETURN
290 '
300 'SUB B-PART
310     GOSUB 600     'PHRASE B1
320     GOSUB 600     'PHRASE B1
330   RETURN
390 '
400 'SUB PHRASE A1
410     GOSUB 1000     'DO
420     GOSUB 1000     'DO
430     GOSUB 1400     'SOL
440     GOSUB 1400     'SOL
450     GOSUB 1500     'LA
460     GOSUB 1500     'LA
470     GOSUB 1400     'SOL
475     GOSUB 1800     'REST
480   RETURN
490 '
```

```
500  'SUB PHRASE A2
510      GOSUB 1300    'FA
520      GOSUB 1300    'FA
530      GOSUB 1200    'MI
540      GOSUB 1200    'MI
550      GOSUB 1100    'RE
560      GOSUB 1100    'RE
570      GOSUB 1000    'DO
575      GOSUB 1800    'REST
580  RETURN
590  '
600  'SUB PHRASE B1
610      GOSUB 1400    'SOL
620      GOSUB 1400    'SOL
630      GOSUB 1300    'FA
640      GOSUB 1300    'FA
650      GOSUB 1200    'MI
660      GOSUB 1200    'MI
670      GOSUB 1100    'RE
675      GOSUB 1800    'REST
680  RETURN
```

Now test the whole program: Type RUN and listen carefully. You should hear all the notes of the song this time.

Now is a good time to add two new tools to the TOOLKIT subroutines. You will often want the computer to go to the graphics or text screen with the screen cleared and the background set to a given color. The SCREEN statement alone will not do the job, but the subroutines below will. **Enter them into the computer now.**

```
1990  '
2000  'SUB TEXT
2010      SCREEN 0
2020      WIDTH 40
2030      CLS
2040  RETURN
2090  '
2100  'SUB GRAPHICS
2110      SCREEN 1
2120      COLOR 0
2130      CLS
2140  RETURN
```

Test the effects of these subroutines by entering GOSUB 2100 and GOSUB 2000 in the immediate mode. They should switch to graphics mode or text mode with a clear screen and a black background. If you are using a color TV, you may prefer the graphics screen to be set to blue. If so, use COLOR 1 in line 2120. If you are using Cassette BASIC, you may not be able to see the left column of characters after the screen changes. This problem has a simple solution. Just add the following line to the two subroutines at lines 2025 and 2125:

```
OUT 980, 2: OUT 981, 44
```

Don't worry about how this remedy works or why. Treat it as a bit of "black magic." This will automatically move the picture one character to the right. (Change the 44 to 43 for a two-character move, and so on.)

When these new subroutines are working, change lines 110 and 150 of your main routine to GOSUB statements that use the new routines. Run the program again. It should work as before.

Save your whole program on cassette or diskette under the name SONG.

Enter the command DELETE 100–680. This tells the computer to erase lines 100–680 from memory. List the program. All that should remain are the TOOLKIT subroutines, including the two new ones you just wrote. **Save the subroutines under the name TOOLKIT. This erases the old version on the cassette or diskette.**

PROJECTS

- Load program SONG back into the computer. Change the PHRASE subroutines so they tell the computer to print a blank line after each phrase is played. Run the new version.

- Sometimes, people repeat the A-part of "Twinkle, Twinkle Little Star" before going on to the B-part. In other words, they change the form to A-A-B-A. What part of program SONG tells the form of the song? Decide what would have to be done to make program SONG play an A-A-B-A song. Then make the necessary changes. Run the new version.

- Make up a song of your own in A-A-B-A form. All you need to do is change the PHRASE subroutines so they contain your melodies. Test each phrase by entering GOSUB statements in the immediate mode. Save your song on cassette or diskette under the name MYSONG.

SUMMARY In this session, you have practiced the top-down method of solving a programming problem. You put the big ideas in the main routine. You put the details in the subroutines. This is sometimes called the "divide and conquer" method: You conquer a big problem by dividing it into small ones. The top-down method does not just work only for programming problems. It also works for any kind of writing, planning, or thinking problem you may face. The main topics of this session are summarized in the table below.

Topic	Description
Debugging message	A PRINT statement put into a program to help understand how it works.
Skeleton subroutine	A subroutine containing only debugging messages.
DELETE *n1* - *n2*	A command to erase program lines with line numbers *n1* through *n2* from memory.

VARIABLES

PART THREE

*I*n Part Two, you learned to solve big programming problems by dividing them into small pieces. You put the major ideas of the program into the main routine. You then put the details into subroutines. This approach to programming—the "top-down" method—lets you deal with each part of the program separately. You don't have to worry about all the parts at once.

At the end of Part Two, you used this method to write a program that tells the computer to play a song. Your program was nearly a hundred lines long. That is a very long program for a beginner to be able to write. But you could do it because you divided the parts of the program into small pieces. You were able to write and test each piece before putting it to work in the program. As you write more programs, you will use the top-down method again and again.

Part Three represents a change of pace. It introduces you to the most important idea in programming: the variable. Until now, each program you have written has told the computer to do one thing and one thing only. Your SONG program, for example, always plays the same song at the same tempo and in the same musical style. You might suppose that the only way to change any of these things is to rewrite parts of the program.

In the next few sessions, you will learn another, much simpler way to change parts of programs. By using variables, you can easily give your programs more variety and make them more interesting. You will soon be able to write programs that do different things every time you run them.

EXPLORING VARIABLES

SESSION 14

Session Goals

- Learn how to use variable names to print things on the screen.
- Learn how to assign meanings to variable names.
- Learn how to use both numeric variables and string variables.
- Discover common errors in using variables.

The LET Statement

In this session, you will learn a new BASIC statement. You will also learn an important new idea. Let's begin with a few experiments at the keyboard. **Start the computer as usual. Then begin these activities:**

```
CLS
NEW
```
Erase the screen and the memory.

```
PRINT 1984
```
You should see 1984 under PRINT.

```
PRINT YEAR
```
Notice the 0. This is new.

```
LET YEAR = 1984
```
This is also new. Watch carefully.

```
PRINT YEAR
```
There is no 0 this time.

```
LET YEAR = 2001
PRINT YEAR
```
You should see 2001 under PRINT.

```
LET YEAR = 1492
PRINT YEAR
```
The same PRINT YEAR statement does different things.

```
PRINT YEAR
```
The computer remembers what YEAR last stood for.

```
NEW
PRINT YEAR
```
Now it has forgotten.

1. You used the statement PRINT YEAR six times. But the same statement printed four different things. Why?
2. What did YEAR stand for after you entered the NEW command?

Another Type of Data

You just explored the use of a **variable**. A variable is information that can *vary*, or change. A variable has a **name** that stands for the information. You used the variable name YEAR. You used the LET statement to specify what information YEAR stood for. In BASIC, such information is a piece of **data**. In this case, the piece of data was a number. Besides numbers, there is also another type of data in BASIC.

```
CLS
PRINT DAY
```
Another 0 should not surprise you.

```
PRINT DAY$
```
The dollar-sign key is the same as (Shift ↑ 4). Only a blank line was printed.

```
LET DAY$ = "MONDAY"
```
Be sure to use quotation marks.

```
PRINT DAY$
```
Note what was printed.

```
LET DAY$ = "BIRTHDAY"
PRINT DAY$
```
Note the new output.

```
NEW
PRINT DAY$
```
DAY$ no longer stands for BIRTHDAY.

Like YEAR, DAY$ is a name that stands for a piece of data. But this time, the data you used are not numbers. Instead, they are words. This type of data is called **string** data because a word is just a string of characters. DAY$ (pronounced "day-string") is the name of a **string variable**. YEAR is the name of a **numeric variable**.

The opposite of a variable is a **constant**. The value of a constant is always the same. In the examples above, the numbers 1984, 2001, 1492, and 0 are **numeric constants**. "MONDAY" and "TUESDAY" are **string constants**.

3. What does the statement LET DAY$ = "BIRTHDAY" tell the computer? Explain in your own words.
4. What does a string variable stand for after you enter the NEW command?

Data-Type Errors

What do you suppose would happen if you accidentally used a string where you should have used a number, or the other way around? Now is a good time to find out.

```
CLS
LET YEAR = 1984
```
That should be OK.

```
LET YEAR = "LEAPYEAR"
```
Oops! That is not allowed.

```
LET YEAR$ = "LEAPYEAR"
```
That's better.

```
LET YEAR$ = 1984
```
No, that won't do.

```
LET YEAR$ = "1984"
```
But that is OK.

YEAR is a numeric-variable name, and 1984 is a numeric constant. YEAR$ is a string-variable name, and "LEAPYEAR" is a string constant. "1984" is also a string constant because of the quotation marks.

5. When did the computer print the message Type mismatch?
6. How do you think the computer tells the difference between a numeric-variable name and a string-variable name?
7. How do you think the computer tells the difference between a numeric constant and a string constant?

Name Errors

We have been using the names YEAR, YEAR$, DAY, and DAY$. How much freedom do you have in picking names? Let's see.

```
CLS
LET A = 5
LET AB = 10
PRINT BEEPER
```
These names are OK.

```
LET 2A = 20
PRINT A+
PRINT WHY?
```
But these names are illegal.

Names must start with a letter of the alphabet. After that, there can be letters or numbers (plus a dollar sign for strings). *Other characters in names are illegal.* Those are the main rules, but there are some exceptions:

```
LET BEEP = 1
PRINT LET
PRINT SOUND
```
Surprise! The computer does not accept these.

These names all start with a letter and contain letters, so they follow the rules above. But the computer complains. The reason is that the words BEEP, LET, and SOUND are part of PCjr BASIC. *You may not use any BASIC word as the name of a variable.* For a list of all BASIC words, see page 413.

8. What kind of character must you use to begin a variable name?
9. Why are each of the names 2X, X*, and NEW illegal for variables?

Using Variables in Programs

Until now, you have been exploring variables by using statements in immediate mode. Let's see what happens in program mode.

```
NEW
CLS
```
Erase the memory and clear the screen.

```
10 PRINT YEAR
20 LET YEAR = 1492
```
What will this program tell the computer to do?

```
RUN
```
Were you right?

```
30 PRINT YEAR
LIST
```
What will this do?

```
RUN
```
Notice both numbers printed on the screen.

```
40 LET YEAR = 2010
50 PRINT YEAR
CLS
LIST
```
What three numbers will be printed now?

```
RUN
```
Right?

10. Just after you typed RUN the first time, what did YEAR stand for?
11. What made YEAR stand for two different numbers later?

SUMMARY

Your experiences in this session have introduced you to variables. The main ideas you have learned about variables are summarized in the table below.

Topic	Description
Data	Pieces of information recognized by a computer.
Constant	A piece of data, such as a number or string, written so that the computer can recognize it. Numeric constants are numbers written in standard decimal notation. String constants are letters, numbers, or other characters written between quotation marks.
Variable	A name that stands for a piece of data. At different times in a program, the same name can stand for different data.
LET	A BASIC statement that tells the computer what a given variable stands for.

HOW VARIABLES WORK

SESSION 15

Session Goals

- Learn more about what variables mean.
- Learn how to assign a value to a variable.
- Use a picture to explain how variables are given values and printed on the screen.
- Recognize that a variable is a place in the memory of the computer.

Variables and Assignment

Your experiments with the computer introduced you to variables. You used a `LET` statement to give a name to a piece of data. After that, the computer dealt with that piece of data simply by using its name. Then you used another `LET` statement to change the meaning of the name. *Giving names to data is the most important idea in computer languages.*

Now is a good time to review what you did in the last session and to think about what it means. **Leave your computer now, find a comfortable chair, and spend the next 15 minutes reading.**

In the last session, when you typed

```
LET YEAR = 1984
PRINT YEAR
```

the result was the same as when you typed

```
PRINT 1984
```

The `LET` statement told the computer what the name `YEAR` stood for. `PRINT YEAR` told the computer to print *whatever* `YEAR` stood for.

There are many everyday examples of this kind of thing. Think about the way we describe a softball game. When we explain the rules, we use variables: the "pitcher," the "catcher," the "batter," and so on. But before the game can begin, we have to say who the pitcher is, who the catcher is, and so on. The captain of a team says, "Susan, you are our pitcher." Using the grammar of BASIC, you would say that sentence this way:

```
LET pitcher = Susan
```

People often use two special words when they talk about variables. They say that the `LET` statement tells the computer "to **assign** a **value** to a variable." For example, `LET YEAR = 2010` tells the computer to assign the value `2010` to the variable named `YEAR`. *The value of a variable is the piece of data that the name stands for.* We often call the `LET` statement the **assignment statement** because it *assigns*, or gives, a value to a variable. (In softball, the captain assigns Susan to the job of pitcher. The value of "pitcher" is Susan.)

You learned in Session 14 that the `NEW` command and the `RUN` command also assign values. `NEW` and `RUN` give every numeric variable a value of `0`. They give every string variable a value of `" "`. This is called the **empty string**, since there are no characters between the two quotation marks.

Every variable has three main properties: its **name**, its **type**, and its **value**. Any `LET` statement in a program tells you all three properties of one of the variables in the program: The name comes after the word LET. The type is *string* if there is a dollar sign after the name, and *numeric* otherwise. The value is whatever is on the right side of the equal sign.

1. What two types of data have you learned about so far?
2. What is the name, type, and value of each variable below?
   a. LET X = 5   *c.* LET Z$ = "2"
   b. LET A$ = "DOG"   *d.* LET P = -3
3. Which variable names below are legal? If a name is illegal, explain why.
   a. FRED   *d.* BEEP
   b. A3   *e.* $C
   c. 3A   *f.* 27
4. Can you think of two LET statements that will cause a Type mismatch error message? Write them.

How Variables Work

Session 14 gave you a lot of first-hand experience with variables. You found out that you could use a LET statement to tell the computer the value of a variable. After that, you could recall the value simply by using the name of the variable. Somehow, the computer *remembered* the value. When you entered the NEW command, the computer *forgot* the old value. Now is the time to understand how the computer remembers and forgets values.

In the last session, you entered and ran the following program:

```
10 PRINT YEAR
20 LET YEAR = 1492
30 PRINT YEAR
40 LET YEAR = 2010
50 PRINT YEAR
```

The computer printed three numbers on the screen: 0, 1492, and 2010. But how did it do that? What was going on inside the computer while the program was running?

The best way to answer these questions is to think again about the memory unit in the computer. The picture introduced in Session 4 will help. On the top of the next page you can see how the computer looks just after you enter the RUN command.

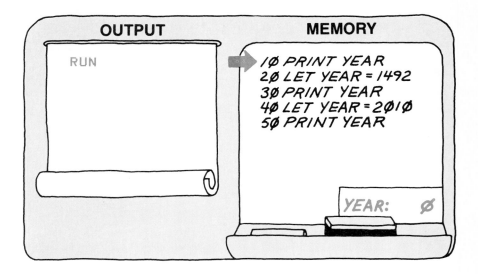

Note the box at the bottom right-hand corner of the chalkboard. It is named YEAR, and it contains Ø at the start. This box is a new feature of the memory chalkboard.

The computer begins by performing the first BASIC statement in the program. That is PRINT YEAR. How does the computer perform it? The answer is simple: The computer first reads whatever is in the memory box named YEAR. It then prints the same thing on the output scroll. Here is the picture afterward:

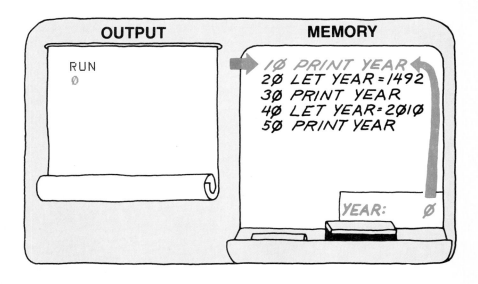

Next, the control crank moves the line pointer down to line 20, the first LET statement. How does the computer perform it? Here are the rules:

The computer's rules for performing the LET statement

1. Find the value of whatever is on the *right* side of the equal sign.
2. Write the value in the box whose *name* is on the *left* side of the equal sign.

The number on the right side of the equal sign in line 20 is 1492. The name on the left side is YEAR. Here is the picture after the computer performs the LET statement:

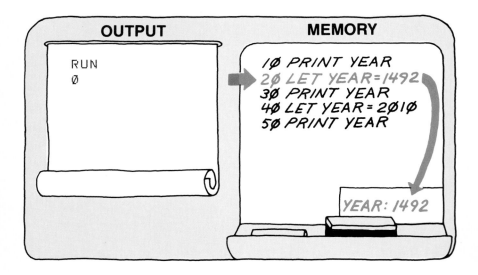

Note that the memory box named YEAR now contains the value 1492. The old value, 0, is forgotten.

Next, the computer moves the line pointer down to line 30. It then performs the PRINT YEAR statement. As before, the computer reads whatever is in the memory box named YEAR. It then prints it on the output scroll. You can see the new picture at the top of the next page.

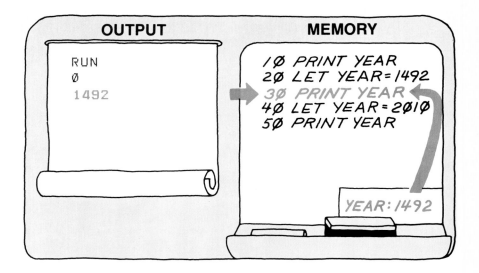

Note that the computer has written 1492 on the scroll. Note also that the YEAR box still contains 1492.

Again, the computer moves the line pointer down. Line 40 contains a LET statement. Thus, the computer performs the rules for it. This time, the right side of the equal sign has the value 2010. Here is the new picture:

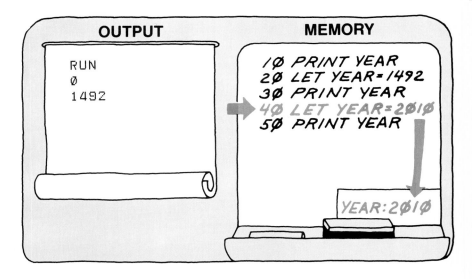

Note the change in the YEAR box in the memory. The LET statement first told the computer to erase the old value (1492) in the box. It then told the computer to write a new value (2010) there. As before, the computer forgets the old value.

Once more, the line pointer moves down. The computer then must perform the PRINT YEAR statement in line 5Ø. Here is the new picture:

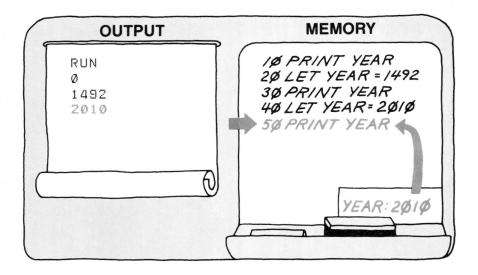

The computer wrote the current value in the YEAR box (2Ø1Ø) on the output scroll. Finally, the computer moves the line pointer down. It finds that there are no more BASIC lines. Thus, it prints Ok on the output scroll and turns on the cursor again. Here is the new picture:

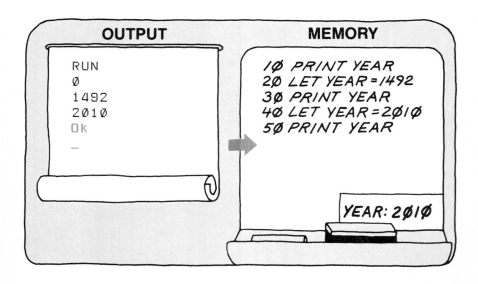

How to Think about Variables

The best way to think about a variable is to imagine that it is a *place in the memory* of the computer. Different places in the memory have different variable names. A place can hold one item of data at a time. A place that holds a number cannot hold a string, and the other way around.

You enter the RUN command to tell the computer to perform a program. But the RUN command also tells the computer something else that is very important: It tells the computer to put Ø in all the places that can hold numbers. It also tells the computer to put " " (the empty string) in all the places that can hold strings. You saw in Session 14 that the NEW command tells the computer to do the same thing.

You can write a variable name anywhere in a program that you have written constants before. When a variable name is used in a PRINT statement, the computer looks in memory for a place with the same name. Then it reads the data value stored there. Finally, it prints that value on the screen.

In a LET statement, a variable name is the *only* thing that can go on the left side of the equal sign (=). The computer first finds the value of whatever is on the *right* side of the equal sign. Then the computer writes the value in the place in memory that has the same name as the variable. The new value erases any data already there.

It is also legal to have a variable name on the *right* side of the equal sign. Here is an example:

```
6Ø LET B$ = A$
```

At first glance, you may think this means to take the data out of location A$ and put it into location B$. That is almost correct, but not quite. According to the LET statement rules, the computer must first "find the value of whatever is on the the right side." This means it must go to the place named A$ and read the data stored there. Then the computer must put a *copy* of the data in the place named B$. *Note that the data in location A$ is not moved or erased. It is just copied and only a copy is moved.*

5. What happens to the values of variables after the computer carries out the NEW command?
6. Look at the last picture of the computer on page 174. What would happen if you now entered the statement PRINT YEAR into the computer?
7. What would the computer print on the screen if you entered the four lines shown below? Use the computer picture to help you explain what would happen.

```
NEW
10 PRINT YEAR
20 LET YEAR = 2000
RUN
```

8. What would the computer print on the screen after it performed the program shown below? Use the computer picture to help you explain.

```
10 LET X$ = "HORSE"
20 LET X$ = "COW"
30 PRINT X$
```

9. What would the computer print on the screen after it performed the program shown below? Use the computer picture to help you explain.

```
10 LET X$ = "HORSE"
20 LET Y$ = X$
30 PRINT Y$
```

10. Suppose the first statement in a program says PRINT N. Explain why the computer prints a 0.
11. What number is in the P and Q memory boxes right after each statement in the program below is performed?

```
10 LET P = 7
20 LET Q = 11
30 LET P = Q
40 LET Q = P
```

SUMMARY

By thinking about a variable as a place in the computer's memory, you can easily understand how variables work. The ideas you have learned about variables are summarized in the table below. Be sure you understand variables: Using variables is the heart of programming.

Topic	Description
Variable	A named place in the memory unit of a computer.
Value	An actual piece of data stored in the memory unit.
Type	The kind of data (string or numeric) stored in the memory unit.
Assignment	Giving a value to a variable.
Empty string	A string containing no characters.

INPUT AND PROCESSING DATA

SESSION 16

Session Goals

- Print things on the screen with different spacing.
- Use your computer to do arithmetic.
- Input numbers on your computer.

Writing a Calculator Program

You've now learned a lot about variables. By using variables, you will be able to write much more interesting programs than before. Most useful programs do three things: First, they take data in from the user of the program. This is called **input**. Second, they do something to the data. This is called **processing**. Third, they give data back to the user. This is called **output**. These three steps happen whenever you use a pocket calculator.

You may not have realized that a pocket calculator really is a computer. Like every other computer, it has an input unit, an output unit, and a memory unit. Like all computers, it also has a part you haven't learned about yet: a processing unit. The main difference between a pocket calculator and your PCjr is the program in memory. Programs that do thousands of different things can be written and entered into the PCjr. But the calculator's memory contains just one program. It tells the computer inside the calculator how to do arithmetic.

If a tiny pocket calculator can do arithmetic, it shouldn't be hard for you to write a BASIC program to tell your PCjr how to do arithmetic. Such a program would have to get two numbers from the user, do the arithmetic, and give out the answer.

The new tool you will need here is a way to get input from the user. We will get to that before long. Let's begin, however, by learning a little more about using the PRINT statement to control the output of the answer.

PRINT with Commas and Semicolons

Until now, you have never used more than one piece of data in a PRINT statement. In this session, you will be using more than one. Now is a good time to learn more about the PRINT statement.

Start the computer in the usual way. Then do the following things in the immediate mode:

PRINT "ABC"
——————————————— No surprises here.

PRINT , "DEF"
——————————————— Notice where the string appears.

PRINT "ABC", "DEF", "GHI"
——————————————— See where the strings are printed.

PRINT "ABC"; "DEF"; "GHI"
——————————————— This is quite different.

PRINT "A"; ; ; ; ; "B"
——————————————— Extra semicolons do nothing.

```
PRINT 2; "PLUS"; 2; "IS"; 4
```
You can mix numbers and strings. Notice the spaces around the numbers.

1. If data in a PRINT statement is separated by commas, how does the computer space the output?
2. If data in a PRINT statement is separated by semicolons, how does the computer space the output?

Doing Arithmetic

Computers solve many arithmetic problems. Let's review arithmetic in BASIC and see how to do arithmetic with variables.

```
NEW
CLS
```
Erase the memory and clear the screen.

```
50 PRINT P , Q
RUN
```
The 0s and their positions should not surprise you.

```
20 LET P = 7
30 LET Q = 3
LIST
RUN
```
Line 50 says to print the value of the variables named P and Q.

```
40 LET R = P + Q
50 PRINT P; "PLUS"; Q; "IS"; R
LIST
```
Check this carefully. Try to guess what the computer will do.

```
RUN
```
Think about how R got its value.

Change the program so that it adds 1234 to 4321. Run the new version. Think about why you saw different numbers this time.

3. What part of your program tells the computer the values of P and Q?
4. What does the + symbol mean in line 40?
5. What does line 40 tell the computer to do? Explain in your own words. (Hint: Think about P, Q, and R as places in the memory unit.)

Using the INPUT Statement

The program now in memory should look like this:

```
20 LET P = 1234
30 LET Q = 4321
40 LET R = P + Q
50 PRINT P; "PLUS"; Q; "IS"; R
```

The program falls nicely into two parts. One part tells the computer what the names P and Q stand for. The other part tells the computer what to do with P and Q, *no matter what P and Q stand for*. When you were writing lines 40 and 50, you did not have to worry about the actual values of P and Q. You just used their names. Lines 20 and 30 assign values, much as you do when you assign Susan to pitch and Larry to catch in a softball game. Lines 40 and 50 are like the rules of the game: The rules are the same no matter who is playing.

Your program is a big step forward. The processing part (line 40) and the output part (line 50) are *independent* of the numbers in the LET statements. Line 40 adds *any* two numbers. Line 50 prints *any* result. There is still one weakness in the program, though: To make it add different numbers, you have to rewrite lines 20 and 30. Let's see how to get around that. **If the program shown above is not in memory, enter it now.**

```
CLS
20 INPUT P
LIST
```
————————————————— Line 20 has a new statement.

```
RUN
```
————————————————— Notice the ? and the flashing cursor.

The computer is waiting for you to type a number and press the (Enter ⏎) key. Do so, as follows:

```
? 5678
```
————————————————— ...and press the (Enter ⏎) key. Notice what was printed.

```
RUN
? 1
```
————————————————— ...and press the (Enter ⏎) key.

```
LIST
```
————————————————— Think about how P got its value.

```
30 INPUT Q
CLS
LIST
```
————————————————— Now both LETs are gone.

```
RUN
? 21
```
————————————————— ...and press the (Enter ⏎) key.

```
? 37
```
————————————————— ...and press the (Enter ⏎) key.

```
RUN
? 12345
? 67890
```
————————————————— Be sure not to use commas in the numbers.

```
20
30 INPUT P, Q
CLS
LIST
```

Now there is only one INPUT statement.

```
RUN
? 21, 37
```

Think how P and Q got values.

```
RUN
? 444, 555
```

That worked too. Now let's make the program more "user friendly."

```
20 PRINT "ENTER TWO NUMBERS"
LIST
RUN
```

...and do what it says.

6. What does the INPUT statement tell the computer to do? Explain in your own words.
7. Your program now contains no data values. Why does that make it better than the old version with LET statements?
8. How does line 20 make the program "friendlier," that is, easier to use?

INPUT Errors

Users sometimes make errors when replying to a request for input. Use your last program to find out what happens when you make such an error. The program should look like this:

```
20 PRINT "ENTER TWO NUMBERS"
30 INPUT P, Q
40 LET R = P + Q
50 PRINT P; "PLUS"; Q; "IS"; R
```

CLS
RUN
? 3   **Enter only one number and press the** (Enter ⏎) **key.** Notice the error message and go on to the next step.

? 3, 4, 5, 6   Note what happens.

? TWO, FOUR   Note what happens.

? 15, 72   Now it works OK.

9. Suppose the input reply does not have as many numbers as there are variables in the INPUT statement. What does the computer do in that case?
10. What does the computer do if there are too many numbers in the input reply?

PROJECTS

● Change the + in line 40 of the last program to a *. You may also want to change PLUS in line 50 to TIMES. Run the new version. Try out some large numbers.

● Change the arithmetic symbol in line 40 of the last program to the / symbol. You might also want to change TIMES to DIVIDED BY in line 50. Run the new version. See what happens when you try to divide by 0.

● Enter this new version of the program above:

```
20 PRINT "ENTER TWO WORDS"
30 INPUT P$, Q$
40 LET R$ = P$ + Q$
50 PRINT P$; " + "; Q$ ;" = "; R$
```

Run the program. See whether quotation marks are needed in the input reply. Experiment with different string inputs.

SUMMARY

By adding the INPUT statement to your arithmetic program, you told the computer how to add *any* two numbers that the user enters. The table below reviews this important statement. Be sure you understand how it works.

Statement	Description
INPUT	A BASIC statement that tells the computer to stop and wait for one or more pieces of data to be entered by the user of the program.
INPUT P, Q	The computer is to wait for two numbers, separated by a comma, to be entered. The first number is assigned to P and the second is assigned to Q.
INPUT P$, Q	The computer is to wait for a string and a number, separated by a comma, to be entered. The string is assigned to P$. The number is assigned to Q.

HOW INPUT AND PROCESSING WORK

SESSION 17

Session Goals

- Learn how to use arithmetic and string operators on the computer.
- Learn what an expression is.
- Learn more about how to input data.
- Use the computer picture to explain how input and arithmetic work.

Review

You will not be using the computer in this session. Find a comfortable chair and read the next few pages.

In Session 16, you found that BASIC gives you ways to input and process data. You used the INPUT statement to tell the computer to accept numbers and strings from the user. You used the LET statement and some new operations to process these data.

At the start of Session 16, you used commas and semicolons in PRINT statements. These punctuation marks do two things: First, they *separate* one item from another in the statement. Second, they say *where* the output is to appear on the screen. A comma tells the computer to print the next output at the start of the next **standard print zone**: There are two standard zones 14 characters apart on the PCjr screen. A semicolon tells the computer that the next output should start wherever the last output ended. You saw that numeric data was printed with an extra space before and after the number.

The +, -, *, and / symbols tell the computer to add, subtract, multiply, and divide numbers. These symbols are called **arithmetic operators**. They usually appear in LET statements, such as these:

```
40 LET R = P + Q
60 LET A = B / C
```

These operators tell the computer to perform an arithmetic operation with two pieces of numeric data, the one to the left of the operator and the one to the right.

There is only one operator that you can use with strings. This is the **link** operator. It tells the computer to join two strings together into a single string. The symbol for the link operator is the plus sign (+). For example, "NOW" + "HERE" tells the computer to join the two strings into the single string "NOWHERE". The link operator is also called the **concatenation** operator.

In every programming language, there is a special word for combinations such as P + Q, B / C, and "NOW" + "WHERE". They are called **expressions**. The main point about an expression is that it has a definite value. *In fact, anything that has a value is an expression.* For example, a single variable has a value. Thus, a variable is also an expression. So is a constant. When people talk about expressions, however, they usually mean combinations of variables, constants, and operators. Every one of the items you see below is an expression:

```
25
"HELLO"
6 + 2
"FAT" + "HER"
X - 4
2 * P + 3 * Q
```

You saw in Session 16 that you can use an expression on the *right* side of the equal sign in a LET statement. In BASIC, there is a simple rule that tells you where you may use expressions: *You may write an expression anywhere it is legal to write a constant in a BASIC statement.* (In Part Six, you will learn the one exception to this rule: the DATA statement.) You have used numeric constants in the LET, PRINT, LINE, SOUND, PLAY, SCREEN, and COLOR statements. So you could also write a numeric expression in any of those statements, as in the following example:

```
COLOR 2 * A + B
```

Variables are also expressions. Thus, you can use their names anywhere you can use an expression. But there are a few places where you may not use anything but a variable name. You have seen the two main ones: Variable names must appear (1) in INPUT statements and (2) on the *left* side of the equal sign in LET statements. You must use variables there because you want to assign values. You cannot assign a value to something unless you name it. For example, the computer will *not* accept these statements:

```
LET 5 = X
INPUT 932
```

1. What are the purposes of commas and semicolons in a PRINT statement?
2. What symbols are used in BASIC for the addition, subtraction, multiplication, and division operators?
3. What does a plus sign between two strings tell the computer to do?
4. What does the term *expression* mean?
5. Where do the rules of BASIC allow you to write an expression?
6. In what two places in BASIC programs can only a variable name appear?

How Input and Arithmetic Work

In Session 16, you experimented with a program that first asked you to enter two numbers and then printed their sum on the screen. Let's take a close look at the steps the computer went through while performing that program. Our picture of the computer needs one more part to explain how your program worked. This part is called the **arithmetic and logic scratchpad**. It stands for the **arithmetic and logic unit (ALU)** in the real computer.

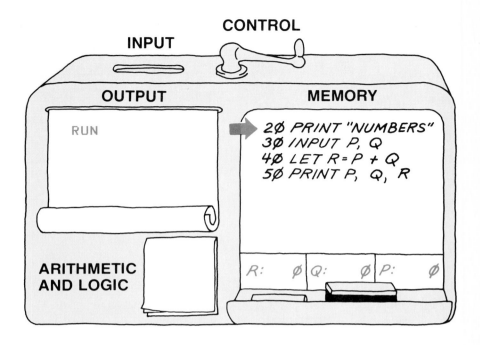

The picture is now complete. *Using a picture with only these five parts, you can understand how the computer performs any program.* The picture shows the computer just after the program has been entered, the screen cleared, and the RUN command entered. *Note the P, Q, and R variable boxes. At first, they have Øs inside.* Here is the picture after the computer performs the first PRINT statement:

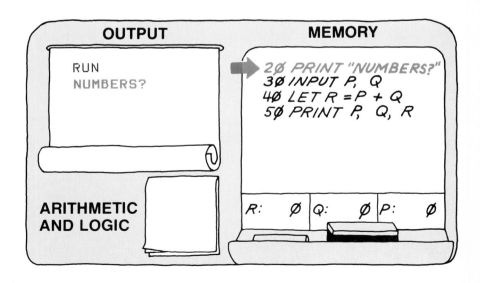

Now the computer moves the line pointer down to line 3Ø and begins to perform the INPUT statement. Here are the rules:

The computer's rules for performing INPUT P, Q

1. Print a question mark on the output screen, turn on the cursor, and stop.
2. Wait for two numbers, separated by commas, to be typed on the keyboard, and for the (Enter ⏎) key to be pressed.
3. Assign the first number to P and the second number to Q.

Below is a picture of the computer while the INPUT statement is being performed. The question mark is on the screen, and the cursor is on. The numbers 234 and 765 are about to be dropped into the input slot.

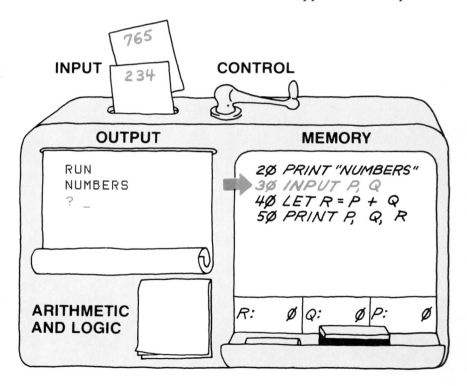

After the two numbers drop into the input slot, the computer does two things: First, it writes them on the output scroll. Second, it also writes them in the P and Q memory boxes. The new picture is at the top of the next page.

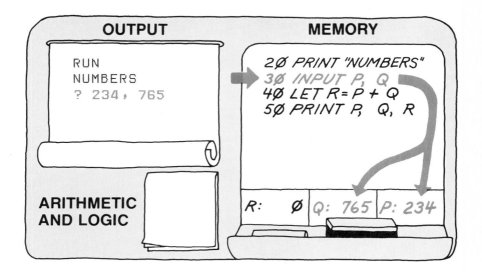

Now the computer must follow the rules for the LET statement. Rule 1 on page 172 says to "find the value of whatever is on the right side of the equal sign." Here is how the computer does that:

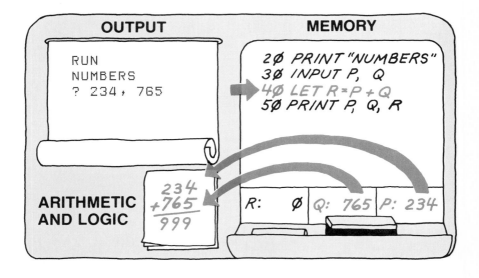

To find the value of P + Q, the computer uses the arithmetic and logic scratchpad. First, it makes copies of the data in the P and Q boxes in memory. Then it adds them together to get 999, which is at the bottom of the scratchpad.

Rule 2 for performing the LET statement says to "write the value (999) in the box whose name is on the left side of the equal sign." Here is how the model looks after the computer performs the LET statement:

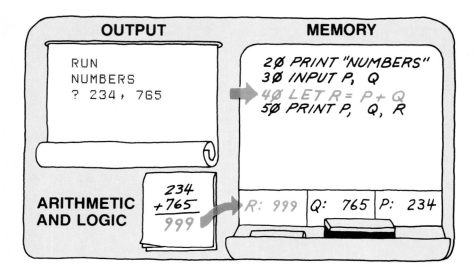

Notice that the R box in memory now contains the answer from the bottom of the scratchpad. This is the value of P + Q. After doing the arithmetic, the computer throws away the scratch sheet. This clears the scratchpad for the next calculation.

Finally, the computer moves the line pointer to the last line. It then performs the PRINT statement there. Here is the picture afterward:

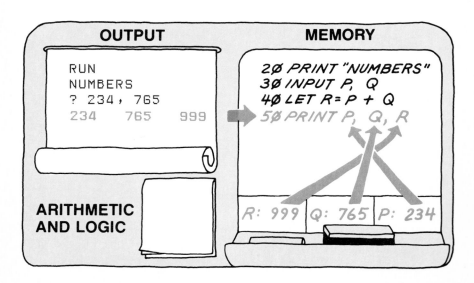

So far, you have seen the computer use the arithmetic and logic unit (ALU) in only one way—to do arithmetic. But the computer also uses the ALU in other ways. It uses the ALU to link strings and to compare one piece of data with another. In other words, the ALU is where the computer processes data. The ALU is the **processing unit** of the computer.

The program line that told the computer how to process the data was line 4Ø, the LET statement. As you have learned, the LET statement is the assignment statement in BASIC. In all computer languages, the assignment statement is nearly always the one that tells the computer how to process the data.

7. What is the computer's arithmetic and logic unit used for?
8. Is it true that the INPUT statement causes something to be output? Explain your answer.
9. While the computer is performing the statement INPUT X, what happens to the number a user enters into the computer?
10. Suppose you run the program shown below and enter the string CAT. What is in the computer's memory afterward?

```
10 LET A$ = "DOG"
20 INPUT A$
```

SUMMARY

In this session, you have taken a close look at input and processing. You have seen what goes on inside the computer at every step. The new topics are summarized below. Make sure you have a clear picture of how input and processing take place in the computer before you go on.

Topic	Description
Standard print zone	A 14-character column on the output screen. A comma in the PRINT statement tells the computer to start the next output in the next print zone. If there is not enough room, part of the output will be printed on the next line of the screen.
Arithmetic operators	The symbols that tell the computer to do arithmetic with two numbers. The symbols +, -, *, and / stand for addition, subtraction, multiplication, and division.
String operator	A symbol that tells the computer to combine two strings. The only string operator in BASIC is +, the link operator. It tells the computer to join the two strings together into a single string.
Expression	Any legal combination of variables, constants, and operators that results in a single value.
Arithmetic & logic unit	The part of a computer in which data is processed.

USING VARIABLES TO CONTROL SUBROUTINES

SESSION 18

Session Goals

- Use a variable to control the duration in the SOUND statement.
- Use a variable to control the tempo of a piece of music.
- Improve the TOOLKIT subroutines.

Play It Again, Sam

In the last four sessions, you have learned about the LET and INPUT statements. You should have a good idea now about variables. You should know what variables are, how they get their values, and how they work. Now it is time to see how you can use variables to make your programs simpler and more interesting.

In Session 13, you wrote a program that told the computer to play "Twinkle, Twinkle Little Star." You saved it in a file named SONG. Suppose you want to hear that tune. All you have to do is load the program back into the computer and enter the RUN command. If you want to hear it again, enter RUN again.

So far, so good. Sooner or later, however, you will get tired of hearing the same song played exactly the same way every time. You will wonder what it would sound like if it were played differently. What if it were played slower or faster? What if the notes ran together? What if they were separated from one another? In other words, you will probably want to *vary* the way the music is played.

You could do that by rewriting the DO-RE-MI subroutines every time you wanted to have the music played in a new way. But there is a much easier way to do the same thing. In this session, you will see how using a BASIC variable can make it easy to change the way the music sounds in program SONG.

Start your computer as usual. Then load program SONG from diskette or cassette. If you did not save the program at the end of Session 13, load the TOOLKIT subroutines and then enter the main routine and five subroutines listed on pages 155–156.

When the program is again in memory, run it a few times. List the main routine. Use it as a directory to the subroutines. List each subroutine. Remind yourself how the program works.

In program SONG, the main routine tells the form of the song. The A-PART and B-PART subroutines tell what musical phrases make up each main part. Subroutines PHRASE A1, PHRASE A2, and PHRASE B1 tell the notes in each phrase. Finally, the DO, RE, MI, etc., subroutines tell the computer how to play each musical note.

List the DO subroutine. It begins at line 1000. If you are using Cartridge BASIC, it should look like this:

```
1000  'SUB DO
1005     PLAY "MF"
1010     SOUND 523, 10
1020     COLOR 1
1030     PRINT "DO"
1035     SOUND 32767, 1
1040  RETURN
```

Look at the four lines that make up the body of this subroutine. Then answer these questions:

1. What do the two numbers in line 1010 tell the computer to do?
2. Why does the computer always play the notes for the same length of time when you run program SONG?
3. What does line 1035 tell the computer to do?

Varying the Length of the Notes

Suppose you wanted the computer to play "Twinkle, Twinkle Little Star" twice as fast. You would have to make the length of each note half of what it now is. That is, you would have to change all the duration numbers in the SOUND statements from 10 clock ticks to 5 clock ticks. Later, if you wanted to change the speed again, you would have to go back and edit all the SOUND statements once more. You would probably tire of this quickly and give up.

Fortunately, there is an easier way. You have learned a very important fact in Part Three: You can use a variable name anywhere in a BASIC program that you can use a constant. For example, you could write line 1010 in subroutine DO like this:

```
1010      SOUND 523, DURATION
```

DURATION is the name of a numeric variable. This statement tells the computer to look into the memory unit and find what number is stored in the place named DURATION. Then it tells the computer to play a frequency of 523 Hz (middle C) for that number of clock ticks.

Suppose that all your DO, RE, MI, etc., subroutines were written like this. That is, suppose they had the name DURATION instead of 10 in the SOUND statements. Now, also suppose that your main routine had this statement at the beginning:

```
115    LET DURATION = 5
```

This assignment statement would tell the computer to start by putting 5 into memory in the place named DURATION. After that, the computer would use 5 for the duration of every note it played. The song would go twice as fast as before. Then, suppose you wanted all the notes to go slower. All you would have to do is change one line: line 115. That is what using variables can do for you.

Now let's explore this idea. **Edit each of your note subroutines, replacing each 10 in a SOUND statement by the name DURATION.** Here, for example, is how the Cartridge BASIC version of subroutine RE should look:

```
1100  'SUB RE
1105     PLAY "MF"
1110     SOUND 587, DURATION
1120     COLOR 2
1130     PRINT "RE"
1135     SOUND 32767, 1
1140  RETURN
```

Be sure to make the same change in your REST subroutine, beginning at line 1800.

Next, add a **LET** statement to your main routine, as follows:

```
100  'PROGRAM SONG
110     GOSUB 2100    'GRAPHICS
115     LET DURATION = 10
120     GOSUB 200  'A-PART
125     GOSUB 200  'A-PART
130     GOSUB 300  'B-PART
140     GOSUB 200  'A-PART
150     GOSUB 2000   'TEXT
160  END
```

Now, run the new version of your program. It should sound exactly the same as before. **Change line 115 so that the value of DURATION is 5. Run the program again and listen. Now change the value to 2 and rerun the program.**

As you have just seen, using the variable name DURATION instead of the constant 10 is very useful. It is now much easier to control the note subroutines. A variable used to control the way a subroutine works is sometimes called a **parameter**. If you have not seen that word before, you will know what it means the next time you see it. In your program, DURATION is the parameter that controls the note subroutines.

4. In your own words, what makes the new versions of your note subroutines better than the old ones?
5. The RE subroutine now tells the computer to print RE whenever it is performed. How would you change the subroutine to have it tell the computer to print different things at different times?

Improving Program SONG

You may have noticed that your program contains a small musical error. As written, the program calls for a rest note as the last note in each of the eight-note phrases of "Twinkle, Twinkle Little Star." For example, the first phrase is now this:

   do, do, sol, sol, la, la, sol, rest

But, as you can see below, there are no rest notes in the actual song. Instead, the last note of each phrase is played twice as long as each of the other notes. Now is the time to fix this musical error.

Twinkle, Twinkle Little Star

Delete the **LET** statement at line **115** of the main routine. Then change your **PHRASE A1** subroutine as follows:

```
400  'SUB PHRASE A1
405     LET DURATION = 10
410     GOSUB 1000   'DO
420     GOSUB 1000   'DO
430     GOSUB 1400   'SOL
440     GOSUB 1400   'SOL
450     GOSUB 1500   'LA
460     GOSUB 1500   'LA
465     LET DURATION = 20
470     GOSUB 1400   'SOL
480  RETURN
```

Notice that the rest-note statement (GOSUB 1800) is now missing. **First, type GOSUB 2100 to move to the graphics screen. Type GOSUB 400 to listen to the subroutine. Listen to the last note.** It should be played twice as long as the other six notes.

Here is how the change works: Line 405 tells the computer to put 10 in the DURATION box in memory. Lines 410–460 tell the computer to perform the note subroutines. Each note subroutine has a SOUND statement containing the variable name DURATION. So the computer looks in the DURATION box in memory. There it finds the number 10. So it plays each note for that amount of time. Then comes line 465. It tells the computer to erase the 10 in the DURATION box and put 20 there instead. Any notes played after that will sound twice as long. That is why the final *sol* was longer than the first six notes.

Using PHRASE A1 as a model, make the same changes in subroutine PHRASE A2. Enter GOSUB 500 to test it. Do the same for subroutine PHRASE B1. When the phrases are correct, run the whole program.

Now you should hear "Twinkle, Twinkle Little Star" played the way you are used to hearing it.

6. Suppose you added the line 475 GOSUB 1300 to your new version of subroutine PHRASE A1. How long would the new note be played?
7. Suppose you accidentally left out the first LET statement in subroutine PHRASE A1. How long would the first six notes of the song be played?

Another Improvement

There is still a problem with your new version of program SONG: It now plays at the same tempo whenever you run the program. To change the tempo, you would have to edit lines 405, 465, 505, 565, 605, and 665. There ought to be an easier way, and there is. Once again, the solution is to use variables.

As things stand now, your three PHRASE subroutines have LET statements that assign 10 and 20 as the values of DURATION. The numbers 10 and 20 are *constants*. That is why the tempo of your song is always the same. It would be easier if you used *variable names* instead. For example, you might think of the first six notes of each phrase as being "quarter notes." Then the seventh note would be a "half note." Using these ideas, you could substitute the name NOTE4 for the number 10. You could use the name NOTE2 for the number 20. On the top of the next page, you can see how subroutine PHRASE A1 would look:

```
400  'SUB PHRASE A1
405     LET DURATION = NOTE4
410     GOSUB 1000    'DO
420     GOSUB 1000    'DO
430     GOSUB 1400    'SOL
440     GOSUB 1400    'SOL
450     GOSUB 1500    'LA
460     GOSUB 1500    'LA
465     LET DURATION = NOTE2
470     GOSUB 1400    'SOL
480  RETURN
```

This version of the subroutine is better than the one now in your computer. First, it is easier to read: It tells you that the first six notes are quarter notes. It tells you that the last note is a half note. Second, you can change the tempo of the music just by changing the values of NOTE4 and NOTE2.

Change the LET statements in the PHRASE A1 subroutine as shown above. In the immediate mode, enter these lines:

```
SCREEN 1
LET NOTE4 = 5
LET NOTE2 = 10
GOSUB 400
```

You should hear the first phrase at twice the tempo as before. **Next, make the same changes in the other two PHRASE subroutines. Then test them in the immediate mode.**

Finally, we must add two LET statements to the main routine. These tell the computer what NOTE4 and NOTE2 stand for. **Add the two lines shown at the top of the next page.**

```
100 'PROGRAM SONG
110    GOSUB 2100   'GRAPHICS
115    LET NOTE4 = 10
116    LET NOTE2 = 2 * NOTE4
120    GOSUB 200 'A-PART
125    GOSUB 200 'A-PART
130    GOSUB 300 'B-PART
140    GOSUB 200 'A-PART
150    GOSUB 2000   'TEXT
160 END
```

Notice that line 116 defines NOTE2 in terms of NOTE4: A half note is twice as long as a quarter note, no matter what the tempo is. **Run the program. Change the 10 in line 115 to 5 and run the program again. Then change the number to 2 and run it again.** You should hear the song in different tempos each time.

8. Which line in the new version of program SONG controls the tempo?
9. Suppose you were writing a song that had eighth notes. These are half as long as quarter notes. What line would you add to the program to define NOTE8 as an eighth note?

A Final Improvement

There is one last musical problem in program SONG. Each note subroutine contains two SOUND statements. Here is subroutine MI, for example, in the Cartridge BASIC version:

```
1200 'SUB MI
1205    PLAY "MF"
1210    SOUND 659, DURATION
1220    COLOR 3
1230    PRINT "MI"
1235    SOUND 32767, 1
1240 RETURN
```

Although the musical note has a variable length, the amount of silence afterwards (line 1035) is always one clock tick. It makes better musical sense to have the amount of silence be shorter if the note is short and longer if the note is long.

The solution is to use a variable that stands for the fraction of the total time that the note is to be played. Let's call this variable HOLD. Then we could write the note subroutine like this:

```
1200 'SUB MI
1210   SOUND 659, HOLD * DURATION
1220   COLOR 3
1230   PRINT "MI"
1235   SOUND 32767, (1-HOLD)*DURATION
1240   RETURN
```

Here is how this works: Suppose you decide that the note should be played for three-fourths of the total time. The rest of the time, there should be silence. In other words, HOLD should have a value of three-fourths. Then 1 – HOLD would equal one-fourth. Now, suppose DURATION stands for eight clock ticks. Three-fourths of eight is six. So line 1210 tells the computer to play the note for six clock ticks. One-fourth of eight is two. So line 1235 tells the computer to be silent for two clock ticks.

Suppose you now change DURATION to four. The note will then be played for three clock ticks (three-fourths of the whole length). The silence will therefore last one clock tick (one-fourth of the whole length).

By varying the value of HOLD, you can change the "connectedness" of the notes. If you set HOLD equal to 1, there will be no silence between the notes. Each note will run into the next without pause. (Musicians call this *legato*.) If HOLD is three-fourths or less, the notes seem very

disconnected. (This is called *staccato*.) You can experiment with these effects by making the changes below.

Using subroutine MI above as a model, change the SOUND statements in all the note subroutines. Then change your main routine to look like this:

```
100  'PROGRAM SONG
110     GOSUB 2100   'GRAPHICS
112     LET HOLD = 7 / 8
115     LET NOTE4 = 8
116     LET NOTE2 = 2 * NOTE4
120     GOSUB 200  'A-PART
125     GOSUB 200  'A-PART
130     GOSUB 300  'B-PART
140     GOSUB 200  'A-PART
150     GOSUB 2000   'TEXT
160  END
```

This tells the computer to play each note for seven-eighths of its length. It also says that the length of a quarter-note is to be eight clock ticks. **Run the program and listen. Now edit line 112. Experiment with different fractions for the HOLD time.**

NOTE *Now you have finished improving this program and its subroutines. Be sure to save all your changes, as explained below. You will need the new versions of the TOOLKIT subroutines in Part Four.*

Save your whole program with the name SONG on cassette or diskette. This should replace the old version of SONG.

Enter the command DELETE 100-680. This tells the computer to erase lines 100-680 from memory. **List the program.** All that should remain are the TOOLKIT subroutines. These include the two new ones you just wrote. **Save the subroutines with the name TOOLKIT.** This erases the old version on the cassette or diskette.

10. If the HOLD value is seven-eighths and the DURATION value is 16, how long will each note sound? How much silence will follow?
11. In the new note subroutines, does changing the HOLD value change the tempo of the music?

PROJECTS

● Load program SONG back into the computer. Edit lines 112–116 to make them the body of a subroutine that begins at line 700. Call it NOTE VALUES. Replace these lines in the main routine with a GOSUB statement to perform the new subroutine. Run the program.

● In your new subroutine, replace the LET statements for HOLD and NOTE4 with a PRINT statement and an INPUT statement. The PRINT statement should ask the user to enter the quarter-note length and the hold value. The INPUT statement should assign the two numbers to NOTE4 and HOLD. You were able to use 7 / 8 for HOLD in your program. However, you must use the decimal form (.875) when entering numbers in response to an INPUT statement. You may want to save this version of program SONG.

SUMMARY

In this session, you have put variables into practice. At the beginning, your SONG program played its tune at the same tempo every time. At the end, the program made it easy for you to vary both the tempo and the "connectedness" of the notes. In the original version, you used constants to say how long to play each note and how long to remain silent. By changing the constants to variables, you were able to write a far more interesting program. Variables give you a powerful way to make the computer do what you want it to.

Topic	Description
Parameter	A variable used to control a subroutine.

THE LOOP BLOCK

PART FOUR

*I*n Part Three, you learned to use variables to give names to pieces of data. You used a new BASIC statement for input and one for assignment. These statements allow you to write programs that tell the computer how to process data, no matter what the actual data values are. Without variables, a program could not tell the computer to accept data from the user, process it, and give a result.

In Part Four, you will learn about another important programming tool: the loop block. Computers are very good at doing things over and over again. Unlike people, computers don't get bored or sloppy. A computer can add a thousand numbers in a second without making a single mistake. In the same time, it can search through a list of a thousand words and tell you whether or not a particular word is in the list.

But how can you tell your computer to add a thousand numbers? How can you tell it to examine a thousand words? You might guess that you need to write a program with at least a thousand statements. Most of these statements would be very much alike. Suddenly, your programming job begins to look very repetitive and very boring. Isn't there a better way?

There is a much better way. In Part Four, you will learn a very simple way to tell the computer to do something again and again. This takes more than one BASIC statement, but not a thousand. You will need to put special statements at the beginning and at the end of the group of statements you want the computer to perform again and again. This entire set of statements is called a "loop block." You will learn about it next.

THE INFINITE-
LOOP BLOCK

SESSION 19

Session Goals

- Use a GOTO statement to tell the computer to skip some of the statements in a program.
- Use a GOTO statement to create an infinite loop.
- Learn how to stop and restart the computer while running a program.
- Use the infinite loop to print strings and explore numbers.

Skipping Statements

Start the computer as usual. Load the TOOLKIT subroutines into the computer from your diskette or tape cassette. If you did not save the TOOLKIT subroutines at the end of Session 18, load program SONG into the computer and delete all lines with line numbers less than 1000. Then go on to the activities below.

```
CLS
100 'PROGRAM SCALE
110    LET DURATION = 10
120    LET HOLD = .8
130    GOSUB 2100   'GRAPHICS
140    GOSUB 1000   'DO
150    GOSUB 1100   'RE
160    GOSUB 1200   'MI
170    GOSUB 1300   'FA
180    GOSUB 2000   'TEXT
190  END
990 '
LIST 100-190
```
Look at the main routine.

```
RUN
```
You should have heard a four-note scale.

This program works like all those you have seen so far: The computer performs the first statement in the main routine. It then performs the second, then the third, and so on. The computer must perform all the statements in the main routine *in order*. Now let's see how to skip some.

```
145    GOTO 160
LIST -190
```
GOTO is a new statement. What do you think the computer will do?

```
RUN
```
One note (*re*) is missing!

```
145    GOTO 170
LIST -190
```
What will this version do?

```
RUN
```
Were you right?

```
145
125      GOTO 190
LIST -190
```
What now?

```
RUN
```
You probably knew nothing would happen.

```
125      GOTO 175
LIST -190
```
Notice that there is no line 175.

```
RUN
```
Does the error message make sense?

```
125
LIST -190
```
Take out the GOTO statement.

```
RUN
```
You should hear four notes again.

 1. In your own words, what does a GOTO statement tell the computer to do?
2. What happens if the computer performs the statement GOTO 380 when there is no line 380 in the program?

Repeating Statements

You have used the GOTO statement to jump forward over statements. Let's find out what happens when you tell the computer to jump backward. Your main routine should look like this:

```
100 'PROGRAM SCALE
110     LET DURATION = 10
120     LET HOLD = .8
130     GOSUB 2100    'GRAPHICS
140     GOSUB 1000    'DO
150     GOSUB 1100    'RE
160     GOSUB 1200    'MI
170     GOSUB 1300    'FA
180     GOSUB 2000    'TEXT
190 END
```

Make any corrections needed in the main routine. Your TOOLKIT subroutines should still be in memory.

```
185      GOTO 130
LIST -190
```
What will this GOTO do?

```
RUN
```
That's a big change!

The GOTO statement at the end of the program told the computer to go back to line 130. The computer started again at line 130, then went to 140, and so on. Finally, the computer got to line 185, which said to go back to 130. This program will never let the computer stop. You have created an **infinite loop**: The program will run forever—or at least until your computer breaks or you do something to stop it.

Here is how to stop the program temporarily: **Press and release the (Fn) key. Then press the (Q) key.** This is the (Pause) function you learned about in Session 10. (Notice that the word "Pause" is in the green stripe below the (Q) key.) By using the (Pause) function, you told the computer to stop the program until further notice.

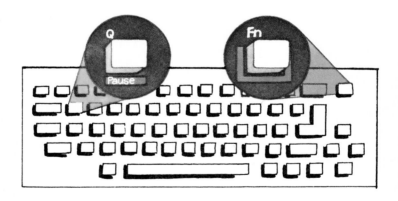

The cursor should be missing from your screen now. This means the computer is not ready for you to enter a command such as RUN. **Press the spacebar or any key in the symbol group.** That should have ended the pause. **Enter the (Pause) function again. Now press another symbol key.**

Next, let's stop the program and get the cursor back on the screen. **Press and release the (Fn) key. Then press the (B) key. This is the** (Break) function you learned about in Session 16.

Notice that the computer has stopped running your program. It printed a message similar to this:

```
^C
Break in line 140
```

Then the computer turned the cursor back on. You cannot restart the program this time by pressing a symbol key.

By changing only the GOTO statement, you have created very different effects. Now let's look at one more change.

185   GOTO 185
LIST -190 _____ What will happen?

RUN _____ Is the computer broken?

Press a few of the symbol keys. Try the (Enter ⏎) key. Your computer seems to be broken. Even though there is a cursor flashing on the screen, the computer is not ready for input. Very strange.

Actually, the computer is still running your program. This is another infinite loop. The computer performed line 185, which said to jump to line 185. So the computer performed line 185 again, which said to jump to line 185, and so on forever. **Use the (Break) function ((Fn) followed by (B)) to stop the program.**

3. How can you tell the computer to repeat all the statements in a program again and again?
4. What is the difference between the (Pause) function and the (Break) function?

Making a Loop That Counts

In this section, you will write a new program that tries to count to infinity. Enter the following lines:

```
NEW
CLS
```
Erase the memory and clear the screen.

```
100 LET N = 1
110 PRINT N
RUN
```
No surprises here.

```
120 LET N = N + 1
130 PRINT N
LIST
```
Think about what line 120 tells the computer to do.

```
RUN
```
You should see 1 and 2 as output.

```
140 LET N = N + 1
150 PRINT N
CLS
LIST
```
What now?

```
RUN
```
Now you should see 1, 2, and 3 as output.

You could make the computer count to 4 by adding another copy of the LET and PRINT statements. More copies would make the computer count higher. However, you would quickly tire of adding such lines to your program. Here is an easier way:

```
DELETE 130-150
130 GOTO 110
CLS
LIST
```
Think about this program.

This program contains an infinite loop. The GOTO statement in line 130 tells the computer to perform line 110 next. Then the computer performs line 120. It next performs line 130, which tells the computer to go back to line 110 again. The computer will stay in the loop until you stop it.

Let's see what the output will look like. **Run the program. Use the** (Pause) **function (**(Fn) **followed by** (Q)**) and symbol keys to stop and restart output. When you have seen enough counting, use the** (Break) **function (**(Fn) **followed by** (B)**) to stop the program and return the cursor. Then list the program.** Here is what it should look like:

```
100 LET N = 1
110 PRINT N
120 LET N = N + 1
130 GOTO 110
```

You learned about variables in Part Three. As a result, you should be able to see exactly what is happening here. Remember that a variable is a *place* in the memory unit. Your program uses a variable named N. Thus, there is a place in memory with the same name. Let's call that place the N-box. Line 100 tells the computer to put 1 in the N-box in memory. Line 110 tells the computer to print whatever is in the N-box. So the computer prints 1.

Line 120 looks tricky at first. However, it is easy to see what it tells the computer to do. Remember the computer's rules for performing the LET statement: First, find the value of whatever is on the right side of the equal sign. Second, assign that value to the variable name on the left side.

The right side of line 120 is N + 1. Thus, the computer must look in the N-box, get the number there, and add 1 to it. The number there is 1, so the *value* of N + 1 is 2. Finally, the computer *assigns* this value back to N. That is the variable name on the left side of the equal sign. So the computer puts the new value 2 into the N-box in memory. When the computer does this, the old value 1 is erased.

Now you know what LET N = N + 1 means. After performing line 120, the computer goes on to line 130. That line tells the computer to perform line 110 next. This time, the computer prints 2, the new value in the N-box.

The computer again arrives at line 120. This time, the N-box contains 2 instead of 1. So the value of N + 1 is 3. The computer puts 3 back into the N-box. As before, the 2 that was there is erased.

Once more, the computer comes to line 130. That line sends it back to line 110, the PRINT N statement. This time the computer prints 3 on the screen. And so the computer repeats these steps forever.

Run the program again. Notice that the computer starts counting at 1. **After a few moments, use the** (Break) **function to stop the program.** Notice that the computer has told you the number of the line at which the program stopped. Let's see what we can learn at this point. The PRINT statement in immediate mode is a good tool for snooping.

PRINT N
_____ This is the value of N when the computer stopped.

CONT
_____ This is a new command.

CONT tells the computer to *continue* running the program where it left off. CONT works a lot like RUN. But there are two differences. With CONT, the computer does *not* set each variable to zero or the empty string. It also does *not* put the line pointer back at the first statement. Let's see what else we can do.

(Break)
PRINT N
_____ Stop the program and print the value of N.

LET N = 10000
_____ In the immediate mode, set the value of N to 10000.

CONT
_____ Continue.

(Break)
_____ Stop the program.

PRINT, LET, and CONT in the immediate mode are very useful for debugging programs.

5. How do you stop a running program and get the cursor back on the screen?
6. How do you restart a program at the place it was stopped?
7. After you stop a running program, how can you find out the value of a variable in it?
8. Suppose the A-box in the memory unit contains the number 5. Then the computer performs the statement LET A = A * 10. What is in the A-box after that?

Standard Form of Infinite Loop

Infinite loops occur often in programs. So it is important to learn how to write an infinite loop clearly.

You created an infinite loop by adding a GOTO statement that sent the computer back to an earlier statement. But people reading through your program would not know at first that it had an infinite loop. They couldn't see it until they reached the GOTO statement. If your program were long, they might have to do a lot of reading before they reached that point.

To make your programs easy to read, begin your infinite loops with a remark statement. That statement should warn the reader that the block of statements that follows forms an infinite loop. The GOTO statement tells the computer to go back to the remark statement at the beginning. It is a good idea to put another remark statement after the GOTO statement. That remark statement should tell the reader that there are no more statements in the loop block. These remark statements are examples of **documentation**. Their only purpose is to make the program easier to read.

You indented the body of a subroutine to make it easy to read. A loop has a body of statements too. You can also make your loops stand out by indenting the body of statements.

Let's put all these good writing ideas together in an outline. You can use the outline below when you write any infinite loop:

```
___   'LOOP FOREVER
___       first body statement
___       second body statement
___       etc.
___
___       GOTO ___
___   'END LOOP
```

The blanks at the beginning of each line and after the word GOTO stand for the actual line numbers you will use. The first line tells the reader that an infinite-loop block is beginning. The body statements are all indented. The final remark statement lets the reader know where the loop ends.

The outline contains a new feature. It is the arrow from the GOTO back to the first remark statement. This is called a **jump arrow**. It reminds you of something important: The number after the word GOTO *must* be the same as the line number of the remark statement at the beginning. You will see jump arrows often in the rest of this book.

The line that the jump arrow points to is called the **target** of the GOTO. In this book, the targets will always be remark statements. The words after the apostrophes in the remark statements explain the reason for the jump. In the infinite-loop outline, the reason for the jump is to repeat the body of the loop forever. *Always use remark statements to explain the jumps in your programs.*

You should always try to make your programs easy to read. That way, other people will know right away what your programs are supposed to do. If other people can read your programs easily, they will be able to make helpful suggestions. Making your programs more readable also helps you. For one thing, well-written programs are easier to change. In addition, you might not read one of your programs for a while. If you go back to it weeks or months later, you will be able to understand it quickly if you have written it clearly.

Bad writing habits can be expensive. People have to write programs. Later, they have to change them and keep them up to date. They might have to rewrite them in order to run them on new computers. Badly written programs make all these jobs much more difficult. Over the long run, it is more expensive to correct badly written programs than to buy new computers.

9. What is the purpose of indentation in the infinite-loop block?
10. What does documentation mean? What is its purpose?
11. What important thing does the jump arrow in a program outline remind you about?

SUMMARY

In this session, you used the GOTO statement to create an infinite loop. You learned the standard form for writing *any* infinite loop. You learned how to stop and restart a running program. These topics are summarized below.

Topic	Description
(Pause) function	(Fn) followed by (Q). Interrupts a running program. Press any key to restart the program.
(Break) function	(Fn) followed by (B). Stops a running program and puts the cursor back on the screen.
GOTO *n*	A BASIC statement that tells the computer to move the line pointer to line *n* next.
CONT	A command that tells the computer to continue performing the program in memory at the place it was stopped.

EXPLORING STRINGS AND NUMBERS

SESSION 20

Session Goals

- Learn the longest string the PC*jr* can handle.
- See how the computer prints very large and very small numbers.
- Learn that there is a largest and a smallest number that the computer can store.
- Learn the order in which the computer does arithmetic operations.
- Learn that the computer does not always give perfectly accurate answers.

Big Strings

The infinite loop is a useful tool for exploring strings on the computer. Let's get started with a loop that joins strings together inside an infinite loop. **Start the computer in the usual way. Then enter the program below:**

```
100 'PROGRAM BIG STRINGS
110    LET A$ = " "
120 '  LOOP FOREVER
130      LET A$ = A$ + "---->"
140      PRINT A$
150      PRINT
160      GOTO 120
170 '  END LOOP
180  END
```

Take a few minutes to study the program. Then answer the following questions:

1. What is the first value assigned to the string variable A$ in program BIG STRINGS?
2. What three actions happen inside the loop in program BIG STRINGS?
3. What does line 130 tell the computer to do to the string in the A$-box in memory?

When you run the program, be ready to stop the computer quickly using the (Pause) function ((Fn) followed by (Q)). **Run the program and do the (Pause) function as quickly as you can.** Each line on the screen shows the string that was in the A$-box in memory during one trip around the loop. Each string is longer than the previous one by an "arrow" five characters long. **Read the program listing above carefully. Be sure you understand how it works.**

Press the spacebar to restart the output. After a few more lines appear on the screen, stop the computer with the (Pause) function. When the string printed on the screen is eight arrows (40 characters) long, it stretches across the whole screen. When the computer adds the next arrow to A$, the string "wraps around" to the next line. But you should think of all 45 characters as part of the same string. This long string was the *value* of A$ when the PRINT A$ statement told the computer to print it on the screen.

How much further can the value of A$ grow? There is one way to find out. **Press the spacebar to restart the computer. This time let the program run until the computer stops.**

The String too long in 130 message shows why the computer stopped. It takes memory to store the value of a string variable. The A$-box in memory has a limit: It can hold only 255 characters. You have just discovered that limit on the PCjr. The last value of A$ took up six full screen lines plus 15 characters on the seventh line. That is a total of 255 characters. When the computer tried to add one more arrow to the value of A$, the length of the new string would have been greater than 255. Thus, the attempt failed. The computer then printed the error message and stopped.

The infinite loop is also a useful tool for exploring numbers on the computer. In the last session you saw how to make a counting loop. This time, let's start with a multiplication loop. **Erase the program in memory. Then enter the program below:**

```
100  'PROGRAM NUMBERS
110     LET P = 1
120  '   LOOP FOREVER
130        PRINT P
140        LET P = P * 10
150        GOTO 120
160  '   END LOOP
170  END
```

You will be running and changing this program throughout this session. Take a moment now to think about what it tells the computer to do.

4. What is the first value assigned to the variable P in program NUMBERS?
5. What two actions happen inside the loop in program NUMBERS?
6. What does line 140 tell the computer to do to the number in the P-box in memory?

Now let's see what the program does. **Clear the screen. Run NUMBERS and do the (Pause) function quickly.** At the top of the screen, the numbers are 1, 10, 100, 1000, 10000, and so on. (The computer does not use commas to group the digits.) Each number is ten times the previous one. Something strange appears after 1000000, though. The next line is 1E+07. But if you multiply 1,000,000 by 10, you get 10,000,000.

7. What number do you get if you move the decimal point in the number 1.0 seven places to the right?

8. What do you think 1E+07 means?

Press the spacebar to restart the program. Watch the output until the computer starts printing error messages. Then use the (Break) function ((Fn) followed by (B)) to stop the computer.

You have just discovered two things about the way your PCjr handles big numbers. First, when numbers get bigger than 9,999,999, the computer uses **E-notation** to print them on the screen. Note the *plus* sign after the E. The symbol E+07 means "move the decimal place seven places to the *right* of where it is." So, 1E+07 means exactly the same thing as 10000000.

The second fact is that some numbers are too big for the computer to handle at all. The number 1E+38 was OK. But then the computer tried to multiply that number by 10 (in line 140). The result was too big to fit in the P-box in memory. So the computer printed Overflow and went on. The term **overflow** means that the data is too big to assign to a variable in the memory unit. (You saw an example of a string overflow in the last section.) Whenever your PCjr finds a number that is too big, it *substitutes* the biggest number it can handle. That number is about 1.7E+38.

If you have used a pocket calculator, you already know about these ideas. There is always some number that is too big for the calculator to handle. Also, the "scientific calculators" use E-notation for big numbers. (E-notation is also called **scientific notation**.)

 9. One of the numbers printed by the computer was 1E+37. What does E+37 mean?

10. How would you write the number 1,300,000,000 in E-notation?

11. About how big is the biggest number the computer can store?

Small Numbers

You have seen how the computer prints very large numbers. You have also seen the error message for a number that is too big to put into memory. Now, let's change the program and explore some very small numbers.

```
140        LET P = P / 2
LIST
```
Check the program.

The / symbol means "divided by." The value of P is divided by 2 each time around the loop. The result of this division is assigned back to P.

The value of P will get smaller and smaller. **Run NUMBERS but use the (Pause) function right away to stop the output.** Notice the first three numbers: They are 1, .5, and .25. Each number is equal to the previous one divided by 2.

This pattern keeps up until the computer reaches the number .0078125. Then, instead of printing .00390625, the computer prints 3.90625E-03. Note that there is now a *minus* sign after the E instead of a plus sign. The E-03 means "move the decimal point three places to the *left* of where it is now."

Press the spacebar to restart the program. After a while, you will see nothing but zeros on the screen. **Use the (Break) function to stop the program.** The PC*jr* has computed a number smaller in size than the minimum it can handle. Whenever this happens, it *substitutes* zero and continues with the program. There is no "underflow" error message.

12. What do you think the number 1E-04 means?
13. What was the *smallest* number the computer printed before it began printing zeros?

Allowed Ranges of Data

You have seen that the computer cannot store every number. Some are too large or too small. Earlier, you learned that there are also limits on strings.

As you saw, the computer could store numbers approximately between 1E-39, or

0.000000000000000000000000000000000000001

and 1E+38, or

100000000000000000000000000000000000000

Numbers smaller or bigger than these seldom appear in real problems. For example, the size of an atom, in feet, is 3.3E-10. The distance from the earth to the sun, also in feet, is 4.9E+11.

There are also limits on string data. After all, the computer has to fit the characters of a string into its memory. The PC*jr* limits you to strings no longer than 255 characters. Suppose you try to join two strings into one string that is too long. If you do so, the computer will print String too long and stop. Can you guess what the shortest string is? It is the empty string. It has no characters.

Accuracy of Numbers

Besides the limits on the size of numbers, there is also a limit on accuracy. The computer handles some numbers, such as 1, 263, and 879432, with perfect accuracy. But the computer cannot handle other numbers, such as 1 / 3, with the same accuracy. If you tell the computer to print the result of dividing 3 into 1, it will print .3333334. (**Try it.**)

This answer is not exactly correct. The computer would need to print an infinite number of 3s after the decimal point to give the correct answer. The P box in memory cannot, of course, store an infinite number of digits. The computer saves only about seven digits, not counting leading or trailing zeros. In other words, the **precision** of numbers in the PC*jr* is about seven digits.

You know that most people count by 10s. This is called **decimal** arithmetic. But the PC*jr*, like most computers, counts by 2s. This is called **binary** arithmetic. When you use your computer, you enter numbers and expect output in **decimal** form. But the PC*jr* handles these numbers internally in binary form. Sometimes, the decimal numbers you enter don't convert exactly to binary form.

Also, the computer's internal binary numbers don't always convert exactly to the decimal form it uses for output. Once in a while, number conversions and rounding lead to tiny errors. These can surprise you. If someone asked you to round one-third off to seven decimal places, you would write .3333333. But your PC*jr* prints .3333334. Numbers in the computer may turn out to be slightly different from what you expected.

Immediate-Mode Arithmetic

As you have seen, the computer can do addition, subtraction, multiplication, and division. You also know that you can enter the PRINT statement in the immediate mode. This gives you an easy way to use the computer as a calculator. Here are some examples:

```
NEW
PRINT 1001 / 13
```
The computer prints the answer immediately.

```
PRINT 3 * 4
PRINT 1 + 2 + 3 + 4 + 5
PRINT 1 * 2 * 3 * 4 * 5
PRINT 9999 - 3456
```
Here are more answers.

Pocket calculators are easier to use than the computer for this kind of problem. Once in a while, however, it is handy to use the computer this way. But typing PRINT each time is slow. So the PC*jr* lets you use a question mark instead. You did this before.

```
?100 / 4
?8 * 7
```
The question mark means the same as PRINT.

Order of Arithmetic

If you want to add 8 + 4 + 2, it doesn't matter which numbers the computer adds first: Starting at the left, the computer adds 8 + 4, which gives 12. It then adds 2, which gives 14. But the computer would get the same answer if it started at the right: 4 + 2 is 6, and 8 + 6 is 14.

Sometimes the order matters. For example, what do you think PRINT 8 - 4 - 2 tells the computer to do? Starting at the left, the computer would do the subtraction 8 - 4, which gives 4. Then it would subtract 2 from 4 to get 2 for the answer. But if the computer started at the right, it would do the subtraction 4 - 2, to get 2. Then it would subtract 2 from 8 to get 6. Which answer does the computer actually give? Let's see.

```
PRINT 8 - 4 - 2
```
Now you know.

```
PRINT 8 - 4 + 2
```
Did the computer start at the left?

```
PRINT 8 / 4 / 2
```
What order did the computer use?

```
PRINT 8 / 4 * 2
```
What was the order?

 14. In what order did the computer perform the arithmetic operations in the last four examples?

When the computer is doing only addition and subtraction, the rule is simple: Go from left to right. The computer uses the same rule when it is doing only multiplication and division. But suppose the computer must add or subtract *and* multiply or divide, all in the same problem. What happens then? Let's see.

```
PRINT 8 * 4 + 2
PRINT 8 * 4 - 2
PRINT 8 / 4 + 2
```
There are no surprises yet.

```
PRINT 8 + 4 * 2
```
This one is different.

```
PRINT 8 + 4 / 2
PRINT 8 - 4 * 2
```
_____ These are also different.

 15. When the computer adds and multiplies in the same program
line, which operation is done first?
16. When the computer adds and divides in the same program line,
which operation is done first?

The computer follows rules to decide which arithmetic operation to
do first when there is more than one to do. You have seen what those
rules are. Now you will see how to change the rules. You can make the
computer do things in the order *you* want. You will need the parenthesis
keys. The left parenthesis is (Shift ↑ 9). The right parenthesis is (Shift ↑ 0).

```
PRINT 8 + 4 * 2
```
_____ The multiplication was done first.

```
PRINT (8 + 4) * 2
```
_____ Notice the different answer.

```
PRINT 8 + (4 * 2)
```
_____ That gave the first answer.

Operations inside parentheses are done before operations outside. The
last example shows you something important: No harm is done when
you put parentheses where they are not needed.

 17. When there are several arithmetic operations in one line, how
can you tell the computer to do one operation before all the
others?

The computer follows a few simple rules when it performs arithmetic
in long expressions. There is one main rule. This rule has two exceptions. The main rule is that the computer starts at the left and works its
way to the right. It does this just as you read the words in a sentence.
Here are the exceptions:

Exceptions to Left-Right Order
1. The computer multiplies and divides before it adds or subtracts.
2. The computer does the arithmetic inside parentheses before
anything else.

The first line below shows a complicated example of arithmetic. Each line after the first shows one step in finding the result. Look for examples of the two rules on the previous page.

```
                10 - 4 * (3 - 1) / (2 + 2) + 3
Step 1:                   ‾‾‾‾‾‾‾
                10 - 4 *    2    / (2 + 2) + 3
Step 2:                             ‾‾‾‾‾‾‾
                10 - 4 *    2    /    4    + 3
Step 3:              ‾‾‾‾‾‾‾‾‾‾‾
                10 -    8         /    4    + 3
Step 4:                 ‾‾‾‾‾‾‾‾‾‾‾‾‾‾
                10 -              2         + 3
Step 5:          ‾‾‾‾‾‾‾‾‾‾‾‾‾‾‾‾‾‾
                  8                        + 3
Result:           ‾‾‾‾‾‾‾‾‾‾‾‾‾‾‾‾‾‾‾‾‾‾‾‾‾‾‾
                                           1 1
```

You found that it was perfectly OK to put parentheses where none were needed. The computer ignored them. Suppose you do not know whether you need parentheses or not. It is better to put extra ones in than to leave necessary ones out.

18. Convert 1000000000 to E-notation.
19. Convert 1.23456E+02 to decimal notation.
20. Why can't the computer handle the number one-third with perfect accuracy?
21. Use the computer's rules for arithmetic to find the answer to the problem below.

    (3 * 5 - 1) + 2 - 8 / (2 + 2)

PROJECTS

- It is easy to change NUMBERS into a program that prints a multiplication table. Suppose you want to make a times table for the number seven. Change your program to look like this:

```
100  'PROGRAM NUMBERS
110     LET N = 7
120  '  LOOP FOREVER
130        PRINT N; "TIMES"; P; "IS"; N * P
140        LET P = P + 1
150        GOTO 120
160  '  END LOOP
170  END
```

Think what this tells the computer to do. Then run the program. Use the (Pause) function to stop output, the spacebar to restart output, and the (Break) function to stop the program.

Make a times table for your age: Change line 110 so that N is your age. Then run the program.

- Make a division table. An interesting value for N is 720720. Change N * P into N / P in line 130. You may also want to change TIMES to DIVIDED BY.

- In this session, you have learned about **single-precision** numbers. There are also **double-precision** numbers. If you would like to learn more about these numbers, read about constants and variables in Chapter 3 of the *BASIC* reference book for your PCjr.

- You have learned about the four arithmetic operators: +, -, *, and /. The BASIC on your PCjr has several more. If you are interested in learning about them, read about arithmetic operators in Chapter 3 of the *BASIC* reference book for your PCjr.

SUMMARY

In this session, you used infinite loops to explore strings and numbers. You found that the PC*jr* can handle strings up to 255 characters long. It can handle numbers from about 3E-39 to 1.7E+38. When doing arithmetic, the PC*jr* reads from left to right, with these two exceptions: First, it multiplies and divides before it adds or subtracts. Second, it does the arithmetic inside parentheses before anything else.

Topic	Description
E-notation	A way of writing very large and very small numbers. The number after E tells how far to move the decimal point. The sign after E tells which direction to move it: A plus sign means move the point right; a minus sign means move it left.
Overflow	A piece of data that is too large to be stored in memory.
Maximum string	The largest string that can be stored in memory. On the PC*jr*, it has a length of 255 characters.
Maximum number	The largest number that can be stored in memory. On the PC*jr*, it has a value of about 1.7E+38.
Minimum number	The smallest number that can be stored in memory. On the PC*jr*, it has a value of about 3E-39.
Precision	The number of digits handled during arithmetic calculations. On the PC*jr*, the normal precision is about seven digits. Double-precision numbers are also available.

THE STANDARD LOOP BLOCK

SESSION 21

Session Goals

- Learn how to use the IF statement.
- Use the IF statement to get out of a loop.
- Learn the general outline form of a loop block.
- Use the loop block to repeat an action a fixed number of times.

Review

In Session 19, you saw the outline of the infinite loop. It looked like this:

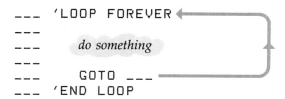

```
___   'LOOP FOREVER
___
___      do something
___
___         GOTO ___
___   'END LOOP
```

Remember that the blanks stand for line numbers. The jump arrow points to the target of the GOTO statement. Notice that the block begins and ends with remark statements. The phrase *do something* stands for one or more BASIC statements. These the computer will perform again and again.

A Standard Loop

Let's begin by writing an infinite loop that puts the words GOOD OLD before any word you enter. **Turn on the computer (if it isn't already on). Then enter the following program:**

```
100 'LOOP FOREVER
110     INPUT A$
120     PRINT "GOOD OLD "; A$
130     GOTO 100
140 'END LOOP
LIST
```
Read the program carefully and see what it does.

```
RUN
? BOY
```
What was printed back?

```
? AARDVARK
```
What happened this time?

```
? DAYS
```
Now you know how the program works.

Use the (Break) function to stop the program. Each time you entered a word, the computer printed GOOD OLD followed by that word. Since these actions were inside an infinite loop, *you* had to stop the program. There ought to be a way to have the *computer* decide whether to leave the loop. Every programming language has such a feature. In

BASIC, the IF statement gives you a way to tell the computer when to stop looping. Let's see how.

```
100  'LOOP
115     IF A$ = "STOP" THEN 140
```

Notice the indentation of the IF statement.

```
RENUM 100
LIST
```

Study the new program for a few moments.

Here is what your program should look like:

```
100  'LOOP
110     INPUT A$
120    IF A$ = "STOP" THEN 150
130     PRINT "GOOD OLD "; A$
140      GOTO 100
150  'END LOOP
```

Run the new program. Each time you see a question mark, enter a word from the following list:

    CAR, HOUSE, TIMES

After you enter each word, you should see GOOD OLD followed by that word. **Finally, enter the word STOP.** That should cause the computer to leave the loop.

A loop that tells the computer to repeat statements until some condition becomes true is called a **conditional loop**, or simply a **loop**. Here is the outline for every such loop:

```
___   'LOOP
___
___      do something
___
___      IF exit condition THEN ___
___
___      do something
___
___      GOTO ___
___   'END LOOP
```

The *exit condition* in the IF statement tells the computer when to stop looping and jump out of the loop. The IF statement is not indented as far as the rest of the statements in the body of the loop. This makes it easier for the reader to find the exit condition. Here is how the loop works:

The computer's rules for performing a loop block

1. Perform the first "do something."
2. Test the exit condition to see whether it is true or false. If it is true, stop looping and move the line pointer to the END LOOP remark statement.
3. If the exit condition is false, perform the second "do something."
4. Move the line pointer back to the LOOP remark statement, and start over with Step 1.

The loop works this way only if it is written correctly. There is nothing magical about the phrases LOOP and END LOOP in the remark statements. They are there to help the reader. The computer ignores them. But the numbers after THEN and GOTO are important: *They must match the line numbers of the two remark statements in the outline.* If they are wrong, Steps 2 and 4 above may not work. It is up to you to get the numbers right.

There is one important difference between the two "do something" blocks in a loop: The computer must perform the first one at least once. However, it may never get to the second one at all. This happens if the exit condition is true at the start.

In some loop blocks, one or the other "do something" parts may not be there at all. In other words, the IF statement may be the first statement inside the loop. Or, it may be the last, except for the GOTO statement. You will see some examples of this later.

1. What kind of statement should be at the beginning of a loop block? What kind should be at the end?
2. What statement in a loop block tells the computer when to stop looping?
3. What is the main difference between the two "do something" blocks in a loop?

Why Loops?

You may be wondering why you are spending so much time on the loop block. After all, how many loop problems can there be? You will probably be surprised to find out how often loops occur. This is true in everyday life as well as in programming.

Think of the following directions from a cookbook: "Bring the water to a boil." That may not sound like a loop, but it is. Below are the directions needed to tell a very dumb assistant how to boil a pot of water. The directions are written partly in English and partly in BASIC.

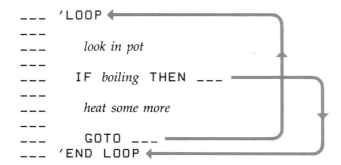

The same cookbook says to "add salt to taste" when you season a stew. That may not sound like a loop, but it is. Here is how to tell the helper to do the job:

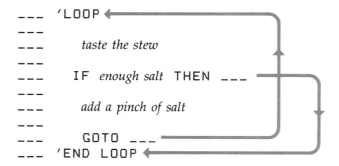

4. A recipe says "beat the egg whites until they are stiff." How would you write these instructions in the form of a loop block?
5. Think of an everyday event and write a description of it in the form of a loop-block outline.

Using a Loop to Average Numbers

What is the average age of the people in your family? To find out, you must add all the ages and then divide that sum by the number of people. Let's see how to tell the computer to do the work for you.

Suppose you enter the numbers 10, 12, 34, and 36. The computer must add the numbers, getting 92. The computer must also count the numbers as they are entered, getting 4. Then it must divide 92 by 4 and get the average, 23.

The computer has five main jobs. The first is to get the numbers from the user. The second is to find the sum. The third is to count the numbers. The fourth is to divide the sum by the count. The last is to print the result. You will see that the first three jobs can be combined easily. As each new number comes in, the computer can add it to the sum so far and also add 1 to a counter. The last two jobs can also be combined. Here is the main routine:

```
100 'PROGRAM AVERAGE
110     GOSUB 200    'SUM AND COUNT
120     GOSUB 400    'OUTPUT AVERAGE
130 END
```

The first subroutine must tell the computer to ask for input, one number at a time. Let's use N as the name of the variable that stands for each number the user gives. The program must also tell the computer to add the numbers and to count them. Let's call the sum SUM and the count COUNT.

The idea here is to build up SUM and COUNT as each new number N is entered. These statements will build up the sum and keep track of the count:

```
LET SUM = SUM + N
LET COUNT = COUNT + 1
```

Repeating these statements with each new number N will do the job. A loop is the answer. Before the loop starts, SUM and COUNT both have to be set to 0.

Of course, you have to tell the computer that there are no more numbers to average. One way to do that is to mark the end of the list with a number that will never be part of the data. This is called a **flag**. For example, you could use -999 as the flag. The loop should stop as soon as N is -999. In other words, the loop exit condition should be N = -999.

The average is the final sum divided by the final count. It can be expressed as SUM / COUNT. The computer needs to calculate the average after the loop ends. Finally, it needs to print the result.

As always, the best way to begin is to write the subroutines in a mixture of English and BASIC. Here is how the outline should look:

```
200  'SUB SUM AND COUNT
210      set SUM to zero
215      set COUNT to zero
220  '   LOOP
230          ask user for a number
240        IF number equals flag THEN 280
250          add number to SUM
260          add 1 to COUNT
270          GOTO 220
280  '   END LOOP
290    RETURN
390  '
400  'SUB OUTPUT AVERAGE
410      compute average
420      print average
430    RETURN
```

PROJECT

● Finish writing the two subroutines needed to complete this program. Check them carefully and enter the complete program into the computer. Run the program several times and check that it is working correctly. When you are satisfied, save the program with the name AVERAGE.

SUMMARY

In this session, you have learned a standard way to write all loop blocks. You will use this loop outline whenever you want to tell the computer to do something again and again, until some condition becomes true. Here are the main ideas:

Topic	Description
Conditional loop	A block of statements that is performed again and again, until some condition becomes true.
Exit condition	The condition that, when true, tells the computer to stop performing a loop.
IF *condition* THEN *n*	A BASIC statement. It tells the computer to test the condition and find whether it is true or false. If the condition is true, the computer moves the line pointer to line number *n*. If it is false, the computer goes on to the statement after the IF statement.

EXPLORING FUNCTIONS

SESSION 22

Session Goals

- Explore the LEN, MID$, INT, SQR, ABS, INKEY$, and RND functions.

- Use the INT and RND functions to make random integers.

- Learn that a function has a name, a type, and a value.

- Learn that a function usually takes in a value and always returns a value.

- Understand that a function is a process.

Review

You used the infinite loop to study numbers. Now you will use the conditional loop to explore something new: **functions**. Your goal for now is to discover what functions do and how they work. Later, you will see how to put functions to work in your programs.

Start the computer as usual. Erase the memory. Then enter the following program:

```
100 'PROGRAM FUNCTIONS
110 '  LOOP
120     INPUT P$
130    IF P$ = "STOP" THEN 160
140     PRINT P$
150     GOTO 110
160 '  END LOOP
170  END
```

Run the program. Enter any word you want and see what happens. Do it again. Then enter the word STOP. The program should stop. **Clear the screen and list the program.**

Your program has only a main routine. Notice that the body of the main routine is a single conditional loop. It goes from line 110 through 160. Like every other conditional loop, it has one or two "do something" parts and an exit condition.

The first "do something" is the INPUT statement in line 120. It tells the computer to wait for the user to enter a string. Next comes the exit condition. The IF statement tells the computer to see whether the string just entered is STOP. If it is, the computer should stop the loop. After the IF statement, there is another "do something." It is a PRINT statement. Finally, the GOTO statement in line 150 tells the computer to keep looping.

You will be using conditional loops like this one all through this session. **Be sure you understand this program well before you go on to the next section.**

The LEN Function

Let's begin with a small change to your program. **List the program. Then make the changes in the three lines shown below:**

```
100  'PROGRAM FUNCTIONS
110  '  LOOP
120        INPUT P$
130      IF P$ = "STOP" THEN 160
135        LET N = LEN(P$)
140        PRINT N
145        PRINT
150        GOTO 110
160  '  END LOOP
170   END
```

Line 135 contains an example of a **function**. The name of this function is LEN, which stands for "length." Notice that P$ appears both in the INPUT statement and as part of the LEN function. Let's see how the LEN function works.

Run the program and enter each of these strings: **DOG, AARDVARK, MISSISSIPPI, 5280, and Z. After each input, press the (Enter ⏎) key. Look carefully at what the computer does. See what happens when you press (Enter ⏎) without having typed input. When you finish, enter the word STOP.**

1. What do you think LEN(P$) tells the computer to do? Explain in your own words.
2. If the value of A$ is TELEVISION, what is LEN(A$)?

The MID$ Function

Let's go on to another function. **Change lines 135 and 140 of program FUNCTION to look like this:**

```
100  'PROGRAM FUNCTIONS
110  '  LOOP
120        INPUT P$
130      IF P$ = "STOP" THEN 160
135        LET A$ = MID$(P$, 3, 1)
140        PRINT A$
145        PRINT
150        GOTO 110
160  '  END LOOP
170  END
```

Notice that P$ appears both in the INPUT statement and as part of the MID$ function. Line 135 tells the computer to assign the value of the MID$ function to A$. **Run the program. Enter the following strings: ABCDEF, **C**, CHARLIE, SKYSCRAPER, and 1234567. Remember to press (Enter⏎) after typing each string. See what the computer prints in response.**

Now for a small change. **Enter STOP to stop the program. Then edit line 135 to look like this:**

```
135        LET A$ = MID$(P$, 2, 4)
```

Run the program again. This time, enter the strings TWINKLE, BLIMP, and PRICES. Watch what happens in each case. Enter STOP to leave the loop.

3. What does the MID$ function do? Explain in your own words. (Hint: MID$ stands for "middle string.")
4. If the value of W$ is HOWDY, what is MID$(W$, 2, 1)?
5. If the value of B$ is PARTNER, what is MID$(B$, 1, 4)?

The INT Function

You have used two BASIC functions that do things with strings. Let's look next at some functions that deal with numbers.

Make the following changes in lines 120 through 140 so that program FUNCTIONS looks like this:

```
100  'PROGRAM FUNCTIONS
110  '  LOOP
120       INPUT A
130      IF A = -999 THEN 160
135       LET N = INT(A)
140       PRINT N
145       PRINT
150       GOTO 110
160  '  END LOOP
170   END
```

Line 120 tells the computer to accept a number from the user. Line 135 tells it to assign to N the INT of that number. Line 140 tells the computer to print the value of N. **Run the program for each of the following inputs: 1, 2, 3, 3.5, 3.999, 4, and 53.7. Press the (Enter ⏎) key after each input. See what the computer prints each time.**

6. What the does INT function do? (Hint: INT stands for "integer.")

Your computer should still be running the program. If not, run it again. **Type each of the following values: 0, -1, -2, -2.1, -2.9, -3, -3.1, and -45.1. Press (Enter ⏎) after you type each value. See what the computer prints each time. Enter -999 to stop the program.**

7. You may wish to change your answer to question 6. How would you answer question 6 now?
8. What is the value of INT(153.21)?
9. What is the value of INT(-153.21)?

The SQR Function

Now, let's look at a new function. **Change line 135 of program FUNCTIONS to look like this:**

```
100 'PROGRAM FUNCTIONS
110 '  LOOP
120       INPUT A
130      IF A = -999 THEN 160
135        LET N = SQR(A)
140        PRINT N
145        PRINT
150        GOTO 110
160 '  END LOOP
170  END
```

Let's see what the SQR function does. **Run the program. Enter the numbers 4, 9, 25, 49, 100, 2, and -25. Press the (Enter↵) key after you type each number. See what the computer prints each time.**

10. What the does the SQR function do?
11. What is SQR(36)?
12. What happens if the computer tries to use SQR with a negative number?

The ABS Function

Now, let's look at another function. Change line 135 of program FUNCTIONS to look like this:

```
100 'PROGRAM FUNCTIONS
110 '  LOOP
120       INPUT A
130      IF A = -999 THEN 160
135        LET N = ABS(A)
140        PRINT N
145        PRINT
150        GOTO 110
160 '  END LOOP
170  END
```

The new function is ABS, which stands for "absolute value." Let's see what it does. **Run the program and enter the numbers 5, -5, 1.58, -1.58, 245, and -124. Press the (Enter⏎) key after you type each number.** See what the computer prints each time. **Enter -999 to stop.**

13. What does the ABS function do? Explain in your own words.
14. What is ABS(-76.23)?
15. What is ABS(346.92)?

The INKEY$ Function

Suppose you wanted to control a program by pressing individual keys on the keyboard. You could use an INPUT statement. However, as you have seen, the INPUT statement stops the program until the computer receives input from the keyboard. You might not want to stop the program. Luckily, there is another way to do this.

Your computer can inspect the keyboard "on the fly." The program keeps on running. But the computer takes a look to see if a key has been pressed. The function that does this is called INKEY$. You will learn about this function next. **Change your program to look like this:**

```
100 'PROGRAM FUNCTIONS
110 '   LOOP
120       LET K$ = INKEY$
130      IF K$ = "S" THEN 160
140       PRINT K$
150        GOTO 110
160 '   END LOOP
170 END
```

Notice three things: First, lines 135 and 145 should be missing. Second, line 120 contains the INKEY$ function. Third, the exit condition is now K$ = "S". Let's see how it works.

Run the program. Nothing seems to be happening except that the screen has gone blank. That is because you haven't pressed a key yet. **Now press a few keys and watch the screen.** As you press each key, you can watch the corresponding letters scroll quickly up the screen.

The INKEY$ function is working all the time. If no key is down on the keyboard, INKEY$ assigns the *empty* string to K$. But the empty string produces a blank line when it is printed on the screen. That is why you see nothing on the screen most of the time. **Press (S) to stop the program. Change line 140 to look like this:**

```
140      PRINT LEN(K$) , K$
```

This line tells the computer to print the *length* of the string K$ as well as the string itself. **Run the program. Press a few keys. When you have seen enough, press Ⓢ to stop the program.**

This version of the program shows more clearly what is taking place. When no key is down, the value of INKEY$ is the empty string. The length of the empty string is zero, since there are no characters in it. That was the reason for the line of zeros that scrolled up the screen. As soon as you pressed a key, things changed. Instead of zeros, you saw a 1. That is because the length of a single character is 1. You also saw the character corresponding to the key you pressed. It appeared in the second print zone.

16. How are the INKEY$ function and the INPUT statement alike? How are they different?
17. If a key is pressed on the keyboard, what is the value of the INKEY$ function?

The RND Function

We will look at a very important function next. **Change program FUNCTIONS to look like this:**

```
100 'PROGRAM FUNCTIONS
110 '  LOOP
120       LET K$ = INKEY$
130       IF K$ = "S" THEN 160
135       LET N = RND
140       PRINT N
150       GOTO 110
160 '  END LOOP
170  END
```

Line 135 tells the computer to assign the value of RND to N. Line 140 tells the computer to print this value on the screen. Lines 120 and 130 tell the computer to quit looping when the user presses Ⓢ.

RND stands for "random number." The RND function is unusual: It produces numbers that seem to have no pattern or design. **Run the program. Stop the computer with the (Pause) function. Look carefully at the output on the screen. Think about the questions at the top of the next page. Start and stop the program several times. When you understand what is happening, stop the program with the Ⓢ key.**

18. What was the largest number you saw on the screen?
19. What was the smallest number you saw on the screen?
20. Was there any pattern to the numbers?

Using Functions

Now that you know how some BASIC functions work, let's see how to put them to use. The RND function makes **random numbers**. INT turns numbers into integers. There ought to be a way to combine RND and INT to get random integers. There is a simple way. **Enter the change shown below:**

```
100 'PROGRAM FUNCTIONS
110 '   LOOP
120       LET K$ = INKEY$
130       IF K$ = "S" THEN 160
135       LET N = 40 * RND
140       PRINT N
150       GOTO 110
160 '   END LOOP
170   END
```

Run the program. Stop the output with the (Pause) function. Restart the output by pressing any key. Start and stop the program several times. Look carefully at the numbers on the screen each time you stop the output. When you have seen enough, use the (S) key to stop the program.

Now let's combine RND with INT. **Edit line 135 so it looks like this:**

```
135       LET N = INT(40 * RND)
```

Think about what line 135 tells the computer to do. **Run the program. Stop and restart the output with the (Pause) function, as before. Take a good look at the numbers produced by the program. Use the (S) key to stop the computer.**

21. What was the largest number you saw?
22. What was the smallest number you saw?
23. What does this version of the program do? Explain in your own words.

The Form of Functions

You have just learned about a few of the most useful functions in BASIC. There are many other such functions. However, they all work the same way as the ones you have used here. Instead of exploring each one, let's think about what a function is and what it does.

Nearly all programming languages come with built-in words called *functions*. Functions are important because they give you new ways to tell the computer to process data. You already know how to tell the computer to add, subtract, multiply, and divide numbers and to join strings. But without functions, how would you tell the computer to take the square root of a number? How would you tell it to print the first character of a string? How would you tell it to print the length of a string? You have just seen how to use functions to do those things.

In BASIC, most functions have the same form. First comes the name of the function. Then there is a left parenthesis. Next comes an expression, such as the name of a variable, a constant, or a combination of variables and constants. Some functions, such as MID$, need more than one expression. Each expression is separated from the next by a comma. Finally, there comes a right parenthesis. Here are examples of correctly written functions:

```
LEN("AARDVARK")
INT(100 / 3)
SQR(49)
MID$(W$, 1, J)
```

There is a special word for the expressions between parentheses in functions. They are called **parameters**. Sometimes, they are called **arguments**. In the previous examples, "AARDVARK" is the parameter of the LEN function. The number 49 is the parameter of the SQR function.

Some functions in BASIC have no parameters. RND and INKEY$ are two examples.

One more special term is used to describe functions: **result**. The result is the value to which the function is equal. The result of SQR(49) is 7. The result of INT(100 / 3) is 33. People also say that a function "returns" its result: LEN("AARDVARK") returns 8 as the result.

Like variables and constants, functions also have a *type*: either numeric or string. The type of a function is the same as the type of the data it returns. For example, INT returns a number. Thus, it is a *numeric* function. MID$ returns a string. Thus, it is a *string* function. What type do you think LEN is? LEN has a string parameter. However, it returns a number. The kind of data returned is what determines the type of a function. Thus, LEN is a numeric function.

You learned in Session 17 that an expression is anything with a value. Variables, constants, and operators can be combined into expressions. Since a function also has a value, you can use a function in an expression. You may be glad to know that the list of things that can go into expressions is now complete. Here are examples of correct expressions that include functions:

```
40 * RND
LEN("SNAIL") / 2
MID$("RUNNER", 1, 4) + "ING"
INT(SQR(10))
```

Look over the expressions above. Think carefully about what each means. The last example shows a function used as the parameter of another function. That is OK, since a function is an expression and any expression can be a parameter. The computer first finds the square root of 10 (about 3.16). It then finds the integer part of that number (3).

24. What is the value of LEN("YIPPEE")?
25. What is the parameter of ABS(-254)?

Functions as Processes

Like variables, each function has a name, a type, and a value. For example, the name of the string-length function is LEN. Its type is numeric. Its value is the number of characters in the string written in parentheses after LEN. But there is one big difference between functions and variables.

Suppose you use the variable N in a program. It too has a name, which is N. It has a type, which is numeric. It has a value, which is whatever is stored in the N-box in the computer's memory. As you learned in Session 15, a variable is a *place* in memory. Variables get their values by assignment. For example, LET N = 10 tells the computer to put 10 in the place named N. INPUT P tells the computer to take the number entered by the user and put it in the place named P.

Functions are *not* places in memory. It would be incorrect to write LET INT(2.3) = 17. There is no place in memory named INT(2.3). Thus, it makes no sense to try to assign 17 to it. Functions are *processes* that produce results. For example, the LEN function carries out a process with these steps: First, it counts the characters in the string parameter. Second, it returns the number of characters as the result.

A function behaves more like a subroutine than a variable. Both tell the computer to carry out the steps of a process. The difference is that a function returns a value, but a subroutine does not.

You may be wondering how the computer knows the steps of the LEN function or the SQR function. The steps of a subroutine are just statements in BASIC that *you* write. But the steps of these built-in functions are instructions in machine language. These instructions are stored on the same memory chips that contain all the other instructions that tell your computer how to perform a BASIC program.

26. How are functions and subroutines alike? How are they different?
27. What is the major difference between a variable and a function? Explain in your own words.

Value-in, Value-out Tables

Every function returns a value. Usually the value depends on the parameter (or parameters) that appear in parentheses after the function name. For example, SQR(9) returns the value 3, and SQR(16) returns the value 4. Think of the parameter as the value that goes *into* the function. Think of the result as the value that comes *out of* the function. The function *takes in* one or more items of data, *processes* the data, and *puts out* one item of data.

A very good way to find out how a function works is to look carefully at what goes in and what comes out. The following table should help you understand some of the functions you have been studying:

Function	Value(s) In	Value Out
LEN	"AVERYLONGWORD"	13
	"ROCKET"	6
	"Z"	1
	""	0
MID$	"COMPUTER", 4, 3	"PUT"
	"COMPUTER", 6, 1	"T"
	"COMPUTER", 2, 0	""
INT	2.1	2
	2	2
	1.999	1
	1.1	1
	1	1
	0.1	0
	0	0
	-0.1	-1
	-1	-1
SQR	100	10
	64	8
	2	1.414214
	0	0
ABS	6.98	6.98
	-6.98	6.98

The RND and INKEY$ functions are not included in the value-in, value-out table. That is because neither has a value in (a parameter). As you have seen, RND returns random numbers between 0 and .9999999. The numbers seem to be scattered as if by chance. The INKEY$ function constantly samples the keyboard to see if a key has been pressed.

There are many other functions in the version of BASIC for your PC*jr*. As you become better at programming, you will need some of them. You should read Chapter 4 in the *BASIC* reference book for a complete list of the functions that are available.

Making Random Integers

We close this session with two simulations that use functions. The RND and INT functions are used very often in programs to generate random integers. For example, you might make the integers 1 and 2 stand for the two sides of a coin. If you want to "flip the coin" in a fair way, the computer must return these two integers at random. Random integers from the set 1, 2, 3, 4, 5, and 6 can stand for the roll of a die. In this session, you have seen examples of random integers. Let's return for a closer look.

Suppose you want a computer to simulate a tossed coin by returning integers at random from the set 1 and 2. The following expression will do that:

```
INT(2 * RND) + 1
```

Here is how the expression works. RND returns a random number between 0 and 0.9999999. Next, the computer multiplies that number by 2. The result, a number between 0 and 1.999999, is the "value in" of INT. So INT returns 0 if the number is between 0 and 0.9999999. It returns 1 if the number is between 1 and 1.999999. The last step is to add 1. This will give a value of either 1 or 2 as the value of the whole expression.

Suppose you wanted to simulate picking one card at random from a deck. There are 52 cards in a deck, so you need a random integer between 1 and 52. This expression is just what you need:

```
INT(52 * RND) + 1
```

You should be able to figure out how this works. For example, see what value comes out when RND returns 0.1. Try again with 0.5. You should get card number 6 and card number 27 as the two results.

SUMMARY

In this session, you learned how to use functions. You saw that the best way to describe functions is in terms of "value in" and "value out." The key ideas are summarized below:

Topic	Description
Function	A process that produces a piece of data. The data produced is the value of the function. The type of the data produced is the type of the function.
Parameter	The data that goes into the function. A function may have any number of parameters or none at all.
Result	The data that comes out of the function. A function returns only one value.

THE FOR/NEXT ABBREVIATION

SESSION 23

Session Goals

- Learn how to write a counting loop.
- Use FOR and NEXT statements to rewrite a counting loop.
- Explore the FOR and NEXT statements.
- Explore the exit values of a loop variable.

The Loop Block

You have learned that the loop block gives you a way to tell the computer to perform some action again and again. It tells the computer to do something over and over until the exit condition from the loop becomes true.

In Session 21, you learned how to write a standard outline for the loop block. This outline uses a mixture of English and BASIC to describe the structure of the loop block. Here it is again:

```
___   'LOOP
___
___       do something
___
___       IF  exit condition  THEN ___
___
___       do something
___
___       GOTO ___
___   'END LOOP
```

The BASIC loop block contains two control statements: The IF statement tells the computer when to exit from the loop. The GOTO statement tells the computer to keep looping.

As you have seen, the jump arrows in the loop block show the targets of the IF and GOTO statements. In the loop-block outline, the targets are remark statements. These explain the purpose of the jumps.

A Loop That Counts

Sometimes one of the "do somethings" in the loop block is missing. Such a loop block is called an **abbreviated loop block**. Here is a loop block with the first "do something" missing:

```
___   'LOOP
___       IF  exit condition  THEN ___
___
___       do something
___
___       GOTO ___
___   'END LOOP
```

A counting loop is an example of an abbreviated loop block. The purpose of a counting loop is to perform some action (to "do something") a fixed number of times. The counting loop needs one statement before the loop block. That statement sets the counter to its first value.

Here is the outline of any counting loop:

```
___   LET  C  =  first value
___   'LOOP
___      IF  C  >  last value  THEN  ___
___
___      do something
___
___      LET  C  =  C  +  1
___      GOTO  ___
___   'END LOOP
```

Let's see how to use the counting loop to tell the computer to print the numbers from 50 to 100. In the outline, the words "first value" stand for 50. The words "last value" stand for 100. The words "do something" stand for PRINT C. Here is the outline for this example:

```
___   LET  C  =  50
___   'LOOP
___      IF  C  >  100  THEN  ___
___      PRINT  C
___      LET  C  =  C  +  1
___      GOTO  ___
___   'END LOOP
```

The first line in the outline says to assign 50 to C. Inside the loop, the IF statement tests C to see if it is already greater than 100. It is not, so the computer performs the PRINT statement. Thus, 50 appears on the screen. Next, the LET statement adds 1 to C. It then assigns the sum, 51, to C. Finally, the GOTO statement sends the line pointer back to the beginning of the loop. Each time the computer goes through the loop, it tests to see if C has become greater than 100. Sooner or later, the condition becomes true. As a result, the loop stops. Until that happens, the PRINT statement prints each number through 100.

1. How would you change the outline above to have the computer print the numbers from 0 to 1000?
2. How would you change the outline above to have the computer count by 2s?
3. In the outline above, what is the value of C after the computer exits from the loop?

Experiments with the Counting Loop

Now, let's experiment with a program that contains a counting loop. **If the computer is on, enter the NEW command. Otherwise, start the computer. Then enter the following program:**

```
100 'PROGRAM COUNT
110    PRINT "FIRST & LAST VALUES"
120    INPUT F, L
130    LET C = F
140 '  LOOP
150     IF C > L THEN 190
160       PRINT C
170       LET C = C + 1
180       GOTO 140
190 '  END LOOP
200  END
```

Notice the counting loop. It is in lines 140 through 190. Line 130 tells the computer what to use for the first value of the counter, C. Line 150 tests to see whether the counter is bigger than the last value. Let's see how the program works.

RUN ——————————————— Answer the question.

? 5, 10 ——————————————— Note the list of numbers.

RUN
? 90, 100 ——————————————— Note this list.

RUN
? -10, 10 ——————————————— This list began at -10.

RUN
? 5, 5 ——————————————— There is only one number this time.

RUN
? 5, 4 ——————————————— There are no numbers this time.

Look at the program again.

4. Which variable in program COUNT stands for the first value of the counting loop?
5. Which statement sets the counter equal to the first value?
6. What is the exit condition in this loop?
7. Which statement adds 1 to the value of the counter?

The FOR/NEXT Abbreviation

You just experimented with a program that asked you to enter a first value and a last value. It then printed a list of numbers that started with the first value and increased by 1 each time. The program looked like this:

```
100  'PROGRAM COUNT
110     PRINT "FIRST & LAST VALUES"
120     INPUT F, L
130     LET C = F
140  '  LOOP
150      IF C > L THEN 190
160       PRINT C
170       LET C = C + 1
180        GOTO 140
190  '  END LOOP
200   END
```

There is a simpler way to write this same program. **Change the program so that it looks like this:**

```
100  'PROGRAM COUNT
110     PRINT "FIRST & LAST VALUES"
120     INPUT F, L
140     FOR C = F TO L
160       PRINT C
190     NEXT C
200   END
```

The new FOR statement is a shorthand way of writing lines 130, 140, and 150 in the original version of COUNT. The new NEXT statement replaces lines 170, 180, and 190 in the original version. Notice also that the variables F and L appear in the FOR statement. Suppose F equals 5 and L equals 10. What do you think the program says to do? Let's find out.

Go back and enter each pair of numbers you used with the original version of program COUNT. You should find that the new version of the program works exactly the same way as the old one did.

8. Which three statements in the original version of program COUNT does the FOR statement replace?
9. Which three statements in the original version of program COUNT does the NEXT statement replace?

Exit Values

The loop variable C has some value after the loop stops. That value is its **exit value**. Let's explore exit values next. **List your program. Add the following line right after the NEXT statement:**

```
195     PRINT "EXIT VALUE = "; C
```

Think about what line 195 tells the computer to do. What do you think will be printed if F is 5 and L is 10? **Run the program again. Enter the same pairs of numbers for F and L that you did before. Pay close attention to the exit value each time.**

10. How is the exit value of the loop variable C related to the last value L?
11. Look at line 150 in the original version of program COUNT. Why is the exit value of C equal to 11 if L is 10?

Changing the Step

So far, all your counting loops have counted by 1s. Next you'll see how to make them count by 2s and other numbers. **Clear the screen and list the program. Change the FOR statement to this:**

```
140     FOR C = F TO L STEP 2
```

Note the STEP phrase. Now do these new experiments:

```
RUN
? 0, 20
```
_____ Note the numbers *and* the exit
value.

```
RUN
? 0, 21
```
_____ Think about these results.

```
RUN
? 0, 21.9999
RUN
? 0, 22
```
_____ Think about these results, too.

Next, let's try another STEP phrase in the FOR statement in line 140.
List the program. Change the FOR statement to this:

```
140    FOR C = F TO L STEP 10
```

List the program again and check it. Then do these new experiments:

```
RUN
? 0, 100
```
_____ Note the numbers and the exit
value this time.

```
RUN
? 1, 100
```
_____ Think about these results.

12. What does the STEP phrase in a FOR statement tell the
    computer to do?
13. What one change would you have to make in the original
    version of program COUNT (page 256) to make it count by 10s?

Counting Down

So far, all your experiments have resulted in lists in which the numbers
got bigger. You can also tell the computer to count backward. **List the
program. Change the 10 after STEP to −1.** The FOR statement should
look like this:

```
140    FOR C = F TO L STEP −1
```

List the program and check it. Then do these new experiments:

RUN
? 10 , 5

Look carefully at the list and at the exit value.

RUN
? 20 , 0

Think about these numbers.

14. What does a negative value in the STEP phrase of a FOR statement tell the computer to do?
15. How is the exit value of C related to L when there is a negative STEP value?

A Few Details

You have only a few more details to learn about the FOR/NEXT abbreviation for counting loops. **Change the program to this:**

```
100  'PROGRAM COUNT
140     FOR C = 3 + 4 TO 3 * 4
160        PRINT C
190     NEXT C
195     PRINT "EXIT VALUE" = "; C
200  END
```

Think what this changed program tells the computer to do. Then run the program and see if you are right.

You just saw that the computer calculates the first and last values of a FOR/NEXT loop before it starts the loop. Let's see whether you can change the last value from inside the loop. **Change the program to this:**

```
100  'PROGRAM COUNT
120     LET L = 10
140     FOR C = 1 TO L
160        PRINT C
165        LET L = 5
190     NEXT C
195     PRINT "EXIT VALUE = "; C
200  END
```

Notice that L starts out as 10. But inside the loop, L is changed to 5. Do you think the program will count to 10 or to 5? **Run it and find out. Afterward, type PRINT L in immediate mode. That will tell you what L is equal to.**

The last experiment shows you something important: *The first and last values of a FOR/NEXT loop are computed only once, before the loop starts. They cannot be changed from inside the loop.* You *can* change L inside the loop. However, that change will not affect the last value of the loop variable C.

16. When does the computer decide what numbers to use for the first and last values of the loop variable in a FOR/NEXT loop?
17. Can a LET statement inside the body of a FOR/NEXT loop change the last value of the loop variable?

PROJECTS

- Write a FOR/NEXT loop that prints the integers from 0 to 20. Next to each integer, the program should print the square root of that integer. Use the function SQR.

- Write a FOR/NEXT loop that tells the computer to print the integers from 0 to 100. For each number N, the computer should print the square (N * N) and the cube (N * N * N) of the number.

- Write a FOR/NEXT loop that counts from 50 to 10000. Let FREQ be the loop variable. Put the statement SOUND FREQ, .2 inside the loop. Run the program. Then add the phrase STEP 5 to the FOR statement. Run the program again. Then change the FOR statement to count backwards from 10000 to 50.

SUMMARY

In this session, you have learned how to write a loop that repeats for a fixed count. Then you learned to use the FOR and NEXT statements to make any counting loop easier to write.

Topic	Description
Counting loop	A block of statements that is performed a fixed number of times.
Loop variable	The variable that acts as the counter in a counting loop. The computer adds to or subtracts from the loop variable each time it goes through the loop.
Exit value	The value of the loop variable immediately after the computer leaves the loop.
FOR/NEXT loop	A shorthand way to write a counting loop in BASIC.
FOR	A BASIC statement used to begin a counting loop. It tells the computer the first and last values of the loop variable. If there is a STEP phrase, it tells what number to add to the loop variable each time through the loop. If there is no STEP phrase, the step amount is 1. The computer begins the loop by testing the exit condition.
NEXT	A BASIC statement used at the end of a counting loop. It tells the computer to add the STEP amount to the loop variable and repeat the exit test.

LOOP-BLOCK APPLICATIONS

SESSION 24

Session Goals

- Use the loop-block outline to solve a programming problem.
- Review the `INKEY$`, `RND`, and `INT` functions.
- Learn more about graphics on the PC*jr*.

Planning a Program with Loops

You have learned all there is to know about the loop block. You know how to write it. You know how it works. And you know how to use the FOR and NEXT statements to make counting loops easier to write. Now it is time to put the things you have learned to use.

In Session 7, you learned about the PSET and LINE statements for drawing points and lines on the graphics screen. In Session 10, you learned to use the SOUND statement to make musical tones. In Session 22, you used the RND function to get random numbers. You know enough now to write a dazzling program that uses all these features of your PCjr at the same time.

Your goal is to plan a program that very rapidly draws random points, lines, and rectangles on the screen. The colors should also be picked at random. As each figure is drawn, a random musical note should be played. The whole process should repeat again and again until you press the Ⓢ key.

The phrase "repeat again and again until" tells you that the program will be based on the loop block. As always, the best way to start work on a program is to write the main routine first. You should begin with the usual mixture of English and BASIC. Here is an example:

```
___   'PROGRAM DAZZLER
___   '   LOOP
___           check the keyboard
___           IF  key is S  THEN  ___
___           get some random numbers
___           output graphics and sound
___           GOTO ___
___   '   END LOOP
___   END
```

Before converting this program completely into BASIC, let's make sure it is correct. The entire body of the main routine is a loop block. The first action inside the loop is to check the keyboard and see whether a key has been pressed. Next, the computer tests to see if the key was the Ⓢ. If so, the computer will exit from the loop and the program will stop. If not, the computer does the next two actions: First, it gets some random numbers. Second, it uses them to produce graphics and sound. Finally, the GOTO statement sends the computer back to the beginning of the loop.

The program seems OK so far. Now let's go on to the next step of the top-down method of programming: Let's convert the English words to BASIC statements. We can have the computer "check the keyboard" in two different ways: We can use the INPUT statement. Or we can use the INKEY$ function. Which is best? The main difference between them is that the INPUT statement stops the computer and waits for input, but the INKEY$ function does not. If no key has been pressed, INKEY$ simply returns the empty string. The computer then goes on to the next statement. Since your purpose is to dazzle, you want the computer to keep going on. So INKEY$ is best.

Thus, "check the keyboard" becomes LET KY$ = INKEY$. Now the exit condition is easy to convert to BASIC: So "key is S" becomes KY$ = "S". The remaining two phrases, "get some random numbers" and "output graphics and sound," are not easy to convert into one or two BASIC statements. In this case, the rule is to use GOSUB statements for them. Here is the complete main routine:

```
100 'PROGRAM DAZZLER
110 '   LOOP
120        LET KY$ = INKEY$
130        IF KY$ = "S" THEN 170
140        GOSUB 400    'RANDOM NUMBERS
150        GOSUB 600    'OUTPUT
160        GOTO 110
170 '   END LOOP
180    END
```

The next step in the top-down method is to plan and write the subroutines. At this early stage, it is a good idea to keep the subroutines simple. That way, you will soon have something to enter into the computer and test. With that idea in mind, let's limit the RANDOM NUMBERS subroutine to picking only two random numbers. Then the OUTPUT subroutine can simply print them on the screen. Here are the simple versions of the two subroutines:

```
390 '
400 'SUB RANDOM NUMBERS
410     LET X1 = RND
420     LET Y1 = RND
430  RETURN
590 '
600 'SUB OUTPUT
610     PRINT X1, Y1
620  RETURN
```

At this point, you have a complete BASIC program. The next step is to enter it into the computer and get it running. **Start the computer as usual. Enter the main routine and both subroutines. Run the program. Fix any lines with syntax errors.** You should see two columns of numbers scrolling up the screen. **Now press the ⑤ key.** The program should stop. (If it does not, you will have to use the (Break) function to stop it.) **Fix any errors you find.**

1. In program DAZZLER, what value does KY$ have if no key has been pressed?
2. Program DAZZLER is not very exciting yet. Why is it a good idea to enter this simple version into the computer before adding more lines to it?

Getting Graphics Output

You now have a working program. It doesn't do much yet. However, it is a strong framework on which to build. As you add features to the program, you will not have to worry about the basic structure. It will stay the same. As a result, you can focus your attention on the details.

The next step is to add graphics. In Session 7, you used the PSET statement to draw tiny dots on the screen. For example, PSET (160, 100) tells the computer to draw a dot in the middle of the graphics screen. (Remember, the width of the medium-resolution graphics screen is 320 dots. The height is 200 dots.) You can use PSET in your program to make the computer draw lots of dots at random places on the screen.

Clear the screen and list the two subroutines. Think about the changes you will need to make.

One change is easy: The PRINT X1, Y1 statement will have to be changed to PSET (X1, Y1). But that is not enough. When you ran the first version of your program, it printed the values of X1 and Y1. They were all numbers between zero and one. But now X1 must be a number between 0 and 319. And Y1 must be a number between 0 and 199.

In Session 22, you learned how to use the INT and RND functions together to make random integers. For example, the expression INT(52 * RND) gives a random integer between 0 and 51. (If you need to review this idea, see page 246.) You can use this method of getting random integers in your new program. You will have to use 320 as the multiplier of RND to get the right numbers for X1. Similarly, you will have to use 200 to get Y1.

Use screen editing to make the changes shown on the next page in your two subroutines.

```
400  'SUB RANDOM NUMBERS
410     LET X1 = INT(320 * RND)
420     LET Y1 = INT(200 * RND)
430  RETURN
590  '
600  'SUB OUTPUT
610     PSET (X1, Y1)
620  RETURN
```

Now see what happens when you try to run the new version of your program. The message Illegal function call in 610 tells you that something is wrong. The words of the message are misleading: PSET is a statement, not a function. You may at first think you've misspelled the statement or used the wrong punctuation. But that is not it. Spelling and punctuation errors usually result in a Syntax error message.

Your problem now comes from the fact that your program uses a graphics statement while the computer is on the text screen. You need to tell the computer to go to the graphics screen before you ask it to produce any graphics output. It's also a good idea to end the program by returning to the text screen. **Make these two changes to your main routine:**

```
100  'PROGRAM DAZZLER
105     SCREEN 1
110  '  LOOP
120        LET KY$ = INKEY$
130     IF KY$ = "S" THEN 170
140        GOSUB 400   'RANDOM NUMBERS
150        GOSUB 600   'OUTPUT
160        GOTO 110
170  '  END LOOP
175     SCREEN 0
180  END
```

Then run the program. It should work fine now. You should see many little dots appearing in random places all over the screen. If you are using a color TV, some dots will look blue and others will look orange. The color is not set by the computer. It is a feature of the color TV, itself. The same kind of dot may have a different color even if it is drawn in two places right next to each other.

Press the (S) **key.** That should stop the loop. Then the computer should return to the text screen again. You should see the word OK at the top of the screen. **Run and stop the program a few times.**

The program you have written is more than just a recreation. One of the best ways to test whether a computer's random-number program makes truly random numbers is to do what you have just done: Pick two successive "random" numbers and use them to plot a point on the screen.

3. What would the computer have drawn if you did not make the changes in subroutine RANDOM NUMBERS?
4. What did the message Illegal function call tell you about the PSET statement?

Making Random Lines

Your program now tells the computer to draw randomly placed dots on the graphics screen. It should be easy to make it draw lines between the dots. In Session 7, you used the LINE statement to draw a line between two points. For example,

```
LINE (0, 0) - (319, 199)
```

tells the computer to draw a line from the upper left-hand corner of the screen to the lower right-hand corner.

There is another way to use the LINE statement. You can leave out the first pair of numbers and their parentheses. For example, you could write this statement:

```
LINE - (319, 199)
```

This also tells the computer to draw a line to the lower right-hand corner. However, it does not say where the line should begin. *When you leave out the first pair of numbers in the* LINE *statement, the computer uses the previous point drawn as the beginning of the line.* For example, the four statements below tell the computer to draw a triangle:

```
10 PSET (0, 0)
20 LINE - (0, 199)
30 LINE - (319, 199)
40 LINE - (0, 0)
```

Let's see how to use this new form of the LINE statement to add some interest to program DAZZLER. Your OUTPUT subroutine looks like this now:

```
600  'SUB OUTPUT
610     PSET (X1, Y1)
620  RETURN
```

By changing PSET to LINE followed by a hyphen, you can make the computer draw a line from each random point to the next one. **Make this change in line 610:**

```
610     LINE - (X1, Y1)
```

Run the program. Notice that the *first* point is not defined. However, the computer assumed a point. Can you see where this first point was? **Use ⓢ to quit. Then list the program.**

Now, suppose you do *not* want all the points connected. You would get a different effect if you had the computer pick *two* points at random and then draw a single line between them. The following changes in the subroutines will do the job:

```
400  'SUB RANDOM NUMBERS
410     LET X1 = INT(320 * RND)
420     LET Y1 = INT(200 * RND)
422     LET X2 = INT(320 * RND)
424     LET Y2 = INT(200 * RND)
430  RETURN
590  '
600  'SUB OUTPUT
610     LINE (X1, Y1) - (X2, Y2)
620  RETURN
```

Make the three changes shown above. Run the program. Use ⓢ to quit. This time, you saw random lines like so many sticks tossed on the screen.

5. What does the statement LINE - (0, 199) tell the computer to do?
6. In the last version of the program, why does subroutine RANDOM NUMBERS call for four random integers?

Adding a Tool

Your program now draws each line as quickly as possible. That is exciting, but the program would be more flexible if you could easily stop and restart it. You know one way to do that: Use the (Pause) function to stop and any symbol key to restart. That sounds easy enough, but there is an even easier way. In this section, you will learn how to tell the computer to keep the loop going as long as you hold a key down, and to pause whenever you release the key.

The loop in your main routine now looks like this:

```
110 '   LOOP
120        LET KY$ = INKEY$
130       IF KY$ = "S" THEN 170
140         GOSUB 400   'RANDOM NUMBERS
150         GOSUB 600   'OUTPUT
160         GOTO 110
170 '   END LOOP
```

This loop keeps running because the INKEY$ function does not wait for you to press a key. If there is no key pressed, INKEY$ returns the empty string. You could make the program stop by using the statement INPUT KY$. Then the loop would pause until you pressed the (Enter ⏎) key. By holding the (Enter ⏎) key down, you could use your keyboard's repeat action to keep the loop going.

That sounds good, but there is a problem: The INPUT statement tells the computer to print a question mark on the screen and to turn the cursor on. You probably don't want a lot of question marks on the screen while you are drawing pictures. You need a new tool. Let's call it KEY WAIT. The first step is easy. **Replace line 120 in the main routine with this one:**

```
120        GOSUB 800   'KEY WAIT
```

Next, you must write the subroutine that does this job. But you cannot use the INPUT statement. You want the computer to stay in the subroutine until a key is pressed. This is another job for the loop block. Here is how to outline the loop:

```
___ 'LOOP
___     LET KY$ = INKEY$
___     IF KY$ <> "" THEN ___
___        GOTO ___
___ 'END LOOP
```

The first thing the computer does inside the loop is to assign the value of INKEY\$ to KY\$. The exit condition is that KY\$ is *not* the empty string. The symbol <> means "is not equal to." If KY\$ *is* equal to the empty string, the computer goes on with the loop. There is nothing else to be done inside the loop. The GOTO statement sends the computer back to the beginning of the loop.

There is a shorter way to write any loop in which the second "do something" is missing. You can combine the IF statement with the GOTO that comes right after it. The trick is to change the exit condition into a "keep looping" condition. Here is how your outline would look in the shortened form:

```
___    'LOOP
___        LET KY$ = INKEY$
___        IF KY$ = " " THEN ___
___    'END LOOP
```

This version tells the computer to keep looping as long as KY\$ is equal to the empty string. In other words, the computer should wait for some key to be pressed. When a key is pressed, the loop should stop. At that point, KY\$ should tell what the key was.

The lines below show this loop as the body of the new subroutine you need. Enter all the lines now.

```
790 '
800 'SUB KEY WAIT
810 '   LOOP
820        LET KY$ = INKEY$
830        IF KY$ = "" THEN 810
840 '   END LOOP
850  RETURN
```

Run the program again. No lines should appear on the screen yet. **Press the spacebar once.** You should see a line. **Press any symbol key except (S).** You should see another line. **Hold the spacebar down for a while. Then release it.** Lines should be drawn as long as you hold the spacebar or any symbol key down. **Press the (S) key.** The program should stop.

You should remember the subroutine you learned about here. It is very short, but it is also very useful. It is particularly useful if you want to get input from the keyboard without having any letters or symbols appear on the screen. After you finish this session, you may want to add this subroutine to your TOOLKIT file.

7. In your program now, why is KY$ = " " called a "keep looping" condition?
8. Suppose the user presses a key while the computer is performing the loop in subroutine KEY WAIT. Then the computer performs line 830. What line will be performed next?

Adding Colors and Shapes

You now have more control over how your program works than before. Let's use the new version to add excitement. In Session 7, you used the LINE statement to draw boxes and fill them with color. Let's begin with a simple change. **Enter the command EDIT 610. Use cursor editing to add ,, B to the end of the line.** The line should look like this:

```
610     LINE (X1, Y1) - (X2, Y2),, B
```

Run the program. Hold down the spacebar. You will see boxes printed on the screen. Let the spacebar up to stop output. Use (S) to quit.

Next, let's add color to the boxes. In Session 7, you found out that there are four different foreground colors you can use in the LINE statement. Let's pick the colors at random. You know how to do that. **Add this line to subroutine RANDOM NUMBERS:**

```
426     LET C = INT(4 * RND)
```

List the subroutine and check for errors. Enter the EDIT 610 command again. Insert a C between the two commas in line 610. The line should now look like this:

```
610     LINE (X1, Y1) - (X2, Y2), C, B
```

Now run the program. Start and stop it as before. You should see a little more color on your TV screen now.

The next step is to add a lot of color. Usually, the colored lines you see on a home TV are disappointing. But colored areas can be very interesting on a TV. You can easily change your OUTPUT subroutine to draw solid boxes in different colors. All that you need to do it is to change B to BF in the LINE statement.

Use the EDIT 610 command again. Use the (End) function to move the cursor to the end of the line. Type an F. Press the (Enter ⏎) key. List the OUTPUT subroutine and check line 610 for BF at the end of the line. Then run the program as before.

9. What do the symbols B and BF mean in the LINE statement?
10. Explain how the new version of the program tells the computer what color to use for the boxes it draws.

More Color and Sound

The boxes you have just seen on your TV screen have four colors: black, cyan, magenta, and white. The boxes were drawn against a black background. It is easy to choose a different background color, using the COLOR statement. You have done this many times before. To make the background color dark blue, you must use the number 1 in a COLOR statement. **Add this line to your main routine:**

```
107     COLOR 1
```

Run the program. Notice the four colors of the boxes. Then stop the program. What colors did you see?

This time, three colors are the same as before: cyan, magenta, and white. But there are no black boxes this time. Instead, you see blue boxes. What is going on?

The answer is simple. The value of the C variable tells the computer what color to use for the boxes. There are four possible values for C. If C is 1, the color is cyan. If C is 2, the color is magenta. If C is 3, the color is white. These three colors are called **foreground** colors. But what happens when C is 0? In that case, the box is drawn in the *background* color, *whatever the background color is.* Later, if you tell the computer to change the background color, everything drawn with C equal to 0 suddenly changes color.

This is fun to do. On page 34 is a table showing the 16 possible background colors. So let's have the computer choose one at random each time it goes through the loop. **Add these two statements to your subroutines now:**

```
428     LET BACK = INT(16 * RND)
605     COLOR BACK
```

List the subroutines and check for errors. Line 428 picks a random background-color number between 0 and 15. Line 605 tells the computer to set the background color to that number. **Run the program. Press the spacebar once. Press it several more times. Notice the background.** You should see it change color each time you press the spacebar. At the same time, boxes drawn in the old background color should switch to the new color. **Press ⓈS to stop.**

There is another interesting thing you can do with colors. In medium-resolution graphics, your PC*jr* has two different sets of foreground colors. Each set is called a **palette.** In art, a painter's palette is a board containing globs of paint the artist wants to use. The artist picks a color by putting a brush in the right place on the palette.

On your PC*jr*, you picked a foreground color by telling the computer the value of C. In other words, the value of C is like a *place* on the painter's palette. The color you get on the screen depends on the color of the "paint" at that "place" on the palette. If C is 3, the "paint" is white, and you get a white box.

This is true on palette 1, the set of foreground colors used so far. But there is another palette. It is called palette 0. If C is 3 on this palette, the "paint" in that "place" is brown, not white. The table below tells the colors on each palette:

Place Number	Palette 0 Color	Palette 1 Color
0	Background	Background
1	Green	Cyan
2	Red	Magenta
3	Brown	White

Now, how can you tell the computer to use palette 0 instead of palette 1? That is easy: Just add another number to your COLOR statement. The first number picks the background color. The second number picks the palette. **Edit line 107 to look like this:**

```
107     COLOR 1 , 0
```

This line tells the computer to begin with background color number 1 (dark blue) and foreground palette number 0. **Run the program now. Press the spacebar and watch the new foreground colors. Press (S) to stop.**

Let's make a final improvement to your program by adding some sounds. You have used the SOUND statement to make musical notes on your PCjr. The first number in the statement tells the computer what frequency to play the note at. The second number tells the computer how long to play the note. Let's keep the length of each note the same and make it very short—say, one clock tick. But let's pick the frequency at random. **Add these two statements to your subroutines now:**

```
429     LET FREQ = 50 + INT(1000 * RND)
615     SOUND FREQ , 1
```

Line 429 picks a random frequency between 50 Hz and 1049 Hz. Line 615 tells the computer to play the note for one clock tick.

If you are using Cassette BASIC, the program is now complete. If you are using Cartridge BASIC, you need to set "foreground" music mode. In that case, add this statement to the main routine:

```
109     PLAY "MF"
```

List the main routine and subroutines. Check for errors. Run the program. Hold down the spacebar. Adjust the volume control on your TV if necessary. Stop and start the program as usual. Use (S) **to quit.** Your final program (in Cartridge BASIC) should look like this:

```
100 'PROGRAM DAZZLER
105    SCREEN 1
107    COLOR 1, 0
109    PLAY "MF"
110 '  LOOP
120       GOSUB 800   'KEY WAIT
130      IF KY$ = "S" THEN 170
140       GOSUB 400   'RANDOM NUMBERS
150       GOSUB 600   'OUTPUT
160       GOTO 110
170 '  END LOOP
175    SCREEN 0
180  END
390 '
400 'SUB RANDOM NUMBERS
410    LET X1 = INT(320 * RND)
420    LET Y1 = INT(200 * RND)
422    LET X2 = INT(320 * RND)
424    LET Y2 = INT(200 * RND)
426    LET C = INT(4 * RND)
428    LET BACK = INT(16 * RND)
429    LET FREQ = 50 + INT(1000 * RND)
430  RETURN
590 '
600 'SUB OUTPUT
605    COLOR BACK
610    LINE (X1, Y1) - (X2, Y2), C, BF
615    SOUND FREQ, 1
620  RETURN
790 '
800 'SUB KEY WAIT
810 '  LOOP
820       LET KY$ = INKEY$
830      IF KY$ = " " THEN 810
840 '  END LOOP
850  RETURN
```

11. In medium-resolution graphics mode, what does the second number in the COLOR statement tell the computer?

PROJECTS

● Program DAZZLER is a good one to save on a cassette tape or diskette. However, before you do so, there is one other thing you should do: Now is the time to renumber the lines to make room for any other changes you may want to make in the future. Start with the command RENUM 100. Then list the beginning of the program: say, lines 100 through 300. Read the main routine. Find the line number of subroutine RANDOM NUMBERS. Renumber the program from that line on, making the first new line number 400. In other words, if the first renumbering makes subroutine RANDOM NUMBER begin at line 240, you should enter the command RENUM 400, 240. Then list the main routine again. Repeat the procedure above with each of the other two subroutines. Renumber them so that they begin at lines 600 and 800. When the line numbers are OK, save the program. If you have a printer, use the LLIST command to print a listing.

● Your PCjr has many different screen modes. There are three in Cassette BASIC. There are four more in Cartridge BASIC. (You may need additional memory in your computer to use some screen modes.) If you are interested in exploring these modes, program DAZZLER will help you. For example, to explore SCREEN 3 all you need to do is this: Change 320 to 160 in the LET X1 and LET X2 statements. There are 16 foreground colors in this mode. Thus, you can also change 4 to 16 in the LET C statement. If you are interested in these modes, read about them in Chapter 4 of the *BASIC* reference book for your PCjr. Read first about the SCREEN statement and then about the COLOR statement.

● Subroutine KEY WAIT is very useful in many situations. Add it to your TOOLKIT file. Load TOOLKIT into memory. Then type the lines of the subroutine, using line numbers beginning with 3000. Finally, save the subroutines again under the same name.

SUMMARY

In this session, you have used two BASIC loop blocks to control a program with graphics and sound output. The loop in the main routine told the computer to keep drawing rectangles and making sounds until the (S) key was pressed. The loop in the KEY WAIT subroutine told the computer to check the keyboard again and again until any key was pressed. These are just two of thousands of possible uses of the loop block.

Topic	Description
Palette	A set of colors. In medium-resolution graphics mode, there are two palettes. Each palette has four colors, numbered 0 through 3. In both palettes, color 0 is the same as the current background color.
COLOR b, p	A BASIC statement that, in medium-resolution graphics, sets the background to color b and the palette to number p. This statement means different things in other screen modes.

THE BRANCH BLOCK

PART FIVE

I *n Part Four, you learned about the BASIC loop block. You used it to tell the computer to repeat some action until a condition became true. You found out how to write a counting loop. You learned how to use the* FOR *and* NEXT *statements as a shortcut for writing counting loops. Along the way, you used loops to explore strings, numbers, and functions.*

Before you read Part Four, you wrote only programs in which all the statements were performed one after the other. No statements were repeated. Such a straight-line sequence of statements is called an "action block." In this block, each statement tells the computer to perform some action. The main actions are input, assignment, and output. After the computer completes the action, it goes on to the next action in the block.

In Part Five, you will learn about a third kind of program block. It is called a "branch block." This block tells the computer to do either one thing or another thing. You will not need to learn any new BASIC statements to build a branch block. It is made out of the same parts as the loop block. However, the loop and the branch work differently. The loop tells the computer to repeat something. The branch tells the computer to choose between two things.

At this point, you may be wondering how many more kinds of program blocks you will have to learn about. The answer is simple: none. Every programming task can be done using only three kinds of blocks: actions, loops, and branches. This is a good fact to keep in mind when you have a programming problem. Instead of looking around for the next statement to write, ask yourself which kind of block you need. There are dozens of kinds of statements. But there are only three kinds of blocks.

THE STANDARD BRANCH BLOCK

SESSION 25

Session Goals

- Learn to use compound conditions in the branch block.
- Learn the structure of the branch-block outline.
- Use the branch-block outline to describe everyday events.

Comparison Operators in the IF Statement

You won't need to use the computer for this session. **Find a comfortable chair. Spend the next 20 minutes or so reading this session.** You have used the IF statement in the loop block. It told the computer when to exit from the loop. You will be using the IF statement for a different purpose in Part Five. Now is a good time for you to learn more about the IF statement.

The condition in the IF statement is made up of one or more comparisons. A comparison is always made up of two pieces of data separated by a **comparison operator**. You know that the symbols +, -, *, and / are arithmetic operators. They tell the computer to perform the rules of arithmetic on the numbers to the left and right of the operator. The six symbols =, < >, >, > =, < =, and < are comparison operators. They tell the computer to compare the two pieces of data and decide whether the comparison is true or false.

There are six ways to compare two numbers. The table below tells the meaning of the operators when they are used to compare two numbers.

Comparison Operators

Operator	Meaning When Applied to Numbers
=	is equal to
< >	is not equal to
>	is greater than
> =	is greater than or equal to
< =	is less than or equal to
<	is less than

The terms *greater than* and *less than* refer to a number's position on the number line.

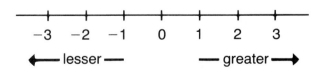

For example, 2 is greater than 1, and it is also greater than -3. On the number line, 2 is to the right of 1 and also to the right of -3. Notice also that -1 is greater than -2. That is because -1 is "more positive," or to the right of, -2.

The table below contains the same six comparison operators. It gives their meaning when they are used to compare two strings. The words "earlier" and "later" refer to dictionary order.

Comparison Operators

Operator	Meaning When Applied to Strings
=	is equal to
< >	is not equal to
>	is later than
> =	is later than or equal to
< =	is earlier than or equal to
<	is earlier than

Of course, not all possible strings are words in the dictionary. However, the rules of dictionary order apply to nonwords as well. The comparison "AARRGH" > "AARDVARK" is true. That is because AARRGH, if it were a word, would appear later in the dictionary than AARDVARK.

Strings can also contain punctuation marks, spaces, and numbers. You can think of all these as letters in one big alphabet: The space comes first, then most of the punctuation marks, then the numbers, and finally the letters. It is OK to compare "ABC" to "123". Since both are enclosed in quotation marks, both are strings. But you cannot compare "ABC" to 123. The latter is a numeric constant. If you try to compare a string to a number, you will get a Type mismatch error message.

1. The operator > can be used to compare either strings or numbers. What is the difference in meaning between the two cases?
2. Are the following comparisons true or false?
   a. 4 * 5 >= 16 + 2
   b. "KIT" > "KITTYCAT"
   c. 350 >= 250
   d. "ABACUS" < "COMPUTER"

Compound Conditions

The condition in an IF statement can have more than one comparison. Such a condition is called a **compound** condition. In compound conditions, the comparisons must be separated by the words OR or AND. Here is an example of a compound condition using OR:

```
IF N = 7 OR A$ = "YES" THEN 50
```

The condition in the IF statement is compound because there are two comparisons between IF and THEN. They are separated by the word OR. The compound condition is this:

```
N = 7 OR A$ = "YES"
```

The compound condition is true if either part is true. That is, if N is 7, *or* if A$ is YES, *or* if N is 7 *and* A$ is YES, the condition is true. The whole condition is false *only* if N is not 7 *and* A$ is not YES. In this example, there are only two comparisons in the condition. However, there can be more than two comparisons in a compound condition. When the word OR is used between the parts of a compound condition, the whole condition is true if any *one* of the parts is true.

The comparisons in a compound condition can also be separated by AND. Here is an example of such a condition:

```
A$ > B$ AND X = Y
```

This compound condition is true only if *both* comparisons are true. It is false if either comparison is false. A compound condition can have several comparisons separated by AND. Here is an example:

comparison 1 AND *comparison 2* AND *comparison 3*

All the comparisons must be true for this compound condition to be true. If any one of the comparisons is false, then the compound condition is false.

Both AND and OR can be used to separate the comparisons in certain compound conditions. Here is an example:

```
A$ > B$ AND X = Y AND C > 0 OR W1$ = W2$
```

The logic of this compound condition is hard to follow. There are four comparisons in the condition. Is the condition true if the first three comparisons are true *or* the last one is true? Is the condition true if the first two comparisons are true *and* either the third *or* fourth is true? You probably aren't sure.

Since complicated compound conditions that use both AND and OR are hard to understand, it's best to avoid them. However, if you have to use both AND and OR, there is a way you can make your meaning clearer. You can use parentheses. For example, the condition

```
(A$ > B$ AND X = Y AND C > 0) OR W1$ = W2$
```

is easier to understand because of the parentheses. It is true if the first three comparisons are all true, if the last comparison is true, or if all the comparisons are true. Otherwise, it is false.

It is important to remember that the IF statement uses a condition to determine what statement the computer performs next. It makes no difference whether the condition is simple or compound. It does not matter whether numbers, strings, or both are used in the comparison. If the condition is false, the computer goes on to the next line after the IF. If the condition is true, the computer jumps somewhere else.

3. What is a compound condition?
4. Are the following conditions true or false?
   a. 4 > 2 OR "DOG" > "CAT"
   b. 3 > 4 OR 10 > 12 OR "A" > "B"
   c. 4 > 2 AND "DOG" > "CAT"
   d. 3 < 4 AND 10 < 12 AND "A" < "B"

Branch-Block Outline

In Session 21, you learned how to write an outline of the loop block. You used a mixture of English and BASIC words. In this session, you will write a similar outline for the **branch block**.

A loop block is used to do something over and over until a condition becomes true. A branch block is used in an either-or situation. In a branch block the computer begins by testing a condition to see whether it is true or false. The condition can be a single comparison or a compound condition. If the condition is true, the computer performs one group of statements. If the condition is false, it performs a different group of statements. In either case, the computer goes on to the next statement in the program after completing the branch block.

The first part of a branch block is an IF statement. It contains the condition to be tested. After that, there must be one group of statements for the computer to perform if the condition is true. There must be another group for the computer to perform if the condition is false. There must be a GOTO statement *between* the two groups. It tells the computer to skip the second group if it has already performed the first. Here is the branch-block outline:

```
___    IF condition THEN ___ ELSE ___
___    ' THEN
___
___        do something
___
___        GOTO ___
___    ' ELSE
___
___        do something
___
___    'END IF
```

As in the loop-block outline, the blanks show where line numbers will be used. The jump arrows remind you that the numbers after THEN, ELSE, and GOTO must match the line numbers of the targets of the jumps. Remark statements tell the reader of the reasons for the jumps. *Condition* can stand for a comparison, such as A1 > 5. It can also stand for a compound condition, such as A$ = "YES" AND C < 10. The indented phrase *do something* stands for one or more BASIC statements. Here is how the computer performs a branch block:

The computer's rules for performing a branch block

1. Test the condition to see whether it is true or false.
2. If the condition is true, move the line pointer to the THEN remark. Then perform the first "do something" block. If the condition is false, move the line pointer to the ELSE remark. Then perform the second "do something" block.
3. Move the line pointer to the END IF remark. Then exit from the branch block.

The outline shows that the branch block is very different from the loop block. In the loop block, there is a jump arrow from the GOTO statement at the end *all the way back to the beginning*. In the branch-block outline, both jump arrows go *forward*.

The IF statement appears in both kinds of blocks. However, it has completely different purposes in the two blocks. In the loop block, the IF statement tells the computer when to exit from the loop. In the branch block, the IF statement tells the computer which "do something" to perform.

The GOTO statement also appears in both kinds of blocks. But as with the IF statement, it has totally different uses in the two blocks. In the loop block, the GOTO statement at the end tells the computer to loop back to the beginning. In the branch block, the GOTO statement tells the computer to skip the ELSE "do something" if it has performed the THEN "do something."

5. Why must a jump arrow go backward in a loop block but not in a branch block?
6. What is the purpose of the IF statement in the branch block? In the loop block?
7. What is the purpose of the GOTO statement in the branch block? In the loop block?
8. What do the three remark statements in the branch-block outline on page 284 tell someone who is reading the program?

Branches in Everyday Life

Branches are not just used in computer programs. You probably use branches often in telling other people how to do things. You also find many branches in the instructions for doing everyday tasks. Let's look at an example now.

Think about these sentences: "The right lane on a highway is the slow lane. People drive slowly in the right lane." *Slow* is an adjective in the first sentence. *Slowly* is an adverb in the second sentence. You can change the adjective to the adverb by adding *ly*. But is that rule always true? *Speedy* is also an adjective. If you add *ly*, you get *speedyly*, which is obviously wrong. The correct way to spell the adverb is *speedily*.

In school, you learned the following spelling rule for changing adjectives to adverbs. "If the adjective ends in *y*, change the *y* to *i* and add *ly*. Otherwise, just add *ly*."

If you think of this spelling rule as a program block, you'll see that it is not a loop. Nothing gets done again and again. The block is a branch: Either one thing gets done or another thing gets done. Here is how you could write the spelling rule, using a mixture of English and BASIC:

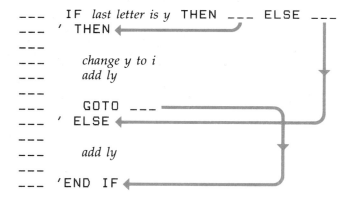

```
___     IF last letter is y  THEN  ___  ELSE  ___
___     ' THEN

___
___         change y to i
___         add ly

___
___         GOTO ___
___     ' ELSE

___
___         add ly

___
___     'END IF
```

Paul Revere faced a problem we can describe with a branch block. This example is interesting because it needs an action and a loop block as well as a branch block.

Paul Revere's mission was to warn the Minutemen at Lexington whether the British forces were coming by land or by sea. His instructions to a fellow patriot might have been these: "Climb up in the tower of Old North Church, where you can see what the British are doing. If they come by land, hoist one signal lantern. If they come by sea, hoist two. Once I see the signal, I'll ride and spread the alarm."

There are three separate parts to Paul's instructions. First, climb the tower. Second, wait until you see the British. Third, give one alarm or the other. Here is a BASIC outline of the orders:

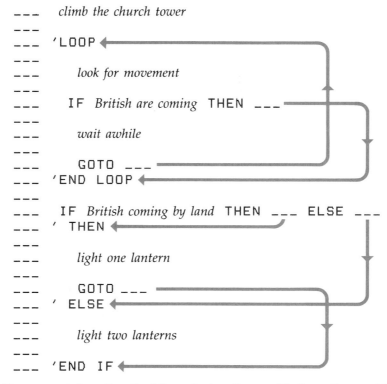

```
___    climb the church tower
___
___    'LOOP
___
___        look for movement
___
___        IF British are coming THEN ___
___
___        wait awhile
___
___        GOTO ___
___    'END LOOP
___
___    IF British coming by land THEN ___ ELSE ___
___    ' THEN
___
___        light one lantern
___
___        GOTO ___
___    ' ELSE
___
___        light two lanterns
___
___    'END IF
```

You cannot describe all of these instructions with the action and loop blocks alone. You need the branch block too. *Using just these three kinds of blocks, you can give any instructions, no matter how complicated they are. This is true whether you are giving instructions to a person or to a computer.*

9. A friend telephones you and says: "Let's go on a picnic Saturday. If it rains, we'll go to a movie instead." Rewrite this suggestion in the form of a BASIC branch outline.

10. Make up your own either-or situation. Write instructions for it in the form of a BASIC branch outline.

SUMMARY

In this session, you learned about the branch block. This is the last of the structures you need to learn about to solve *any* programming problem. The key ideas are outlined in the table below.

Topic	Description
Branch block	A program structure used to tell the computer to perform *either* one block of statements *or* another block of statements. The choice depends on whether some condition is true or false.
Comparison operators	The symbols =, < >, >, > =, < =, and <. These symbols are used to form comparisons between numbers or between strings.
Compound condition	A condition containing more than one comparison. The comparisons must be separated by the BASIC words AND or OR.
OR	A BASIC word used to separate comparisons in compound conditions. In a compound condition with two comparisons separated by OR, the condition is true if either of the comparisons or both are true. The condition is false if both the comparisons are false.
AND	A BASIC word used to separate comparisons in compound conditions. In a compound condition with two comparisons separated by AND, the condition is true only if both comparisons are true. The condition is false if either comparison is false.

NESTING PROGRAM BLOCKS

SESSION 26

Session Goals

- Write a branch block that simulates the toss of a coin.
- Nest a branch block inside a loop block.
- Change the coin-tossing simulation to stop after a fixed number of heads have occurred in a row.

Writing a Coin-Tossing Branch Block

Now that you have seen how the branch block works, we will write a program that uses one. The job is to make the computer behave like a coin tosser. A program that does this kind of thing is called a **simulation**: The computer does not toss a coin, but in some ways it can act like it is doing so. Your program will print HEADS or TAILS after each "toss." You will use the RND function to get the random numbers needed to decide which word to print.

As always, the best way to begin the program is to start at the top. What are the main things that have to be done? The program could run as an infinite loop. Or it could be a conditional loop—a loop with an exit. We choose the conditional loop because it gives the user of the program more control. What condition shall we use? Let's have the loop run for a fixed count. This means that there will be two main parts to the program: First, the computer will ask the user how many coins to toss. Second, the computer will simulate the proper number of tosses. For each toss, the outcome (either HEADS or TAILS) will be written on the screen.

Here is the main routine, written partly in English and partly in BASIC:

```
100  'PROGRAM COINS
110       ask how many coins to toss
120       toss coins and print outcome
130  END
```

Now look at each English phrase in the body of the main routine. If one or two BASIC statements will carry out the task, put them in the main routine. If not, put in a GOSUB statement to a subroutine where the job will be done. Don't let yourself get bogged down in details. Think at as high a level as possible.

In this program, both main tasks are complicated enough to need GOSUB statements. Once we have put them in, we have finished the main routine. Here is how it should look:

```
100  'PROGRAM COINS
110       GOSUB 200    'HOW MANY
120       GOSUB 400    'TOSS COINS
130  END
```

Turn on your PC*jr* and enter the main routine.

The next step is to write outlines of the subroutines that we will need. You can see from the main routine that one subroutine begins at line 200. Another begins at line 400. We'll begin with skeleton subroutines. These will contain simple debugging messages. **Enter the changes shown below:**

```
100 'PROGRAM COINS
110    GOSUB 200   'HOW MANY
120    GOSUB 400   'TOSS COINS
140 END
190 '
200 'SUB HOW MANY
210    PRINT "HOW MANY"
380 RETURN
390 '
400 'SUB TOSS COINS
410    PRINT "TOSS COINS"
580 RETURN
```

Now you have a skeleton of the final program. **Run the program. Make sure it prints the messages in the right order.**

Next, let's turn to the bodies of the two subroutines. The rule for writing subroutine bodies is the same as for the main routine. If you can do the job with one or two BASIC statements, do it. If not, use a GOSUB statement to another subroutine that will contain the detailed steps. Again, don't let yourself get bogged down in these details.

The body of the first subroutine is easy to write. It should clear the screen. It should next ask the user how many coins to flip and then wait for input. **Enter the following lines:**

```
210    CLS
220    PRINT "TOSS HOW MANY COINS"
230    INPUT N
240    CLS
```

Before starting the body of the second subroutine, let's think a bit about what is required. First, the subroutine is to simulate tossing a coin. This action will have to be repeated again and again. What kind of structure is needed to do this? Clearly, it is *not* a branch. A branch deals with an either-or situation. A loop block is needed to do something (such as toss a coin) again and again. You used the variable N in line 230, so the coin is to be tossed N times. You will need a counting loop. The FOR/NEXT abbreviation for the loop is ideal.

Now, what goes in the body of your loop? You must tell the computer to toss a coin and print the result. That may seem difficult, so let's put the details off. For now, we can use a GOSUB as the body of the loop. We can decide later how to tell the computer to toss a single coin.

Change the body of subroutine TOSS COINS as shown below. Also, add the skeleton version of subroutine ONE TOSS. Run the program. Make sure your counting loop works correctly.

```
400 'SUB TOSS COINS
410    FOR COUNT = 1 TO N
420       GOSUB 600   'ONE TOSS
430    NEXT COUNT
580  RETURN
590 '
600 'SUB ONE TOSS
610    PRINT "ONE TOSS"
780  RETURN
```

The only part of the program left to write is the body of subroutine ONE TOSS. Here is where the coin-toss simulation will be done. What kind of structure is needed? It is *not* something that is done again and again. Thus, a loop block won't work. It is an either-or situation.

```
600 'SUB ONE TOSS
610    IF condition THEN 620 ELSE 650
620 '    THEN
630         print "heads" message
640       GOTO 670
650 '    ELSE
660         print "tails" message
670 '  END IF
780  RETURN
```

The two "do somethings" in the branch block are easy to convert to BASIC. But what should we use for the condition? If the simulation is to be fair, we want the two messages to show up in random order. So we need to use the RND function. It returns a random number between zero and one. Let's assume that if the random number is greater than one-half, the toss is "heads." Otherwise, the toss is "tails." Then the condition we need is RND > .5. Here is what the finished subroutine should look like:

```
600  'SUB ONE TOSS
610     IF RND > .5 THEN 620 ELSE 650
620  '    THEN
630        PRINT "HEADS"
640        GOTO 670
650  '    ELSE
660        PRINT "TAILS"
670  '  END IF
780  RETURN
```

Enter the subroutine body shown above. In the immediate mode, enter the line GOSUB 600 a few times. You should see either HEADS or TAILS appear on the screen. Now your whole coin-toss simulation is complete.

Run the program. Enter the number of tosses you want to see. Try it again. When you have seen enough, save the program under the name COINS on either cassette tape or diskette. (Note: You will need this program in Session 32.) If you have a printer, use the LLIST command to print a listing.

1. What is the purpose of the RND function in the coin-tossing simulation?
2. If you told the computer you wanted to toss a coin 1000 times, how many HEADS would you expect to get? Why?

Nesting Program Blocks

In both the loop and branch blocks, you have seen the phrase "do something." These words mean that any block of BASIC statements can go in that place. You have learned that there are only three fundamental program blocks: the action block, the loop block, and the branch block. In other words, the phrase "do something" really stands for one or more of these blocks.

Suppose the "do something" in a loop or a branch is *another* loop or branch block. In that case, the inner block is said to be **nested** inside the outer block. In this book, we have stressed using indentation in programs. One reason is that indenting helps you see nested program blocks more easily.

Here is the subroutine beginning in line 400 in program COINS:

```
400 'SUB TOSS COINS
410    FOR COUNT = 1 TO N
420      GOSUB 600    'ONE TOSS
430    NEXT COUNT
580  RETURN
```

Notice that GOSUB 600 is nested inside the loop block beginning in line 410. But if you look at the body of the subroutine beginning in line 600, you see that it is a branch block. Thus, the branch block is really nested inside the loop block in subroutine TOSS COINS.

There is another way to write subroutine TOSS COINS. Instead of using the GOSUB statement in line 420, you could have put the whole branch block there. Here is how that would look:

```
400 'SUB TOSS COINS
410    FOR COUNT = 1 TO N
420       IF RND > .5 THEN 421 ELSE 424
421 '       THEN
422           PRINT "HEADS"
423           GOTO 426
424 '       ELSE
425           PRINT "TAILS"
426 '      END IF
430    NEXT COUNT
580  RETURN
```

If you look at the subroutine this way, it is quite clear that the branch block is nested *inside* the loop block. If you scan up and down in the subroutine, you can see where the subroutine begins and ends. Further to the right, you can see the beginning and end of the loop block. Looking even further to the right, you can see where the branch block begins and ends. Finally, still further to the right, you see the PRINT statements.

Notice that the PRINT statements are the only action statements in the entire subroutine. All the other statements are there to control these two actions. The branch block tells the computer which action to perform. The loop block tells the computer how many times to perform the branch block.

Which version of subroutine TOSS COINS is better? It is largely a matter of taste. Both versions work equally well. Ultimately, it boils down to which program is easier to read. Judged this way, the first version probably wins. Indentation helps you understand nested blocks. But when the nesting gets deep, indenting the inner blocks does not help as much as using separate subroutines for them.

3. What can replace the "do somethings" in the outlines of the loop block and branch block?
4. What is meant by a *nested program block*?

A Series of "Heads"

Programs that are easy to read are easy to change. Program COINS was written with careful attention to top-down planning. In addition, it used only action, loop, and branch blocks. Thus, it should be easy to change the program to do something else.

Here is an experiment you can try yourself: See how many times you must flip a coin in order to get a series of, say, five "heads" in a row. Each time you get a "tail," you must start counting the series again.

Let's change program COINS to simulate this experiment. First, the computer should ask how long the series of "heads" should be. Then it should simulate tossing coins, counting each toss, and quitting when the series of "heads" happens. After that, the computer should print the total number of tosses that were required to get the string of "heads."

If program COINS is not in your computer, load it now. Let's examine the main routine to see if any changes are needed. Here it is:

```
100  'PROGRAM COINS
110     GOSUB 200   'HOW MANY
120     GOSUB 400   'TOSS COINS
130  END
```

Think about the problem. You should be able to see that some changes should be made. First, the name of the program is a little vague. Let's change it to SERIES. Second, there needs to be a new subroutine. It will report how many tries it took to get the desired series of "heads."

The main routine, with these changes, is shown below. **Enter the changes into your program now.**

```
100 'PROGRAM SERIES
110    GOSUB 200   'HOW MANY
120    GOSUB 400   'TOSS COINS
125    GOSUB 800   'RESULTS
130 END
```

Now list the first subroutine. Only the PRINT message needs to be changed in subroutine HOW MANY. **Change line 220 as shown below:**

```
200 'SUB HOW MANY
210    CLS
220    PRINT "HOW MANY HEADS IN A ROW"
230    INPUT N
240    CLS
380 RETURN
```

List the subroutine beginning at line 400. Subroutine TOSS COINS needs the most work. Here is the old version:

```
400 'SUB TOSS COINS
410    FOR COUNT = 1 TO N
420       GOSUB 600   'ONE TOSS
430    NEXT COUNT
580 RETURN
```

This is a counting loop: The body of the loop is performed exactly N times. For our new program, we cannot tell in advance how many times the computer should perform the loop. We know only that the loop should stop as soon as the series of "heads" is equal to N. For example, if N is 4, we might be lucky and get 4 "heads" in a row on the first 4 tosses. More likely, it will take 10 or 20 tosses.

So the counting loop is the wrong one for this program. That means we cannot use the FOR/NEXT abbreviation for the new loop. Instead, we need to use the full form of the loop block. Here is an outline:

```
400  'SUB TOSS COINS
410  '  LOOP
420       GOSUB 600    'ONE TOSS
425       IF exit condition THEN 430
429          GOTO 410
430  '  END LOOP
580   RETURN
```

As before, this loop tells the computer to perform the GOSUB 600 statement again and again. Now we must decide what the exit condition should be. That is easy. Suppose that HEADS is the name of a variable that tells how many "heads" have been tossed since the last "tails." The loop should stop when HEADS is equal to N, the number entered by the user. So the exit condition is HEADS = N.

The new loop has one other job: It must tell the computer to count *all* the tosses. Let's use COUNT as the name of the variable that holds the count. Inside the loop, there must be a LET statement telling the computer to add 1 to this variable.

Last, we must tell the computer what to use as the starting value for HEAD and COUNT. This process is called **loop initialization**. *You must always remember to initialize outside a loop the variables that change inside the loop.* **Enter the new body statements in the subroutine, as shown below:**

```
400  'SUB TOSS COINS
402     LET HEADS = 0
404     LET COUNT = 1
410  '  LOOP
420        GOSUB 600    'ONE TOSS
425        IF HEADS = N THEN 430
427        LET COUNT = COUNT + 1
429           GOTO 410
430  '   END LOOP
580   RETURN
```

Next, let's look at subroutine ONE TOSS. Here is the old version:

```
600 'SUB ONE TOSS
610    IF RND > .5 THEN 620 ELSE 650
620 '    THEN
630        PRINT "HEADS"
640        GOTO 670
650 '    ELSE
660        PRINT "TAILS"
670 '   END IF
780   RETURN
```

In the new versions, we want the computer to *count* "heads," not *print* HEADS. So line 630 has to be changed to the proper LET statement. What about the other PRINT statement in this block? What should the computer do if the toss is "tails"? The answer is simple: It should reset the "heads" counter to zero. **Make the changes shown below:**

```
600 'SUB ONE TOSS
610    IF RND > .5 THEN 620 ELSE 650
620 '    THEN
630        LET HEADS = HEADS + 1
640        GOTO 670
650 '    ELSE
660        LET HEADS = 0
670 '   END IF
780   RETURN
```

The last thing to do is to write a subroutine to print the results. The problem is to flip N heads in a row. When that is true, the total number of coins flipped is equal to the value of COUNT. **Enter this new subroutine:**

```
800 'SUB RESULTS
810    PRINT "IT TOOK"; COUNT; "TOSSES"
820    PRINT "TO GET"; N; "HEADS"
830    PRINT "IN A ROW"
840   RETURN
```

That completes the changes you need. Here is the finished program:

```
100 'PROGRAM SERIES
110    GOSUB 200    'HOW MANY
120    GOSUB 400    'TOSS COINS
125    GOSUB 800    'RESULTS
130  END
190  '
200 'SUB HOW MANY
210    CLS
220    PRINT "HOW MANY HEADS IN A ROW"
230    INPUT N
240    CLS
380  RETURN
390  '
400 'SUB TOSS COINS
402    LET HEADS = 0
404    LET COUNT = 1
410  '  LOOP
420      GOSUB 600    'ONE TOSS
425    IF HEADS = N THEN 430
427      LET COUNT = COUNT + 1
429      GOTO 410
430  '  END LOOP
580  RETURN
590  '
600 'SUB ONE TOSS
610    IF RND > .5 THEN 620 ELSE 650
620  '    THEN
630      LET HEADS = HEADS + 1
640      GOTO 670
650  '    ELSE
660      LET HEADS = 0
670  '  END IF
780  RETURN
790  '
800 'SUB RESULTS
810    PRINT "IT TOOK"; COUNT; "TOSSES"
820    PRINT "TO GET"; N; "HEADS"
830    PRINT "IN A ROW"
840  RETURN
```

Run the program. Make sure it works like it's supposed to. Enter 4 for the number of "heads." Run the program again using 6. Try again with 5. Use 5 again. Use 5 one more time.

You have just discovered a problem with the random-number generator: It always generates the same sequence of numbers after you enter the RUN command. There is a way to change the sequence, though. **Add this statement to your main routine:**

```
105     RANDOMIZE
```

Run the program. Reply to the first question by typing a number in the range shown in the message. Then use 5 again as the number of "heads." Run the program again, using a different number for the first question, and 5 again for the second one. You should get different results each time.

The RANDOMIZE statement tells the computer to start the series of random numbers in a different way. The series you get is different for each different number you enter when asked to do so. Having to enter a number each time is a nuisance. You can avoid it by using this form of the statement:

```
105     RANDOMIZE 128*INP(64) + INP(64)
```

You should think of this as a bit of "black magic." It works, but it would take too much time to explain how it works. This statement allows you to get a different series of numbers from the RND function every time you run a program. You are not asked to enter a number. **Change line 105 as shown above. Run the program some more.** You should get different results each time you ask for five heads in a row. **Increase the number of heads little by little. See if you can guess how many extra tries it will take each time you ask for one more head. If you enter a number that is too big, use the (Break) function to stop the program.**

After you are finished, save the program in a file named SERIES on either cassette tape or on diskette.

5. How would you change the exit condition in the loop in subroutine TOSS COINS to tell the computer to leave the loop when either the number of heads in a row is N or when the number of coins tossed is 1000?
6. Suppose you made the change described in question 5. What kind of block would you need to write to find out why the computer left the loop?
7. What is the purpose of the RANDOMIZE statement?

PROJECTS

- Change your main routine so that the last two GOSUB statements are inside a loop. Use the INKEY$ function to decide when to exit from the loop.

- Suppose you want program COINS not only to "toss coins" but also to count the *total* number of heads and the *total* number of tails. You then want the computer to print the two counts when the tossing loop is over. Make these changes. Use HEADTOTAL and TAILTOTAL for the new variables. Be careful to initialize each one outside the loop.

- Change your program so that the "coin" comes up heads 60 percent of the time and tails 40 percent of the time, on the average.

SUMMARY

In this session, you have used the branch block to simulate the toss of a coin. You also reviewed the loop block and the top-down method of programming. You saw how to nest one block of statements inside another block. The table below summarizes the important new ideas you have learned. Read the table carefully. Make sure you understand each topic thoroughly before going on to the next session.

Topic	Description
Simulation	A computer program that causes the computer to behave like some real event or activity.
Nesting	Putting one program block inside another block.
Loop initialization	Setting variables to their first values before they are changed by statements in the body of a loop.
RANDOMIZE	A BASIC statement used to vary the sequence of numbers returned by the RND function.

VARIATIONS ON BRANCHES

SESSION 27

Session Goals

- Make a three-way branch out of two two-way branches.
- Learn shortcuts for writing certain branches.
- Learn the standard case-block form.

A Three-Way Branch

In Sessions 25 and 26, you learned how to write a branch block. If the computer must decide which of two "do somethings" to perform, the standard branch block is just what you need. But what if you need more than a two-way branch? What if there are three different choices?

You may be thinking that you will need a totally new type of block for every different number of branches. Luckily, that is not so. The trick is to put one two-way branch block inside another one. Remember, the "do something" in a branch block can be *any* program block: It can be an action block, a loop, a branch, or any combination of these three.

In this session, you will learn how to make a three-way branch out of two two-way branches. Your problem is to write a program that begins by asking the user to enter two words. The program must tell the computer to find which of three things is true: Are the two words the same? If not, is the first earlier in the dictionary than the second? Or is the first later in the dictionary than the second?

It is always best to begin with a main routine written partly in English and partly in BASIC. The English phrases should describe the things to be done. Here is the top-level description of the main routine:

```
100  'PROGRAM WORDS
110      input two words
120      compare words and output results
130  END
```

It will take more than one or two BASIC statements to do the things described in both English phrases in the main routine. So the best plan is to substitute GOSUB statements and put the details into subroutines. The completed main routine and two skeleton subroutines are shown below. **Turn on your PC***jr* **and enter the program. Then run the program. Make sure the debugging messages are correct.**

```
100  'PROGRAM WORDS
110      GOSUB 200    'GET WORDS
120      GOSUB 400    'TEST WORDS
130  END
190  '
200  'SUB GET WORDS
210      PRINT "GET WORDS"
380  RETURN
390  '
400  'SUB TEST WORDS
410      PRINT "TEST WORDS"
580  RETURN
```

Subroutine GET WORDS is easy. It tells the computer to print a prompting message and wait for two words to be typed. **Enter the new body statements shown below:**

```
200  'SUB GET WORDS
210     CLS
220     PRINT "ENTER TWO WORDS"
230     PRINT "SEPARATED BY A COMMA"
240     INPUT A$, B$
380  RETURN
```

Subroutine TEST WORDS is a good deal more complicated. Let's write this subroutine little by little. We'll start at the top, or outer, level of the subroutine. Let's have the computer decide first whether the two words that the user types are the same or not. The action block won't work here. Neither will the loop block. This is an either-or situation. It calls for a branch block. Here is an outline of subroutine TEST WORDS showing the branch block in place:

```
400  'SUB TEST WORDS
410     IF A$ = B$ THEN 420 ELSE 450
420  '   THEN
---
---         print message saying words are same
---
440        GOTO 570
450  '   ELSE
---
---         decide which word is earlier
---
570  '   END IF
580  RETURN
```

If A$ = B$, the words are the same. Thus, the computer will perform the first "do something." What type of program block is needed here? The loop or branch blocks won't do. An action block with a single PRINT statement is what we need.

What about the second "do something"? That is a more complicated problem. Let's put it off. We'll just substitute a debugging message for now. **Enter the new body statements for the subroutine, as shown below. Run the program. Enter two words that are the same. Then run the program again with two different words. Fix any errors you find.**

```
400  'SUB TEST WORDS
410     IF A$ = B$ THEN 420 ELSE 450
420  '    THEN
430        PRINT "BOTH WORDS ARE "; A$
440        GOTO 570
450  '    ELSE
460        PRINT "WHICH WORD IS EARLIER?"
570  '  END IF
580   RETURN
```

Now let's deal with the second "do something." The English phrase "which word is earlier" is a clue to what kind of program block is needed. We need *another* branch block nested inside the outer branch block. This new branch block must enable the computer to decide which of the two words comes earlier in the dictionary. We will need to use the expression A$ > B$ as the condition in the new branch block.

You could bury these details in another subroutine. But this time, let's see what happens if you write the second branch inside the first one. It will seem very complicated at first. Later, you will see how to make it simpler. Here is how the whole subroutine looks:

```
400  'SUB TEST WORDS
410     IF A$ = B$ THEN 420 ELSE 450
420  '    THEN
430        PRINT "BOTH WORDS ARE "; A$
440        GOTO 570
450  '    ELSE
460        IF A$ > B$ THEN 470 ELSE 500
470  '      THEN
480          PRINT A$; " IS LATER THAN "; B$
490          GOTO 520
500  '      ELSE
510          PRINT A$; " IS EARLIER THAN "; B$
520  '     END IF
570  '  END IF
580   RETURN
```

The new part is in lines 460–520. If you look only at those lines, you will see that they form a regular, two-way branch block. The condition is in line 460. The two "do somethings" are the PRINT statements in lines 480 and 510. **Enter the new lines shown at the bottom of the previous page. Run the program several times. Test words that are the same and words that are different.** If you choose the right words, you should see all three possible messages printed on the screen.

The subroutine is beginning to look complicated. The indentation shows which blocks are nested inside what other blocks. But this time the indentation hides the fact that this is really a three-way branch. The program would be easier to read if the three PRINT statements were all indented the same amount. In addition, the two END IF remarks are repetitive. Here is a better way to write the three-way branch.

```
400 'SUB TEST WORDS
410    IF A$ = B$ THEN 420 ELSE 450
420 '    THEN
430       PRINT "BOTH WORDS ARE "; A$
440       GOTO 570
450 '    ELSE
460    IF A$ > B$ THEN 470 ELSE 500
470 '    THEN
480       PRINT A$; " IS LATER THAN "; B$
490       GOTO 570
500 '    ELSE
510       PRINT A$; " IS EARLIER THAN "; B$
570 '  END IF
580   RETURN
```

The main change here is that there are two fewer spaces of indentation in the inner branch block. In addition, one of the END IF remarks (line 520) is gone. Also, the GOTO in line 490 now jumps to the other END IF remark in line 570. **Use screen editing to make these changes in the subroutine. Run the program. Check for errors.** Your whole program should now look like the one at the top of the next page.

```
100 'PROGRAM WORDS
110    GOSUB 200    'GET WORDS
120    GOSUB 400    'TEST WORDS
130  END
190 '
200 'SUB GET WORDS
210    CLS
220    PRINT "ENTER TWO WORDS"
230    PRINT "SEPARATED BY A COMMA"
240    INPUT A$, B$
380  RETURN
390 '
400 'SUB TEST WORDS
410    IF A$ = B$ THEN 420 ELSE 450
420 '   THEN
430      PRINT "BOTH WORDS ARE "; A$
440      GOTO 570
450 '   ELSE
460    IF A$ > B$ THEN 470 ELSE 500
470 '   THEN
480      PRINT A$; " IS LATER THAN "; B$
490      GOTO 570
500 '   ELSE
510      PRINT A$; " IS EARLIER THAN "; B$
570 '  END IF
580  RETURN
```

**Run the program several times with different pairs of words. Be
sure the program works correctly. When you are through, save the program under the name WORDS on either cassette tape or diskette.** You
will need to use this program again later in this session.

1. Is the three-way branch you just wrote a new kind of block? Or is
   it built from other kinds of blocks?
2. In the last version of the three-way branch above, how does the
   indentation make the meaning clearer than in the original version?
3. In the three-way branch above, under what condition will line
   430 be performed? Line 480? Line 510?

Branch-Block Abbreviations

You can solve *any* programming problem by using only three structures: the action block, the loop block, and the branch block. However, sometimes the same block can be written in more than one way. For example, you learned the FOR/NEXT abbreviation for the counting loops. The FOR/NEXT abbreviation is not necessary, merely convenient. Anything that you can do with FOR and NEXT statements you can do with the standard loop block. (The reverse is not true!)

In this session, you will learn some shortcuts for writing branch blocks. Let's begin with a very common situation: the empty branch. You want to tell the computer to do *something* or else to do *nothing*. These English sentences show how often people give this kind of instruction:

If it is raining, take your umbrella.
If you have the money, go to a movie.
If you have the BASIC cartridge, plug it in.

Here is how to write the first sentence above as a BASIC branch block:

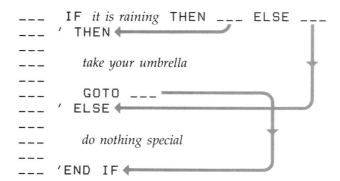

```
___    IF it is raining THEN ___ ELSE ___
___    ' THEN

___
___        take your umbrella

___
___        GOTO ___
___    ' ELSE

___
___        do nothing special

___
___    'END IF
```

The first half of the branch outline above is useful. But the second half looks a little silly: If there is nothing to be done, why say anything at all? Here is the solution to this problem:

```
___    IF it is raining THEN ___ ELSE ___
___    ' THEN

___
___        take your umbrella

___
___    'END IF
```

This version is not just easier to write: It is also easier to read and understand. The rule is this: *When there is a "do nothing" branch, leave it out. In the* IF *statement, make sure the number after* ELSE *is the same as the line number of the* END IF *remark.*

Sometimes, branches like this can be written in an even simpler way. Suppose the "do something" is just a single statement, such as this:

```
200   IF X > 319 THEN 210 ELSE 230
210 ' THEN
220     LET X = 319
230 'END IF
```

This branch tells the computer to keep X from getting bigger than 319. Such a branch would be useful in a graphics program. There you would want to make sure that the things being drawn on the screen are inside the boundaries of the screen. This branch would keep X from getting too big. Here is a simpler way to write this useful branch:

```
200   IF X > 319 THEN LET X = 319
```

You are allowed to put any BASIC statement after THEN in the IF statement. The statement will then be performed if the condition in the IF statement is true. Otherwise, the computer will skip the statement.

There is a tricky way to put more than one statement after THEN, but we don't recommend this practice. If you put a lot of statements after THEN, your programs will become hard to read. Sometimes, they will do unexpected things. Instead, when the "do something" takes more than one statement, use the longer form of the branch block.

4. Rewrite this sentence in the long form of the BASIC branch-block outline: "If you have a diskette drive, read Session 6."
5. Rewrite the sentence in question 4 in the one-line form of the BASIC branch block.

Making a Case Block

In this section, you will learn how to use the one-line form of the branch block to build a **case block**. This is not a new type of block. It is just a shorthand way of writing a series of branch blocks, one right after the other. There is nothing you can do with the case block that you can't do with the longer forms of the branches.

The case block is useful when you want the computer to do only one of many possible things. Your program will be easy to read if all the possibilities appear close together in the program listing. The case-block outline below shows a good way to do that:

```
___  'CASE
___      IF  condition 1  THEN  statement 1
___      IF  condition 2  THEN  statement 2
___      IF  condition 3  THEN  statement 3
___      IF  condition 4  THEN  statement 4
___      IF  condition 5  THEN  statement 5
___
___      etc.
___
___  'END CASE
```

What happens when the computer performs a case block? If *condition 1* is true, then *statement 1* is performed. Whether or not *condition 1* is true, the computer goes on to the second IF statement. If *condition 2* is true, then *statement 2* is performed. Then the computer goes to the third IF statement, and so on. The computer performs every IF statement in the case block. The CASE and END CASE remarks tell the reader where the block begins and ends.

How is the case block used? Normally, you want the computer to do *only one* of the cases in the block. That is the whole idea of a case block. To make that happen, you must be very careful about the conditions you put in the IF statements. *There must be no overlap between two conditions in a case block.* Let's see what "overlap" means.

Suppose the first IF statement in a case block has the condition N = 5, and the second IF statement has the condition N > 2. These conditions are said to overlap because both can be true at the same time. If N has the value 5, then the computer will decide that both conditions are true. So the computer will perform both the first case and the second case in the block. That is *not* how a case block is supposed to work.

It is up to you to make sure that no two of the conditions in a case block overlap. Usually, this is easy to do. Most case blocks use the value of one variable to decide which case to do. Such blocks usually have this form:

```
___  'CASE
___      IF  N  =  constant 1  THEN  statement 1
___      IF  N  =  constant 2  THEN  statement 2
___      IF  N  =  constant 3  THEN  statement 3
___      IF  N  =  constant 4  THEN  statement 4
___      IF  N  =  constant 5  THEN  statement 5
___
___      etc.
___
___  'END CASE
```

In the example on the previous page, N is the name of the variable. Each condition tests whether N is *equal* to a constant, such as 5 or 37. If all the constants are different, then none of the conditions will overlap: The computer will perform only one of the cases in the case block.

Thus, it is usually easy to write case blocks in which the conditions don't overlap. Remember, though, that the computer will test every condition in the block. If two conditions do overlap, both cases will be done.

6. Which IF statements in a case block does the computer perform?
7. Why must no two of the conditions in a case block overlap?

Using a Case Block

Let's look at a familiar branch and see whether it can be rewritten as a case block. Earlier in this session, you wrote a three-way branch. It told the computer to decide these three things: Are two words the same? If not, is the first earlier in the dictionary than the second? Is the first later than the second? Here is the subroutine you wrote:

```
400  'SUB TEST WORDS
410     IF A$ = B$ THEN 420 ELSE 450
420  '    THEN
430        PRINT "BOTH WORDS ARE "; A$
440        GOTO 570
450  '    ELSE
460     IF A$ > B$ THEN 470 ELSE 500
470  '    THEN
480        PRINT A$; " IS LATER THAN "; B$
490        GOTO 570
500  '    ELSE
510        PRINT A$; " IS EARLIER THAN "; B$
570  '  END IF
580   RETURN
```

Reading from the top, you can see that the first PRINT statement is performed if A$ = B$. If that condition is not true, the computer goes to line 450. The next statement is the start of a two-way branch. You can see that if A$ > B$, the computer performs the second PRINT statement. Otherwise, the computer goes to line 500 and performs the third PRINT statement.

Let's think for a minute about that third PRINT statement. If the computer performs it, what can you say about A$ and B$? First, they cannot be equal. (If they were, only the first PRINT statement would have been performed.) Nor can A$ > B$ be true. (If it were, only the second PRINT statement would have been performed.) There is only one possibility left: A$ < B$ must be true.

The three conditions are A$ = B$, A$ > B$, and A$ < B$. Do they overlap? No, there is no way that any two of them can be true at the same time. Each one is a different case.

That means you *can* write this whole branch block in the form of a case block. Here is what it looks like:

```
400 'SUB TEST WORDS
405 '   CASE
410     IF A$ = B$ THEN PRINT "BOTH WORDS ARE "; A$
460     IF A$ > B$ THEN PRINT A$; " IS LATER THAN "; B$
500     IF A$ < B$ THEN PRINT A$; " IS EARLIER THAN "; B$
570 '   END CASE
580 RETURN
```

If program WORDS is not in your PC*jr* now, load it into memory at this point. Then change the body of subroutine TEST WORDS as shown above. The long lines will fold over to the next line of the screen as you type them. **Be sure to press (Enter ⏎) after you type or edit each line.** Then, run the program. Experiment with different pairs of words.

You should get exactly the same results this time that you did before. If both versions do the same job, which form is the best one to use? There is no simple answer. The case block is usually much easier to read than the nested branch block. In the case block, however, *you* must be sure that no two of the conditions overlap. Remember, the computer performs all the IF statements in the block. Your nested branch block is different: If the first condition is true, the next IF is skipped completely.

If you decide to use a case block, you may have another problem: You may want the computer to do more than one statement if a case is true. If so, your best solution is to use a GOSUB statement, such as in the following line:

```
850   IF P = 7 THEN GOSUB 1100   'CASE 7
```

You then put the actual statements for the case in the body of the subroutine.

There is one last shortcut that you may want to use when writing certain branches. It uses a new statement called the ON statement. Here is an example:

```
320   ON J GOSUB 400, 600, 800, 1000
```

The numbers after GOSUB are the line numbers of subroutines. There can be from 1 to 16 numbers after GOSUB. The example above means exactly the same thing as the following set of IF statements:

```
320   IF J = 1 THEN GOSUB 400
321   IF J = 2 THEN GOSUB 600
322   IF J = 3 THEN GOSUB 800
323   IF J = 4 THEN GOSUB 1000
```

The only time you can use an ON statement is when the cases are defined by a variable that can take on the values 1, 2, 3, and so on. This fact puts tight limits on the use of the ON statement. (There is another form of the ON statement in which GOSUB is replaced by GOTO. It too is exactly equivalent to a series of IF statements. The ON/GOTO statement tells the computer to jump to one of the lines in the list after GOTO, depending on the value of the variable.)

8. Is the case block a new kind of block, or is it a shortened form of other blocks?
9. What is the main advantage of using the case-block form?
10. What is the main disadvantage of using the case-block form?
11. What limits the use of the ON/GOSUB abbreviation for the case block?

SUMMARY

This session began by showing you how to nest one branch block inside another. You used this method to create a three-way branch. You then learned how to write a branch in which one of the "do somethings" was actually an instruction to do nothing. Finally, you learned a simple way to write a case block. The table below summarizes these important ideas. Be sure you understand them fully before you go on to the next session.

Topic	Description
Empty branch	A branch block in which one of the "do somethings" is the instruction to do nothing.
Case block	A list of actions, only one of which is to be performed.
IF *condition* THEN *statement*	A short way to write an empty branch block. The statement is performed only if the condition is true.
ON *variable* GOSUB *list*	A BASIC statement that tells the computer to perform one of a list of subroutines. The numbers in the list after GOSUB are the line numbers of the first statements in the subroutines. The value of the variable tells which subroutine to perform.

BRANCH-BLOCK APPLICATIONS

SESSION 28

Session Goals

- Use the case block for a word-processing application.
- Use the case block for a music application.
- Use the case block for a graphics application.

An Application of the Case Block

In the last session, you learned some shortcuts for writing certain branch blocks. You do not *need* to take the shortcuts, of course. As we have said many times, all branching problems can be solved by using only the two-way branch. You can handle three-way and four-way branches, for example, by nesting one branch inside another.

A very useful shortcut is the case block, which you just learned about. It tells the computer to do only one out of several possible actions. Now it is time to put the case block to work. In this session, you will write three programs: The first is a word-processing program. The second is a music program. The third is a graphics program.

Your first problem is this: The user of the program will type words, sentences, or paragraphs on the keyboard. The program should tell the computer to count how many times each of the five vowels (a, e, i, o, and u) occurs. (Word-processing programs, which help you with writing jobs, use case blocks similar to the one you will write.)

We'll need a separate counter for each vowel. The counters will all have to be set to 0 at the start. Then we'll need a loop to check the keyboard again and again. Inside the loop, we'll use the case block to add 1 to a counter if the key was a vowel key. We'll need to pick one key for the exit condition from the loop. Finally, we'll need to have the computer print the results.

As always, let's begin with a top-level description of the program:

```
100  'PROGRAM VOWELS
110      initialize all variables to zero
120      process keys pressed by the user
130      output the totals
140  END
```

The three necessary parts of the main routine are described by the English phrases. Each of these parts will probably need more than one or two BASIC statements. Thus, we should use GOSUB statements. The finished main routine and skeleton subroutines are shown at the top of the next page. **Start the computer as usual. Enter the program into your PC*jr*. Run it and fix any errors.**

```
100  'PROGRAM VOWELS
110     GOSUB 200    'INITIALIZE
120     GOSUB 400    'PROCESS KEYS
130     GOSUB 600    'OUTPUT TOTALS
140  END
190  '
200  'SUB INITIALIZE
210     PRINT "INITIALIZE"
380  RETURN
390  '
400  'SUB PROCESS KEYS
410     PRINT "PROCESS KEYS"
580  RETURN
590  '
600  'SUB OUTPUT TOTALS
610     PRINT "OUTPUT TOTALS"
680  RETURN
```

Next, consider subroutine INITIALIZE. There must be a variable to keep a count of each of the vowels as they are entered from the keyboard. Let's use the name CA to stand for the "counter for a's," CE for the e's, and so forth. In subroutine INITIALIZE, each of these variables must be set equal to 0. Here is the subroutine:

```
200  'SUB INITIALIZE
210     LET CA = 0
220     LET CE = 0
230     LET CI = 0
240     LET CO = 0
250     LET CU = 0
380  RETURN
```

Enter the changes shown above into your computer. Be sure to use the letter O when you type the name CO. Enter GOSUB 200 in the immediate mode. Check for any syntax errors.

Subroutine PROCESS KEYS is next. Let's think carefully about what is needed. The computer must check the keyboard again and again as the user types. If a vowel key is pressed, 1 must be added to the proper counter. If the exit key is pressed, the subroutine should return control back to the main routine. What is needed is a loop block. The outline is at the top of the next page.

```
400 'SUB PROCESS KEYS
410 '   LOOP
420        check the keyboard
430        IF  exit key  THEN 570
---
---        if a vowel key, add 1 to a counter
---
560        GOTO 410
570 '   END LOOP
580  RETURN
```

You want the computer to "check the keyboard" without having the user press the (Enter ⏎) key after each letter. That means you will have to use the INKEY$ function. Next, let's decide on the "exit key." The user will be typing words and sentences, so the (S) key is a poor choice here. Let's use the ($) key this time. Here is the subroutine with these parts converted to BASIC:

```
400 'SUB PROCESS KEYS
410 '   LOOP
420        LET KY$ = INKEY$
430        IF KY$ = "$" THEN 570
---
---        if a vowel key, add 1 to a counter
---
560        GOTO 410
570 '   END LOOP
580  RETURN
```

Now let's think about the phrase that remains: "If a vowel key, add 1 to a counter." What does that mean?

You know what it means, but the idea is complex. You have to break it into smaller pieces to convert it into BASIC. The main idea falls into five pieces: "If the letter is 'a,' add 1 to the counter for a's; if the letter is 'e,' add 1 to the counter for e's; and so forth." In other words, there are five separate *cases*. You need a BASIC case block. The complete subroutine is at the top of the next page.

```
400  'SUB PROCESS KEYS
410  '   LOOP
420        LET KY$ = INKEY$
430        IF KY$ = "$" THEN 570
440  '     CASE
450           IF KY$ = "A" THEN LET CA = CA + 1
460           IF KY$ = "E" THEN LET CE = CE + 1
470           IF KY$ = "I" THEN LET CI = CI + 1
480           IF KY$ = "O" THEN LET CO = CO + 1
490           IF KY$ = "U" THEN LET CU = CU + 1
500  '     END CASE
560        GOTO 410
570  '   END LOOP
580  RETURN
```

Enter the new body of this subroutine. The long lines will fold over to the next line on the screen as you type them. **Run the program and test the loop exit. Run the program again and press each of the vowel keys once. Then press the ⑤ key and use the immediate mode statement PRINT CA; CE; CI; CO; CU. You should see five 1s on the screen.**

The program would be better if the computer printed the symbol for each key as the user pressed the key. That sounds easy: Just put the following line into the loop:

435   PRINT KY$

Now run the program. Type a few keys. Whoops! That is not what we wanted. Remember, the INKEY$ function does not tell the computer to wait for input. **Press the ⑤ key.** Here is what happened: Each time around the loop, the computer printed a line. Most of the time, the value of KY$ was the empty string, so you saw many blank lines.

The program would be nicer if it printed KY$ every time but did *not* print a new line each time. There is a simple way to tell the computer *not* to start a new line after printing something: Just put a semicolon (;) at the end of the PRINT statement. **Use cursor editing to put a semicolon at the end of line 435, as shown below:**

435   PRINT KY$;

Since KY$ equals the empty string most of the time, this statement tells the computer to print nothing on the screen. The semicolon tells the computer not to start a new line. When the user presses a symbol key, the computer will print the symbol. However, it will not start a new line after printing the symbol. **Run the program again. Type a word. Then enter the ⑤ key.** You should see the letters you typed this time.

Finally, we must complete subroutine OUTPUT TOTALS. That is easy. **Enter the changes shown in the subroutine below:**

```
600  'SUB OUTPUT TOTALS
610     PRINT
620     PRINT "THERE WERE"; CA; "A'S"
630     PRINT "THERE WERE"; CE; "E'S"
640     PRINT "THERE WERE"; CI; "I'S"
650     PRINT "THERE WERE"; CO; "O'S"
660     PRINT "THERE WERE"; CU; "U'S"
680  RETURN
```

Enter the statement **GOSUB 600** in the immediate mode. Fix any errors. You should see a five-line message saying that there were zero vowels. **Now run the whole program. Enter a word. Press the ⑤ key to exit.** You should see a correct count of the vowels in your word. **Run the program again. Type a long sentence this time. Press ⑤ again.** You should see the correct number of vowels. **Now list the complete program. If you have a printer, use the LLIST command to print the program.** It should look like the one on the next page.

```
100 'PROGRAM VOWELS
110    GOSUB 200   'INITIALIZE
120    GOSUB 400   'PROCESS KEYS
130    GOSUB 600   'OUTPUT TOTALS
140  END
190 '
200 'SUB INITIALIZE
210    LET CA = 0
220    LET CE = 0
230    LET CI = 0
240    LET CO = 0
250    LET CU = 0
380  RETURN
390 '
400 'SUB PROCESS KEYS
410 '  LOOP
420      LET KY$ = INKEY$
430    IF KY$ = "$" THEN 570
435      PRINT KY$;
440 '    CASE
450        IF KY$ = "A" THEN LET CA = CA + 1
460        IF KY$ = "E" THEN LET CE = CE + 1
470        IF KY$ = "I" THEN LET CI = CI + 1
480        IF KY$ = "O" THEN LET CO = CO + 1
490        IF KY$ = "U" THEN LET CU = CU + 1
500 '    END CASE
560        GOTO 410
570 '  END LOOP
580  RETURN
590 '
600 'SUB OUTPUT TOTALS
610    PRINT
620    PRINT "THERE WERE"; CA; "A'S"
630    PRINT "THERE WERE"; CE; "E'S"
640    PRINT "THERE WERE"; CI; "I'S"
650    PRINT "THERE WERE"; CO; "O'S"
660    PRINT "THERE WERE"; CU; "U'S"
680  RETURN
```

When you are finished, save the program under the name VOWELS on either cassette tape or diskette.

1. In program VOWELS, what does subroutine PROCESS KEYS tell the computer to do if the user enters a letter that is not a vowel?
2. In program VOWELS, will the computer print a $ if the user presses the $ key? Why, or why not?

A Music Example

You can use the case block to tell the computer to treat the keyboard as a set of piano keys. You can tell the computer to play the notes of the piano depending on what key is pressed.

You will be using your TOOLKIT subroutines to play the musical notes. You may remember that we added two variables, HOLD and DURATION, to control these subroutines. (Such variables are called parameters.) The program will have to assign values to these parameters before the subroutines are used. Here is a top-level description of the program:

```
100 'PROGRAM PIANO
110     set graphics mode
120     assign values to sound parameters
130     check keyboard and play notes
140     set text mode
150 END
```

Your TOOLKIT file already has subroutines for setting graphics and text modes. You will need to write only two new subroutines. Let's start with skeleton subroutines. **Load your TOOLKIT subroutines from cassette or diskette. Then enter the main routine and skeleton subroutines below:**

```
100 'PROGRAM PIANO
110     GOSUB 2100    'GRAPHICS
120     GOSUB 200     'SOUND PARAMETERS
130     GOSUB 400     'PROCESS KEYS
140     GOSUB 2000    'TEXT
150 END
190 '
200 'SUB SOUND PARAMETERS
210     PRINT "SOUND PARAMETERS"
380 RETURN
390 '
400 'SUB PROCESS KEYS
410     PRINT "PROCESS KEYS"
580 RETURN
```

Run the program. Fix any syntax errors. The debugging statements were not very useful, since line 140 switched back to text mode and cleared the screen. The main point now is to check for syntax and other errors.

Subroutine SOUND PARAMETERS is easy. You must tell the computer what values to use for DURATION and HOLD. DURATION tells the note subroutines how many clock ticks the note should last. HOLD tells what fraction of that time to sound the note. The rest of the time there will be silence. Let's begin with 2 for DURATION and .9 for HOLD. **Enter the subroutine body shown below:**

```
200 'SUB SOUND PARAMETERS
210     LET DURATION = 2
220     LET HOLD = .9
380 RETURN
```

Enter GOSUB 200 in the immediate mode. Fix any errors.

The main task of this program is in the next subroutine. It must tell the computer to check the keyboard again and again. Thus, the main structure we need is a loop. In fact, it is just like the loop you wrote in program VOWELS. Here is an outline:

```
400 'SUB PROCESS KEYS
410 '   LOOP
420        LET KY$ = INKEY$
430        IF KY$ = "$" THEN 570
---
---        if a note key, sound the note
---
560        GOTO 410
570 '   END LOOP
580 RETURN
```

The only difference in this loop is what goes on inside. This time, the computer must decide which key has been pressed and what sound to make for it. So we will need some kind of branch.

As before, we can use the case block. Suppose we pick one row of keys on the computer keyboard to stand for the white keys in one octave of the piano keyboard. Let's use the second row of symbol keys: Ⓐ, Ⓢ, Ⓓ, Ⓕ, Ⓖ, Ⓗ, Ⓙ, and Ⓚ. Then it is easy to see how to write the case block. You can see it in lines 440 through 530 at the top of the next page.

```
400 'SUB PROCESS KEYS
410 '  LOOP
420     LET KY$ = INKEY$
430     IF KY$ = "$" THEN 570
440 '    CASE
450       IF KY$ = "A" THEN GOSUB 1000   'DO
460       IF KY$ = "S" THEN GOSUB 1100   'RE
470       IF KY$ = "D" THEN GOSUB 1200   'MI
480       IF KY$ = "F" THEN GOSUB 1300   'FA
490       IF KY$ = "G" THEN GOSUB 1400   'SOL
500       IF KY$ = "H" THEN GOSUB 1500   'LA
510       IF KY$ = "J" THEN GOSUB 1600   'TI
520       IF KY$ = "K" THEN GOSUB 1700   'DO
530 '    END CASE
560       GOTO 410
570 '  END LOOP
580   RETURN
```

Enter the new body of this subroutine. After you type line **450**, you can use cursor editing to make line **460**. Repeat the process for the other cases in the case block. The long lines will fold over to the next line on the screen as you type them. To avoid this, you may wish to leave off the trailing remarks. **Run the program and test the loop exit. Run the program again and press each of the note keys once.** You should hear each note of the scale. You should see the screen background turn to different colors. You should see the name of the note printed on the screen. **When you want to stop, press the $ key.**

When you finish working with this program, save it on diskette or cassette in a file named **PIANO**. If you have a printer, use the **LLIST** command to print a listing. It should look like this:

```
100 'PROGRAM PIANO
110    GOSUB 2100    'GRAPHICS
120    GOSUB 200     'SOUND PARAMETERS
130    GOSUB 400     'PROCESS KEYS
140    GOSUB 2000    'TEXT
150  END
190 '
200 'SUB SOUND PARAMETERS
210    LET DURATION = 2
220    LET HOLD = .9
380  RETURN
390 '
```

```
400  'SUB PROCESS KEYS
410  '   LOOP
420        LET KY$ = INKEY$
430        IF KY$ = "$" THEN 570
440  '     CASE
450           IF KY$ = "A" THEN GOSUB 1000    'DO
460           IF KY$ = "S" THEN GOSUB 1100    'RE
470           IF KY$ = "D" THEN GOSUB 1200    'MI
480           IF KY$ = "F" THEN GOSUB 1300    'FA
490           IF KY$ = "G" THEN GOSUB 1400    'SOL
500           IF KY$ = "H" THEN GOSUB 1500    'LA
510           IF KY$ = "J" THEN GOSUB 1600    'TI
520           IF KY$ = "K" THEN GOSUB 1700    'DO
530  '     END CASE
560        GOTO 410
570  '   END LOOP
580   RETURN
```

3. What is the purpose of subroutine INITIALIZE in program VOWELS?

4. If you wanted to add more white notes to the "piano," what would you have to do to program PIANO?

A Graphics Sketcher

Program PIANO and program VOWELS are very similar. They both use slightly different versions of a subroutine named PROCESS KEYS. The body of the subroutine is a loop. Inside the loop, the computer checks the keyboard and may do one of a list of possible cases. The cases are contained in a case block inside the loop.

This subroutine can be used for many other applications. For example, you can use it in a program that allows the user to draw pictures on the screen by pressing keys. To write such a program, all you have to do is make the changes shown on the next page to your PIANO program. The main changes are in the PROCESS KEYS subroutine.

```
100 'PROGRAM SKETCH
110    GOSUB 2100    'GRAPHICS
120    GOSUB 200     'INITIALIZE
130    GOSUB 400     'PROCESS KEYS
140    GOSUB 2000    'TEXT
150 END
190 '
200 'SUB INITIALIZE
210    LET X = 160
220    LET Y = 100
380 RETURN
390 '
400 'SUB PROCESS KEYS
410 '  LOOP
420       LET KY$ = INKEY$
430      IF KY$ = "$" THEN 570
440 '     CASE
450         IF KY$ = "K" THEN LET X=X+1
460         IF KY$ = "J" THEN LET X=X-1
470         IF KY$ = "M" THEN LET Y=Y+1
480         IF KY$ = "I" THEN LET Y=Y-1
530 '     END CASE
540       PSET (X, Y)
560       GOTO 410
570 '  END LOOP
580 RETURN
```

Here is how this works: If the user presses the Ⓚ key, the computer adds 1 to X. If the user presses the Ⓙ key, the computer subtracts 1 from X. The Ⓜ and Ⓘ keys work similarly, but they change the value of Y. Notice line 540. It tells the computer to draw a dot at location (X, Y). The result is that the user can place dots on the screen by pressing keys on the keyboard.

If your PIANO program is not in the computer now, load it from cassette or diskette. Make the changes shown above. Run it and experiment with the Ⓘ, Ⓙ, Ⓚ, and Ⓜ keys. Use the Ⓢ key to exit from the loop. When you have finished, save the program in a file with the name SKETCH.

PROJECTS

● In program SKETCH, add more IF statements to the case block. The statements should test whether one of the number keys on the top row has been pressed. If so, the corresponding COLOR statement should be performed. For example, one of the statements should be this:

```
510           IF KY$ = "3" THEN COLOR 3
```

Run the program. Use the number keys to change the background color.

● The PSET statement allows you to draw points in other colors besides white. In program SKETCH, change line 540 to this:

```
540     PSET (X, Y), C
```

The value of C, which must be between 0 and 3, tells the computer which color to use. Add four new IF statements to the case block. They should test for the (B), (C), (M), and (W) keys. If the (B) key is pressed, C should be set equal to 0, the background color. If the (C) key is pressed, C should be 1, the number for cyan. If the (M) key is pressed, C should be 2, the number for magenta. If the (W) key is pressed, C should be 3, the number for white. Run the program. Press one of the above keys to pick a color. Then place the dots on the screen as usual.

SUMMARY

In this session, you have used the case block in three different programs. In each one, the computer checked the keyboard again and again. When the key pressed by the user matched one of the conditions in the case block, the computer performed one of the actions in the block: counting vowels in the first program, playing music in the second one, and drawing pictures in the third.

ARRAYS

PART SIX

*I*n Part Five, you learned about the BASIC branch block. You used it to tell the computer to choose between two things and do only one of them. You also learned how to solve complex branch problems by nesting one branch inside another. Finally, you learned a few shortcuts for writing certain branches. The case block is the most useful of these.

You have now learned all the kinds of blocks you wil! need to solve any programming problem. Using only actions, loops, and branches, you can handle every situation that comes up. If you are stumped while writing a program, ask yourself this question: "Do I want the computer to do one thing after another, or do I want it to repeat something again and again, or do I want it to choose between two or more things and do just one of them?" Once you know the answer to that question, you will know which kind of block you should write.

Part Six, the last part of this book, returns to the topic of variables. You first learned about variables in Part Three. Using the tools you learned there, you can write a program that tells the computer to do this job: Ask the user to enter 3 words, one after the other; then print the words in reverse order. But could you write a similar program for 100 words? You could, but it would be very long. It would have 100 variables, many input statements, and many output statements. What if the same program had to work for 2 words, 100 words, or any number between them? That would be a hard program to write with the tools you now have.

The tool you need to work with lists of words or numbers is called an "array." In most ways, an array is like the variables you learned about in Part Three. In Part Six, you will learn the one important way that arrays differ from ordinary variables. You will also see how to use this difference to make your programs easier to write.

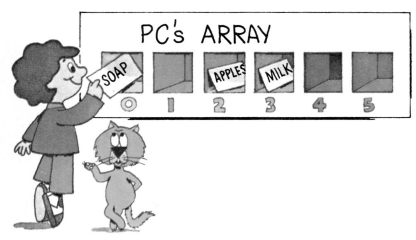

EXPLORING ARRAYS

SESSION 29

Session Goals

- Explore array variables.
- Use a variable as an item number.
- Dimension arrays.

Review

In Part Three, you learned about both string and numeric variables. So far, the name of a variable has always stood for a single piece of data. However, some problems are hard to handle with this kind of variable. Sometimes, a lot of information should be grouped under a single name. Examples of this kind of data would be a list of students in a class, a list of words to be alphabetized, and a list of passengers on an airline flight.

All computer languages have ways to let you use a single variable name to stand for a whole list of data. In BASIC, variables of this kind are called **array variables**, or simply **arrays**. You'll learn about arrays and lists in this session.

String Lists

The best way to begin learning about lists is in the immediate mode.

```
NEW
```
Erase the memory.

```
LET W1$ = "RED"
LET W2$ = "WHITE"
LET W3$ = "BLUE"
```
This gives values to W1$, W2$, and W3$.

```
PRINT W3$, W2$, W1$
```
You should have known in advance what was going to happen, and why.

```
PRINT W2$ + W1$
```
As expected, this joins WHITE and RED.

Now for something new:

```
NEW
CLS
```
Now you have a clear screen. The computer has forgotten about the variables W1$, W2$, and W3$.

```
LET W$(1) = "RED"
LET W$(2) = "WHITE"
LET W$(3) = "BLUE"
```
This is a new way to name variables. The computer didn't complain, so it must know what you mean.

```
PRINT W$(3), W$(2), W$(1)
PRINT W$(2) + W$(1)
```
You got the same results as before.

You've now learned a new way to *name* variables. You have seen that the names W$(2) and W2$ can both be used for a string variable. So far, the two kinds of names have worked the same way. Now let's see how they differ.

```
LET J = 1
PRINT W$(J)
```
J is a variable. It stands for the number of an item in a list. The value of J tells the computer which of the three words in the list to print.

```
LET J = 2
PRINT W$(J)
```
These two statements tell the computer which item to print.

```
PRINT J
```
J is still 2.

```
PRINT W$(J + 1), W$(J - 1), W$(J)
```
Now, the computer must do some arithmetic to find the item numbers.

```
LET J = 4
PRINT W$(J)
```
This time, you got a blank line. You did not tell the computer what W$(4) stood for.

Let's take another look at what you have seen. W1$ and W2$ are the names of ordinary variables. An ordinary variable stands for one piece of data. But W$ followed by parentheses is the name of an array variable. It can stand for a whole list of data. The number inside the parentheses identifies one item in the list. Thus, W$(4) means the fourth item in the list W$. A$(5) means the fifth item in the list A$, and so on.

In most ways, array variables are like ordinary variables: You use LET and INPUT statements to assign values to array variables. You use PRINT statements to print the values of array variables on the screen. In those ways, W1$ and W$(1) are alike.

But array variables differ from ordinary variables in one important way: *With array variables, the thing inside the parentheses can be either a*

number or anything that has a numeric value. For example, you can write
W$(J). To find the value of this expression, the computer does three
things. First, it finds out the value of J. Second, the computer uses that
value as the item number for the list. Third, the computer looks up the
value of that item in the list. Let's explore this in program mode.

```
CLS
NEW
```
———————————————————————— Clear the screen and erase the
memory.

```
500 LET W$(1) = "RED"
510 LET W$(2) = "WHITE"
520 LET W$(3) = "BLUE"
600 PRINT W$(1), W$(2), W$(3)
RUN
```
———————————————————————— This should not surprise you.

```
600 FOR J = 1 TO 3
610    PRINT W$(J)
620 NEXT J
LIST
```
———————————————————————— Think carefully about line 610.
What does it tell the computer to
do?

```
RUN
```
———————————————————————— Were you right?

```
600 FOR J = 3 TO 1 STEP -1
LIST
```
———————————————————————— What will this do?

```
RUN
```
———————————————————————— Now you know.

Line 610 was the same in both versions of your program. But the
computer did different things when you ran each version. Line 610 tells
the computer to print *one* item in the W$ list. The value of J is the item
number. In the first version, J was 1, 2, and then 3. In the second
version, J was 3, 2, and then 1.

You can also use the INPUT statement to assign values to an array.
Let's explore that idea.

```
500 FOR J = 1 TO 3
510    INPUT W$(J)
520 NEXT J
LIST
```
———————————————————————— Think about what line 510 tells
the computer to do.

RUN
_____

Notice the question mark. Give the following answers:

```
?  RED
?  WHITE
?  BLUE
```
_____

What did the computer print? Let's try that again.

```
RUN
?  ROMEO
?  LOVES
?  JULIET
```
_____

You probably guessed what would be printed.

    You can get a better idea of how this program works. Make the two changes below:

```
505     PRINT "WORD"; J,
```
_____

Be sure to type a comma at the end of the line.

```
610     PRINT J, W$(J)
LIST
```
_____

Check the changes.

RUN
_____

Notice the prompting message this time.

    Enter the words SHARKS, EAT, and PEOPLE. The program should work as before. This time, however, the computer prints extra information: It shows the item number of each item in the list.

    This little program tells the computer to accept any three strings from the user. The computer then prints the strings in reverse order. You could have written this program without using an array: You could have used three INPUT statements and six PRINT statements. But suppose you wanted to tell the computer to accept _any number of strings_ and then to print them. You could not do that with ordinary variables. But you can with array variables. **Make the changes shown on the next page in your program.**

```
400 PRINT "REVERSE HOW MANY WORDS"
410 INPUT N
500 FOR J = 1 TO N
505   PRINT "WORD"; J,
510   INPUT W$(J)
520 NEXT J
600 FOR J = N TO 1 STEP -1
610   PRINT J, W$(J)
620 NEXT J
```

Notice lines 410, 500, and 600. The variable N appears in all three lines. Think about what each line tells the computer to do. **Now run the program. Enter 5 as the answer to the first question. Then enter any five words you want in answer to the next five question marks.** You should see the five words printed on the screen in reverse order.

Run the program a few more times. Try reversing two words. Try six words. Will the program work correctly for one word? For zero words? Find out.

1. How does the name of an ordinary variable differ from the name of an array variable?
2. In BASIC, how would you name the 14th member of a list named Y$?
3. What is an array variable used for?
4. Suppose that A$(1) = "TOM", A$(2) = "HARRY", and J = 1. What is the value of A$(J + 1)?

How Many Items?

The program now in memory tells the computer to accept N words from the user and then to print the list backwards. How big can N be? Let's find out.

If the program printed above is not in the computer, enter it now. Run the program. Enter 100 in answer to the first question. This time, instead of words, enter the letters of the alphabet. Be sure to press (Enter ◄─┘) after each letter. Keep doing this until you see an error message.

You should have seen the program work correctly for the first 10 letters. But there was a problem with the 11th letter. You got this message: Subscript out of range in 510.

Let's explore some more. **Add this line to your program:**

```
100 DIM W$(15)
```

Run the program. Again, enter 100 and the letters of the alphabet. This time, the program accepted a list of 15 letters. The error message came with the 16th letter.

DIM is a new BASIC statement. It tells the computer what the largest item number in a list can be. If you leave out the DIM statement, the computer sets the largest item number at 10.

Now let's see what the smallest item number can be. So far, you have counted items in your W$ list starting at item one. Let's see whether we can count from zero.

```
CLS
LIST
```
Notice the 1s in lines 500 and 600.

```
500 FOR J = 0 TO N
600 FOR J = N TO 0 STEP -1
LIST
```
Notice the 0s now.

```
RUN
```
There should be no problems so far.

Enter 3 for the number of words you want to reverse. Then start entering letters of the alphabet.

The results probably surprised you. You said you wanted to enter *three* words. But the computer asked for *four* words. It numbered the items in the list starting with 0. The computer asked for four words because there are four item numbers between zero and three. Now let's see if we can have item numbers that are negative.

Edit lines 500 and 600 so the 0s in the FOR statements are changed to -1s. Run the program and enter 3 again. Then start entering letters.

This time, you should have seen the message Illegal function call in 510 when you entered the first word. *In BASIC, you may not use negative numbers as item numbers in a list.* Zero is allowed as an item number. But you will usually want to start your lists with item number one. That way, you will avoid surprises. The last item number in a list will be the same as the number of items in the list.

Finally, let's see what happens when you try to use numbers with decimal points for item numbers in a list. Here are some immediate-mode experiments:

```
LET A$(1) = "FISH"
LET A$(2) = "GIRL"
```
You now have two strings in memory.

PRINT A$(1), A$(2) — There they are. Now let's try for a mermaid.

PRINT A$(1.5) — What was printed?

PRINT A$(1.49) — What now?

PRINT A$(2.01) — And now?

You just learned two things: First, it is OK to use item numbers that are not whole numbers. Second, if the item number is not a whole number, the computer rounds to the nearest whole number (1.5 is rounded to 2). In the example above, A$(1.5), A$(2.01), and A$(2) all stand for "GIRL".

5. If the computer is asked to print the value of T$(1.4), what will it do first?
6. What is the purpose of a DIM statement?
7. When is a DIM statement needed?
8. What numbers are legal to use as item numbers for an array?
9. What will be the output if the program below is run?

```
100 DIM A$(4)
110 LET A$(1) = "THE"
120 LET A$(2) = "DOG"
130 LET A$(3) = "IS"
140 LET A$(4) = "BROWN"
150 LET J = 2
160 PRINT A$(J + 2), A$(J)
```

PC's PANTRY

PROJECTS

● Your program for reversing a list of words should still be in the computer. Change it so that the computer prints every other word.

● Change the program again. Make it print the length of each word in the list of words entered by the user.

SUMMARY

In this session, you learned about array variables. You found out that an item number locates one of the items of an array. The key ideas about arrays are summarized in the table below. Be sure you understand arrays fully. Arrays are very useful in programming. Using arrays can save you a lot of time and trouble. Review the session if you feel the need.

Topic	Description
Array	A collection of data grouped under a single name. The array may contain either numeric or string data but not both.
Item number	A number used to locate one of the pieces of data in an array.
DIM	A BASIC statement that tells the computer the largest possible item number of an array. If there is no DIM statement in the program, the computer sets the largest item number equal to 10.

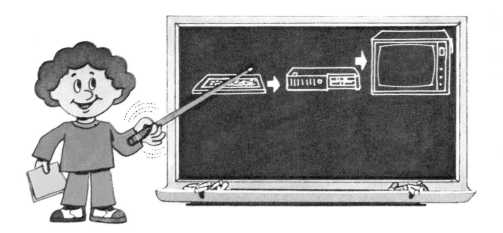

HOW SUBSCRIPTS WORK

SESSION 30

Session Goals

- Review the uses of array variables.
- Learn new words used with array variables.
- Learn that array variables are places in the memory unit.
- Use a simple picture to understand how the computer handles arrays.

Review

In the last session, you wrote a very short program to solve a hard problem. The program told the computer to do three things: First, ask the user how many words are to be entered. Second, accept exactly that many words. Third, print the list of words on the screen in reverse order.

Why is this problem hard? After all, there are other problems much like it that are very easy. For example, it is easy to tell the computer to accept five words and print them back in reverse order. This little two-line program will do the job:

```
10 INPUT W1$, W2$, W3$, W4$, W5$
20 PRINT W5$, W4$, W3$, W2$, W1$
```

But this program works only with lists of exactly five words. You would have to rewrite the program to make it work for a list of three words or one of six words. Also, the program would become very long if it had to handle a list of a hundred words or more.

You found that these problems disappear when you use a new kind of variable called an *array*. Array variables are useful whenever you have a whole list of data items that need to be handled in the same way. Suppose, for example, that you have a list of names that you want the computer to print in a single column. You *could* write a separate PRINT statement for each name. But this three-line loop will do the whole job:

```
100 FOR A = 1 TO NUM
110    PRINT N$(A)
120 NEXT A
```

Line 110 tells the computer to print one name in the list. The value of A tells the computer which name to print. And the FOR/NEXT loop tells the computer to do the same thing over and over again. Each time through the loop, A will have a new value. The loop is to stop when the value of A is greater than the value of NUM.

So far, the only kind of lists you have seen are lists of strings. But there can also be lists of numbers. Like all other variables, an array has a *name*, a *type*, and a *value*. The rules for naming arrays are almost the same as those for ordinary variables. The one exception is that an expression in parentheses must follow the array name. As with other variables, the type of an array is either string or numeric. Other variables have only a single value at a time, but the value of an array is the list of data items it stands for.

We have called the whole list of data an *array*. We have talked about single *items* in the list. And we have used *item numbers* to pick out an item from the list. People sometimes use another set of words to talk about arrays. You will sometimes hear arrays called by another name: **subscripted variables**. A single item is also called a **component**. And what we have called the item number is also known as a **subscript**.

In printing, a subscript is a small number or letter. It is printed just below the line on which the rest of the words and letters are printed. Long before computers were invented, people needed a simple way to write mathematical formulas for handling lists. They had the idea of using a single name for the whole list. They identified each item in the list by printing a number as a subscript after the name. That is why array variables are often called subscripted variables.

You found in your computer explorations that there were limits on the numbers you can use as subscripts. Negative numbers are not allowed. Unless there is a DIM statement in the program, subscripts greater than 10 cause the message Subscript out of range to appear. You may use the DIM statement to set the dimensions of arrays to numbers other than 10. The *dimension* of an array is the largest number allowed for the subscript. The statement

```
100 DIM A(5), B$(100)
```

tells the computer that array A can have six numeric components, including A(0). It also says that array B$ can have 101 string components, including B$(0). It is a good idea to use the DIM statement to dimension all your arrays, even if you will not use subscripts greater than 10.

1. When are array variables useful?
2. What is another name for an array variable?
3. What is a subscript?
4. What is the dimension of an array?

How Subscripts Work

In the next session, you will explore arrays further. You will discover new uses for them. Before going ahead, though, you should make sure that you understand exactly how arrays and subscripts work. A statement like

```
LET G(P + 1) = P - 1
```

can seem very complex at first. But if you spend a few minutes reading the rest of this session, you will discover that its meaning is very simple.

Leave your computer keyboard and screen. Settle into a comfortable chair and read on.

The main idea about an ordinary variable is that it is a *place* in the memory of the computer. Array variables are no different in this respect, as you will soon see. In earlier sessions, you used a simple picture of a computer to understand variables and data. Let's use the same picture again. This time, we'll see how the computer carries out each step of the following program:

```
10 DIM A$(3)
20 LET A$(1) = "CAT"
30 LET A$(2) = "DOG"
40 PRINT A$(2), A$(1)
50 LET J = 1
60 PRINT A$(J)
70 PRINT A$(J + 1)
```

Here is a picture of the computer just after the program has been entered, the screen cleared, and the RUN command entered:

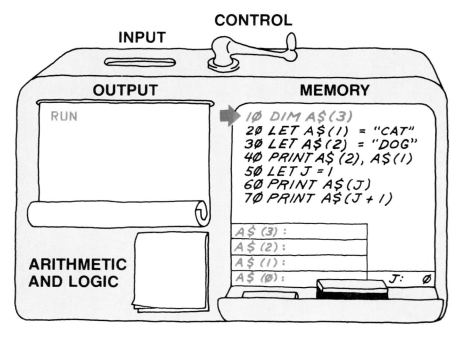

Notice the memory chalkboard in the picture. It contains the seven lines of the BASIC program. It also contains places for the variables. The place named J contains a 0. The other four places, named A$(0), A$(1), A$(2), and A$(3), can contain strings. At first, they each contain the *empty* string. That string has no characters in it. The DIM statement tells the computer to save these four places in memory for the array A$.

This is the picture after the computer has performed the LET statement in line 20. Notice that the memory box named A$(1) has changed.

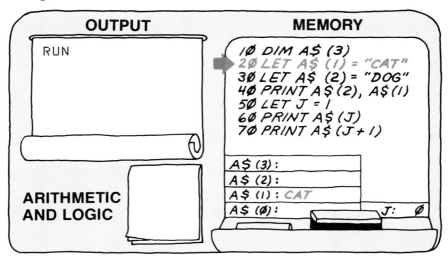

The LET statement tells the computer to do two things: First, find the value of whatever is on the right side of the equal sign. Second, put that value in the place in memory with the same name that appears on the left side of the equal sign. Line 30 is another LET statement. Here is the picture after the computer performs it:

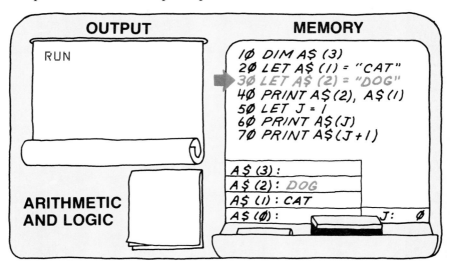

Now we have two words in the A$ array. There are also empty strings in A$(0) and A$(3). Let's look now at the picture after the computer performs the PRINT statement in line 40:

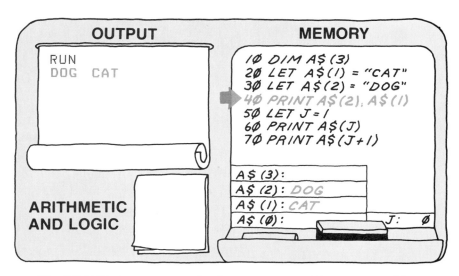

The PRINT statement works the same way with array variables as it does with ordinary variables: The computer uses the variable names to find the places in memory where data is stored. Then it sends that data to the output unit. Let's look at the picture after line 50 is performed:

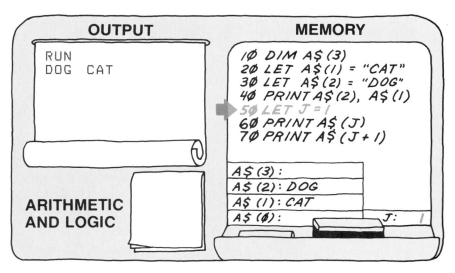

As you have seen before, the LET statement tells the computer to put a new data value in memory. This time the number 1 goes into the memory box named J.

Now let's look closely at line 60. This is a very interesting line. It says to print the value of A$(J) on the output unit. There is a place in memory named J. There are four places with names that begin with A$. But there is no place in memory named A$(J). What does A$(J) mean? The computer needs rules for handling this new kind of name:

The Computer's Rules for Finding Data in Arrays

1. Find the value of whatever numeric expression is written in parentheses after the name of the array.
2. Substitute this number for the expression.
3. Look in memory for a place with the name that results from Rules 1 and 2.

Let's apply these rules to line 60. That line contains the statement PRINT A$(J). Rule 1 says to find the value of the variable named J. The value we need is whatever number is in the J-box in memory. Right now, that value is 1. Rule 2 says to substitute this number for the expression. This means that the computer should use the name A$(1) instead of A$(J). Rule 3 says to look in memory for a place named A$(1). That is where the data to be printed will be found. Here is the picture after line 60 is performed:

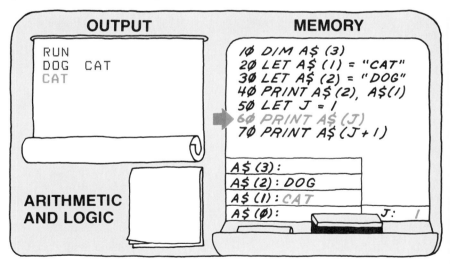

Now you can see how line 60 told the computer to print CAT on the output unit. Next, let's see what line 70 means. It is another PRINT statement. But it is a little different from the one in line 60. What does A$(J + 1) mean? Again, there is no place in memory with this name. But now you know the rules for finding the right place.

Rule 1 says to find the numeric value of J + 1. As usual, the computer uses its arithmetic and logic scratchpad for this job. Here is the picture after the computer has finished following Rule 1:

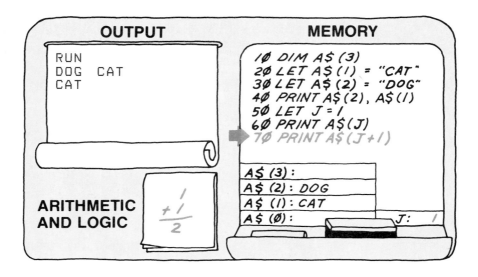

Rule 2 says to substitute this value for the expression in parentheses. So A$(J + 1) becomes A$(2). Finally, Rule 3 says to look in memory for a place named A$(2) and use the data there. Here is the picture after the computer performs line 7Ø:

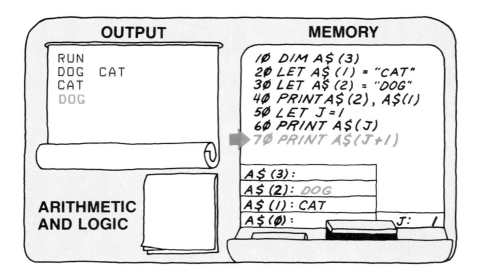

Now the program is finished. You have seen that array variables, like ordinary variables, are named places in the memory of the computer. The main difference between them is that part of the array name is a subscript. Suppose you use a constant, such as 2 or 25, for the subscript. In that case, array variables work exactly the same way as ordinary variables. But you have just seen that it is also possible to use variables and expressions as subscripts. The computer first calculates the numeric value of the subscript. That value tells the computer which data item in memory to use or to assign a new value to.

5. Suppose the P-box in memory contains a 5. What does the statement LET X(2 * P) = 37 tell the computer to do?
6. Suppose the Q-box in memory contains a 3. What does the statement LET X(Q - 1) = Q + 1 tell the computer to do?

SUMMARY This session began with a review of the things you learned in your hands-on explorations in Session 29. You learned some new terms used with arrays. Then you used the simple picture of a computer to understand how arrays and subscripts work. The important ideas introduced in this session are summarized in the table below. Review it carefully before going on.

Topic	Description
Subscripted variable	Another name for an array variable.
Subscript	Another name for the item number of an item in a list.
Component	Another name for an item in a list.
Dimension	The largest whole number that can be used for the subscript of an array. The smallest is zero.

APPLICATION OF ARRAYS

SESSION 31

Session Goals

- Learn to use READ and DATA statements as another way of assigning values to variables.
- Use READ and DATA to initialize array variables.
- Use array variables in a program for building sentences out of phrases.

Review

In Sessions 29 and 30, you learned how to use an item number, or subscript, to locate one piece of data in a list. With arrays and subscripts, you can write programs that are more flexible. In this session and the next, we will develop two programs that will show you ways of using arrays.

Another Assignment Statement

Before we begin writing the new programs, let's experiment with two new statements. These are the READ and DATA statements. **Start the computer as usual. Then enter the lines below:**

```
110 LET A1$ = "THE COW "
120 LET A2$ = "JUMPED OVER "
130 LET A3$ = "THE MOON"
LIST
```
                                    Check out the program.

```
RUN
```
                                    Nothing happened. Or did it?

```
PRINT A2$
```
                                    The computer knows the value of A2$.

```
PRINT A1$; A2$; A3$
```
                                    It knows the value of all three variables.

Nothing was printed when the program was run. That is because there are no PRINT statements in the program. However, as you saw, the computer did put data into its memory unit. That is because you used LET statements to tell the computer to assign values to the variables.

The LET statement is one way to give a value to a variable. For single variables or small arrays, this method works fine. However, suppose you need to assign values to a big array. In that case, your program would need many LET statements. Let's look at a different way to assign values to variables.

```
NEW
CLS
110 READ A1$, A2$, A3$
120 DATA "THE COW ", "JUMPED OVER ", "THE MOON"
LIST
```
                                    Make sure the program is correct.

RUN _____ Again, nothing happened. Or did it?

PRINT A3$
PRINT A1$ _____ The computer knows the value of these variables.

You got the same results you did with the previous program. In both programs, the computer assigned the string constant "THE COW " to A1$. It assigned the string constant "JUMPED OVER " to A2$. Finally, it assigned the string constant "THE MOON" to A3$. In the first program, the assignment was done with LET statements. In the second program, the assignment was done with READ and DATA statements. How do these new statements work?

The READ statement, like the LET statement, tells the computer to assign values to variables. One LET statement, however, can assign a value to only *one* variable. One READ statement can assign many values to many variables. This fact can often save you a lot of typing. This is especially true when you are using array variables.

In some ways, the READ statement is like the INPUT statement: Both words can be followed by a *list* of variable names. The INPUT statement tells the computer to do two things: First, accept several pieces of data from the keyboard. Second, assign the data to the variables named in the list. The READ statement works much the same way. However, in this case the data items are not entered from the keyboard when the program is run. Instead, they are contained in DATA statements within the program. Let's look again at the second program you ran.

```
110 READ A1$, A2$, A3$
120 DATA "THE COW ", "JUMPED OVER ", "THE MOON"
```

Three variables are named in the READ statement. The READ statement tells the computer to assign values to each of these variables. However, instead of getting the values from the keyboard, the computer gets them from the DATA statement. The first piece of data in the DATA statement is assigned to A1$. The second is assigned to A2$. The third is assigned to A3$. Let's explore DATA statements some more.

200 PRINT A1$; A2$; A3$
CLS
LIST _____ This puts a PRINT statement at the end of the program.

```
RUN
```
You should see all three phrases making up one sentence on the screen.

```
120 DATA "THE COW "
130 DATA "JUMPED OVER "
140 DATA "THE MOON"
LIST
```
Now there are three DATA statements. Will the program work the same way?

```
RUN
```
You should see the same sentence.

```
DELETE 120-140
LIST
```
Now there are no DATA statements.

```
100 DATA "THE COW "
120 DATA "JUMPED OVER "
300 DATA "THE MOON"
CLS
LIST
```
Now the DATA statements are scattered.

```
RUN
```
But the program works the same way.

```
300
CLS
LIST
```
Now there are only two pieces of data. What will the computer do?

```
RUN
```
Note the message.

READ and DATA statements give you a handy way to assign data to variables. They are especially useful when you have a lot of data to assign. In addition, they give you an easy way to change the data without having to retype assignment statements: All you have to do is retype the DATA statements.

It makes no difference where the DATA statements are placed in the program. *The line-number order of* DATA *statements is the only thing that matters.* Here is how that works: When you enter the RUN command, the computer does not start performing statements right away. It first goes through the program in line-number order looking for a DATA statement. The computer stops at the first DATA statement it finds. It puts a pointer at the first piece of data in the statement. This pointer is called the **data pointer**. The piece of data it is pointing to is called the **current data item**.

Then the computer starts performing statements. While doing so, the computer reaches a READ statement with a list of several variables. The rules here are very simple: First, assign the current data item to the first variable in the READ statement. Second, move the data pointer to the next piece of data in the DATA statement. Third, do the same thing for the next variable in the READ statement. Repeat these steps until all variables have values assigned to them.

What if the computer runs out of data in the DATA statement it has been using? In that case, it starts looking, in line-number order, for the next DATA statement. If the computer finds one, it puts the data pointer at the first item in the new DATA statement. If there are no more DATA statements, the computer prints an Out of DATA error message.

You can see that the computer handles DATA statements completely differently from the way it handles other statements. All other statements tell the computer to *do* something. DATA statements do *not* tell the computer to do anything. They just list the data items to be *used by* the computer. The location of DATA statements within the program is unimportant. However, their line-number order is very important.

It is true that you have a lot of freedom in placing DATA statements in a program. However, it is wise to place them close to the READ statements so you can easily see what values will be assigned to the variables in the READ statements.

In the example above, the pieces of data were string constants. We will always show string constants inside quotation marks. This makes it clearer where the string begins and ends. BASIC requires you to use quotation marks in LET and PRINT statements. But you are allowed to omit them in DATA statements and in the user reply to an INPUT statement. This saves effort in typing, but can lead to confusion and error. Suppose, for example, that a string contains a comma. In that case, you *must* use quotation marks. Leaving them out will cause an error.

You can also have numbers in DATA statements, or a mixture of numbers and string constants. It is up to you to make sure that when the computer is expecting a string constant, the next piece of data *is* a string constant. Likewise, if the computer is expecting a number, a number must be next in the DATA statements. If your variables and your data do not match, you might expect to get a Type mismatch error. However, you mysteriously get a Syntax error message instead. Be prepared for that.

1. How is the READ statement like the INPUT statement? How is it different?
2. Is the location of DATA statements important? Are the line numbers of DATA statements important? Explain your answer.
3. What happens to the data pointer when you type RUN?
4. What happens if the current data item is a string constant and the current variable in a READ statement is numeric?

A Random-Phrase Generator

Now that you know about array variables and the READ and DATA statements, let's put them to work. The rest of this session uses these new tools. You will learn about another way to use them in the next session.

Here is your problem: Write a program to "mix and match" phrases from sentences. To see how to do this, look at these sample sentences:

The cow	jumped over	the moon.
The fish	swam under	the bridge.
Johnny	ate	bananas.
Martians	landed at	Peoria.

Each of the lines above contains a complete sentence. However, each sentence has been broken into three phrases. These form three columns. You can build many different sentences by selecting one phrase from each column and combining them. If you do this, here are some sentences you might get:

Example: The cow swam under bananas.
Example: Martians ate the moon.
Example: The fish landed at Peoria.

Let's think for a minute about how we might tell the computer to pick one phrase from the first column. The first column is a *list* of phrases. The natural thing to do is to use an array variable to stand for the whole list. Then we can pick one phrase in the list by telling the computer what number to use for the subscript. We will need another array for the list of phrases in column two. We will need a third array for the list in column three.

The problem is to write a program that will tell the computer to do three main things: First, the computer should set up and give values to three arrays. The first array will hold the first phrase in each of the sentences. The second array will hold the second phrase in each of the sentences. The third array will hold the last phrase in each of the sentences. Second, the computer should randomly select phrases from each of the arrays. Third, the computer should put the the phrases together to form a sentence, and print the sentence on the screen.

As always, the best way to begin is with a top-level description of the program. There are three main jobs to be done: First, assign the phrases to the arrays. Second, pick a subscript for each phrase of the sentence. Third, print the sentence. Here is an outline of the main routine:

```
100  'PROGRAM MIX AND MATCH
110      initialize arrays
120      select phrases
130      print the sentence
180  END
```

Erase the program now in memory. Enter the following skeleton program. Run it and fix any errors.

```
100  'PROGRAM MIX AND MATCH
110      GOSUB 200    'INITIALIZE
120      GOSUB 400    'SELECT PHRASES
130      GOSUB 600    'OUTPUT
180  END
190  '
200  'SUB INITIALIZE
210      PRINT "INITIALIZE"
380  RETURN
390  '
400  'SUB SELECT PHRASES
410      PRINT "SELECT PHRASES"
580  RETURN
590  '
600  'SUB OUTPUT
610      PRINT "OUTPUT"
780  RETURN
```

Subroutine INITIALIZE has two jobs to do: First, the arrays should be dimensioned. Second, the computer must assign the sentence phrases to each of the three arrays. Let's call the phrase arrays SU$, VE$, and OB$. (These names remind you that the phrases are the *subject*, the *verb*, and the *object* in the sentence.) These two statements would assign *one* phrase to each array:

```
READ SU$(1), VE$(1), OB$(1)
DATA "THE COW ", "JUMPED OVER ", "THE MOON"
```

But we want the computer to do the same process again and again until all the phrases are assigned. What kind of program block tells the computer to do something again and again? If you are thinking of a loop block, that is the right answer. Let's suppose we have four phrases for each part of the sentence. Then we can use a FOR/NEXT loop. Here is the subroutine:

```
200  'SUB INITIALIZE
210     DIM SU$(4), VE$(4), OB$(4)
220     FOR X = 1 TO 4
230        READ SU$(X), VE$(X), OB$(X)
240     NEXT X
250     DATA "THE COW ", "JUMPED OVER ", "THE MOON"
260     DATA "THE FISH ", "SWAM UNDER ", "THE BRIDGE"
270     DATA "JOHNNY ", "ATE ", "BANANAS"
280     DATA "MARTIANS ", "LANDED AT ", "PEORIA"
380  RETURN
```

Read the subroutine carefully. Think about how it works. Then enter the changes shown above. Be sure to type the letter O in OB\$. The long lines will fold to the next screen line. **Then enter GOSUB 200 in the immediate mode. Fix any errors you find.**

Now for the second subroutine, SELECT PHRASES. How shall we tell the computer to pick the subject, verb, and object phrase to make a sentence? It would be interesting to let the computer pick the phrases at random. You know how to tell the computer to do that.

There are four possible subject phrases: SU\$(1), SU\$(2), SU\$(3), and SU\$(4). Picking a phrase at random means picking a subscript of SU\$ at random. The subscripts are just numbers, and you know how to tell the computer to pick numbers at random. The statement

```
LET P = INT(4 * RND) + 1
```

tells the computer to assign to P a random number in the set 1, 2, 3, and 4. After that is done, the statement

```
PRINT SU$(P)
```

tells the computer to print a phrase with this *random subscript*. The result is a randomly picked phrase.

To build a complete sentence, we need a subject phrase, a verb phrase, and an object phrase. So we must tell the computer to pick *three* random subscripts. The first random number will be used as a subscript to pick a phrase from array SU$. The second random number will pick a phrase from VE$, and so on. Here is subroutine SELECT PHRASES:

```
400  'SUB SELECT PHRASES
410     LET P = INT(4 * RND) + 1
420     LET Q = INT(4 * RND) + 1
430     LET R = INT(4 * RND) + 1
580  RETURN
```

Enter the body of subroutine SELECT PHRASES. Then enter GOSUB 400. Then, in immediate mode, enter the line PRINT P , Q , R. Fix any errors. When the subroutine is correct, your PRINT statement should cause three numbers to be printed. The numbers should be in the set 1, 2, 3, and 4.

Now we come to subroutine OUTPUT. Its job is to tell the computer the following: Use the values of P, Q, and R as subscripts in the phrase arrays. Then put the phrases together. Finally, print the sentence on the screen. Let's also have it put a blank line on the screen before printing the sentence. This will make the output easier to read. Here is the completed subroutine:

```
600  'SUB OUTPUT
610     PRINT
620     PRINT SU$(P); VE$(Q); OB$(R)
780  RETURN
```

Think carefully about how line 620 works. Remember what each variable stands for. Then enter the body of subroutine OUTPUT.

The complete program is shown on the next page. **List the program and check for errors.**

```
100  'PROGRAM MIX AND MATCH
110      GOSUB 200   'INITIALIZE
120      GOSUB 400   'SELECT PHRASES
130      GOSUB 600   'OUTPUT
180  END
190  '
200  'SUB INITIALIZE
210      DIM SU$(4), VE$(4), OB$(4)
220      FOR X = 1 TO 4
230        READ SU$(X), VE$(X), OB$(X)
240      NEXT X
250      DATA "THE COW ", "JUMPED OVER ", "THE MOON"
260      DATA "THE FISH ", "SWAM UNDER ", "THE BRIDGE"
270      DATA "JOHNNY ", "ATE ", "BANANAS"
280      DATA "MARTIANS ", "LANDED AT ", "PEORIA"
380  RETURN
390  '
400  'SUB SELECT PHRASES
410      LET P = INT(4 * RND) + 1
420      LET Q = INT(4 * RND) + 1
430      LET R = INT(4 * RND) + 1
580  RETURN
590  '
600  'SUB OUTPUT
610      PRINT
620      PRINT SU$(P); VE$(Q); OB$(R)
780  RETURN
```

Run the program several times. The phrases in each sentence are
selected at random. Thus, each sentence should usually be different. As
you have seen, that is not true: You get the same three phrases each
time. Your program is not wrong. The problem comes from the fact that
the RND function gives the same series of numbers each time you run
the program. You learned a bit of "black magic" to fix this problem at the
end of Session 26. **Add this statement to your INITIALIZE subroutine:**

205   RANDOMIZE 128*INP(64) + INP(64)

Run the program again a few times. Now you should see different sentences.

But only one sentence is generated each time the program is run.
Let's change the program. Let's have the computer keep on generating
new sentences until the (Break) function is used.

First, what kind of program structure is needed? Second, where should the structure go? By this point in the book, you should be answering these questions yourself. We hope you recognize that a loop is needed. We hope you realize that it should go in the main routine. The last two GOSUB statements form the body of the loop. Here is the new main routine:

```
100 'PROGRAM MIX AND MATCH
110    GOSUB 200   'INITIALIZE
115 '   LOOP FOREVER
120      GOSUB 400    'SELECT PHRASES
130      GOSUB 600    'OUTPUT
140      GOTO 115
150 '   END LOOP
180   END
```

Enter the changes in the main routine. Run the program. Wait until you have seen 30 or 40 sentences scroll by. Then use the (Break) function to stop the program.

Let's make one last change to the program. Let's provide a way out of the loop in the main routine. We need an exit condition. Let's tell the computer to exit from the loop when the sentence in the first DATA statement is generated and printed. That will happen when the computer selects the *first* phrase from each of the arrays. At that time, the values of P, Q, and R will all be 1. Let's also put a message in the program to be printed after the exit from the loop. Here are the changes needed:

```
100 'PROGRAM MIX AND MATCH
110    GOSUB 200   'INITIALIZE
115 '   LOOP
120      GOSUB 400    'SELECT PHRASES
130      GOSUB 600    'OUTPUT
135      IF P = 1 AND Q = 1 AND R = 1 THEN 150
140      GOTO 115
150 '   END LOOP
160    PRINT
170    PRINT "THAT'S THE ONE I'VE BEEN WAITING FOR"
180   END
```

Application of Arrays **359**

Enter the changes. Run the program several times. Notice that the computer may stop after a few sentences are printed on the screen. Sometimes, a large number of sentences appear before the computer stops. That is how things work out when they happen by chance.

When you are through, save the program under the name MIX on either cassette tape or diskette.

5. What changes would you need to make in program MIX AND MATCH so that phrases would be selected from eight sentences?
6. Why was a RANDOMIZE statement added to subroutine INITIALIZE?
7. Suppose you changed line 135 in program MIX AND MATCH to read

    135 IF P = 1 AND Q = 2 AND R = 3 THEN 150

What sentence will be on the screen when the program stops?

PROJECTS

● Add a counter variable to the loop in the main routine. It should keep count of the number of sentences generated as the program runs. Change the OUTPUT subroutine so that it prints the word SENTENCE followed by the number of the sentence just before printing the sentence itself. Thus, the 13th sentence would be preceded by the message SENTENCE 13.

● Change the phrases in the DATA statements to ones that you would like to see the computer build sentences out of. It is better if the sentences have nothing to do with one another. However, they should all have the same subject-verb-object form.

● You can use the idea in this program to make any program you write much more interesting to the user. For example, suppose you have written a program to help a younger person learn arithmetic. The computer will ask questions and check answers. You want the computer to give the person another try if the answer is wrong. Your program might prompt by printing the message Please try again. But that will be a boring message if it is repeated very often. You can avoid boredom by thinking of synonyms for each phrase in the message: You could use "Kindly" or "Let's" instead of "Please." You could use "go" or "answer" instead of "try." You could use "once more" or "another time" instead of "again." Change the DATA statements in your program to let you experiment with these or other synonyms you might think of.

SUMMARY

In this session, you have learned how the READ and DATA statements can be used to assign values to variables. You have written a program that used these statements and the array variables you learned about in Sessions 29 and 30. The two new statements are described in the table below.

Topic	Description
READ *list*	A BASIC statement that tells the computer to assign strings or numbers to the variables in the *list*. The variable names must be separated by commas. The strings and/or numbers to be assigned must appear in DATA statements. The names in the list must match, in number and type, the items in the DATA statements in the program.
DATA *list*	A BASIC statement containing the constants to be assigned to variables appearing in READ statements.

USING ARRAYS FOR BRANCHES

SESSION 32

Session Goals

- Change program COINS to simulate the roll of dice.
- Use an array variable to eliminate a case block.
- Use an array variable and a loop to eliminate similar statements.

Review

In Part Five, you learned about the branch block. You used it to tell the computer to do either one thing or another. Toward the end of that part, you found out how to tell the computer to do only one thing out of a whole list of possibilities. You used a case block for that.

So far in Part Six, you have learned about a new kind of variable: the array. You have seen how to use subscripts to pick out one component of an array. You found that it was easy to control which component the computer picked by using a variable as a subscript.

You probably don't see any special connection between the topics of Parts Five and Six. After all, a branch is a type of *statement* block and an array is a type of *variable*. Statements and variables are totally different things. How can branches and arrays have anything in common?

The example below will show you that branches and arrays have a great deal in common. You will see that many programming problems that can be solved by using branches can also be solved by using arrays. It is important to know when you can use an array in place of a branch. A solution with an array is usually much shorter and simpler than one with a branch.

Coin Tossing Revisited

In Session 26, you wrote a program named COINS. It used the computer to simulate tossing a coin. Let's take another look at that program. The program can be improved by using arrays and subscripts. **Start your PCjr as usual. Then load program COINS from either diskette or cassette tape. If you have not saved the program, enter it now.** Here is how it should look:

```
100 'PROGRAM COINS
110     GOSUB 200    'HOW MANY
120     GOSUB 400    'TOSS COINS
130  END
190  '
200 'SUB HOW MANY
210     CLS
220     PRINT "TOSS HOW MANY COINS"
230     INPUT N
240     CLS
380  RETURN
390  '
```

```
400 'SUB TOSS COINS
410    FOR COUNT = 1 TO N
420       GOSUB 600   'ONE TOSS
430    NEXT COUNT
580  RETURN
590 '
600 'SUB ONE TOSS
610    IF RND > .5 THEN 620 ELSE 650
620 '   THEN
630       PRINT "HEADS"
640       GOTO 670
650 '   ELSE
660       PRINT "TAILS"
670 '   END IF
780  RETURN
```

Take a few minutes to look carefully at the program. Review its key features. Remind yourself how it works. Then run it a few times.

Let's make a few changes in program COINS. First, let's take care of a weakness. When you wrote program COINS, you had not learned about the RANDOMIZE statement. Thus, every time you run the program, you see the same series of heads and tails. You will need a RANDOMIZE statement to tell the computer to produce different results each time you run the program.

Next, let's change the program so that it counts the total number of heads and tails. After all the coins are tossed, the computer should print the two totals. We will need another subroutine for that. Let's start with the changes needed in the main routine. They are as follows:

```
100 'PROGRAM COINS
105    RANDOMIZE 128*INP(64) + INP(64)
110    GOSUB 200   'HOW MANY
120    GOSUB 400   'TOSS COINS
125    GOSUB 800   'OUTPUT
130  END
```

Enter new lines 105 and 125 into the computer now.

Next, we must write a skeleton subroutine for the new OUTPUT subroutine that we will need. **Enter these four lines:**

```
790 '
800 'SUB OUTPUT
810    PRINT "OUTPUT"
980    RETURN
```

Run the program for 10 tosses. Write down the list of HEADs and TAILs. Run the program again for 10 more tosses. Compare the two lists. Do the same thing again.

You should see a different series nearly every time you run the program. You should also see the word OUTPUT at the bottom of the list each time. If both these things are true, the program is working. Also, the skeleton subroutine you just added is OK.

Next, let's not have the program print messages telling which way the "coin" came up. Instead, let's have it count the number of "heads" and "tails." We will need two variables to act as counters. Let's call them HEADS and TAILS. These variables will have to be initialized to equal zero before the coin-tossing loop begins. The loop is in subroutine TOSS COINS. Thus, let's take care of the initialization step there. We will use a GOSUB statement. **Enter the new line 405 shown below. Then enter lines 480 through 520.**

```
400 'SUB TOSS COINS
405    GOSUB 500   'INITIALIZATION
410    FOR COUNT = 1 TO N
420       GOSUB 600   'ONE TOSS
430    NEXT COUNT
480    RETURN
490 '
500 'SUB INITIALIZATION
510    LET HEADS = 0
520    LET TAILS = 0
580    RETURN
```

Run the program and fix any errors you find. The program should work the same way as before. You have not yet told the computer to count instead of printing messages.

The PRINT statements with the messages are in subroutine ONE TOSS. They need to be replaced by LET statements that tell the computer to add 1 to either counter variable. Here are the changes:

```
600 'SUB ONE TOSS
610     IF RND > .5 THEN 620 ELSE 650
620 '    THEN
630         LET HEADS = HEADS + 1
640         GOTO 670
650 '    ELSE
660         LET TAILS = TAILS + 1
670 '   END IF
780 RETURN
```

List subroutine ONE TOSS. Study the two changes shown above. Think about how this branch block will work. Then enter the changes.

Now run the program. Enter 100 for the number of coins to toss. If there were no errors, the only message on the screen should be OUTPUT. It came from the skeleton OUTPUT subroutine.

Enter the statement PRINT HEADS, TAILS in the immediate mode. You should see two numbers that add to 100. They tell you that the computer is counting "heads" and "tails" correctly.

Finally, let's complete the OUTPUT subroutine. Its job is very simple: Tell the computer to print the results of the run. **Make the changes shown below:**

```
800 'SUB OUTPUT
810     PRINT
820     PRINT "HEADS ="; HEADS
830     PRINT "TAILS ="; TAILS
980 RETURN
```

Run the program a few times with different numbers of "coins." The program should now do what we wanted it to do.

Before going ahead, notice how easy it was to make all these changes in program COINS. The main reason for this is that the program was written clearly from the start. You could quickly identify the routine that needed each change. You could make the change without worrying about the effect on other routines. This is the payoff for using the top-down method and limiting your program blocks to three: actions, loops, and branches.

1. What kind of program block is in subroutine ONE TOSS?
2. What is the purpose of the GOSUB 500 statement inside subroutine TOSS COINS?
3. What kind of program block is in subroutine INITIALIZATION?

Simulating Dice

You now have a nice program for exploring a chance event: the toss of a coin. With the program, you can do experiments on a few or many thousands of simulated tosses. At the end of each experiment, the computer will print the number of "heads" and the number of "tails."

Another interesting chance event is the roll of a die. Many games are based on rolling dice. Let's see how to make the computer help you study dice rolls. It should be easy to change program COINS to tell you, after any number of "rolls," how many times each number on the die came up.

What part of program COINS tells the computer to simulate the toss and decide which side of the coin came up? Let's look at the whole program. Here is what should be in your computer now:

```
100 'PROGRAM COINS
105    RANDOMIZE 128*INP(64) + INP(64)
110    GOSUB 200   'HOW MANY
120    GOSUB 400   'TOSS COINS
125    GOSUB 800   'OUTPUT
130 END
190 '
200 'SUB HOW MANY
210    CLS
220    PRINT "TOSS HOW MANY COINS"
230    INPUT N
240    CLS
380 RETURN
390 '
400 'SUB TOSS COINS
405    GOSUB 500   'INITIALIZATION
410    FOR COUNT = 1 TO N
420      GOSUB 600   'ONE TOSS
430    NEXT COUNT
480 RETURN
490 '
500 'SUB INITIALIZATION
510    LET HEADS = 0
520    LET TAILS = 0
580 RETURN
590 '
```

```
600 'SUB ONE TOSS
610    IF RND > .5 THEN 620 ELSE 650
620 '    THEN
630       LET HEADS = HEADS + 1
640       GOTO 670
650 '    ELSE
660       LET TAILS = TAILS + 1
670 '  END IF
780  RETURN
790 '
800 'SUB OUTPUT
810    PRINT
820    PRINT "HEADS ="; HEADS
830    PRINT "TAILS ="; TAILS
980  RETURN
```

The part we need to change is subroutine ONE TOSS. For the coin simulation, you used the expression RND > .5 to decide which side of the coin came up. This was an either/or situation: RND was either greater than one-half or not.

A coin has only two sides, but a die has six. For the die simulation, you need a random number that can be any of six different things. You learned in Session 22 how to tell the computer to generate random *whole numbers*. You used the INT and RND functions. The expression

```
INT(6 * RND) + 1
```

tells the computer to return whole numbers in the set 1, 2, 3, 4, 5, 6. Remember, RND returns a number that is always less than 1. That means that 6 * RND is always less than 6. So INT(6 * RND) is 5 or less. Adding 1 brings the largest whole number up to 6.

Now we know how to make the right set of random whole numbers. What do we do with them? Our goal is to count the number of times each face of the simulated die comes up. We will need six counter variables for this. Let's call them C1, C2, C3, C4, C5, and C6. After each "roll" of the die, we want the computer to add 1 to *only one* of the six counters. When you want the computer to do only one out of many possible things, what kind of block do you need?

If you are thinking of a case block, you are right. Now you should have a good idea of how to rewrite subroutine ONE TOSS. It should first tell the computer to generate a random whole number from 1 to 6. Then it should use a case block to decide which counter to add 1 to. The new version of the subroutine is at the top of the next page.

```
600 'SUB ONE TOSS
610    LET R = INT(6 * RND) + 1
620 '   CASE
630       IF R = 1 THEN LET C1 = C1 + 1
640       IF R = 2 THEN LET C2 = C2 + 1
650       IF R = 3 THEN LET C3 = C3 + 1
660       IF R = 4 THEN LET C4 = C4 + 1
670       IF R = 5 THEN LET C5 = C5 + 1
680       IF R = 6 THEN LET C6 = C6 + 1
690 '   END CASE
780 RETURN
```

Take a careful look at this new subroutine. Notice that no two of the conditions in the IF statements overlap. Thus, this really is a case block. **Now enter the new subroutine body into the computer. Then enter GOSUB 600 and check for error messages. As a final test, enter this line in the immediate mode:**

PRINT C1; C2; C3; C4; C5; C6

You should see a total of five 0s and one 1 appear on the line after the PRINT statement.

Two more jobs remain: First, we must have the computer initialize the new counter variables. Second, we must make it print the final values. **List subroutine INITIALIZATION. Think about how to change it.**

You probably decided to make the new version of subroutine INITIALIZATION look like this:

```
500 'SUB INITIALIZATION
510    LET C1 = 0
520    LET C2 = 0
530    LET C3 = 0
540    LET C4 = 0
550    LET C5 = 0
560    LET C6 = 0
580 RETURN
```

But there is an easier way to assign values to many variables at once. You learned about it in the last session. This is how:

```
500 'SUB INITIALIZATION
510    READ C1, C2, C3, C4, C5, C6
520    DATA  0,  0,  0,  0,  0,  0
580 RETURN
```

Next, we must change subroutine OUTPUT. **List it and think about what needs to be done.** You probably thought of something like this:

```
800 'SUB OUTPUT
810    PRINT
820    PRINT "ONES   ="; C1
830    PRINT "TWOS   ="; C2
840    PRINT "THREES ="; C3
850    PRINT "FOURS  ="; C4
860    PRINT "FIVES  ="; C5
870    PRINT "SIXES  ="; C6
980 RETURN
```

Enter your changes in both these subroutines. Debug them by entering GOSUB 500 and GOSUB 800. Fix any errors you find.

Now run the program and "roll" a "die" a few hundred times. Run the program again. Run it a few more times. You should see the six sides come up with about the same frequency each time. They won't be exactly the same. That is because chance events don't happen that way.

When you ran the program, you found that it was still printing messages about coins and tosses. We need to make a few "cosmetic" changes. These are changes that affect only messages and remarks but do not affect the way the computer works. **Edit the following lines:**

```
100 'PROGRAM DICE
120    GOSUB 400   'ROLL DICE
220    PRINT "HOW MANY ROLLS"
400 'SUB ROLL DICE
420       GOSUB 600   'ONE ROLL
600 'SUB ONE ROLL
```

Run the program once again. It should work the same way as before.

4. What makes the block in subroutine ONE ROLL a true case block?
5. What kind of block is the body of subroutine OUTPUT?

Rolling Several Dice at Once

You have now succeeded in changing your coin-tossing simulation into a die-rolling simulation. You made the changes in simple steps. You always decided first what subroutine needed changing. Then you thought about how to make the changes needed.

In the final section, you will improve this program in a very important way. When it was a coin-tossing program, it could handle only two possible cases: heads or tails. When you changed it to a die-rolling program, it could handle exactly six possible cases. How would you make the program handle *any number* of cases? What if the die had eight sides? Twelve sides? What if there were two dice to roll? In each one of these cases, you would have to do a lot of rewriting to handle the new situation. The program would be better if these changes were easy to make. That is the important improvement that lies ahead.

Let's look at the current version of your program. **If the following lines are not in your computer, enter them now:**

```
100 'PROGRAM DICE
105    RANDOMIZE 128*INP(64) + INP(64)
110    GOSUB 200   'HOW MANY
120    GOSUB 400   'ROLL DICE
125    GOSUB 800   'OUTPUT
130 END
190 '
200 'SUB HOW MANY
210    CLS
220    PRINT "HOW MANY ROLLS"
230    INPUT N
240    CLS
380 RETURN
390 '
400 'SUB ROLL DICE
405    GOSUB 500   'INITIALIZATION
410    FOR COUNT = 1 TO N
420       GOSUB 600   'ONE ROLL
430    NEXT COUNT
480 RETURN
490 '
```

```
500  'SUB INITIALIZATION
510     READ C1, C2, C3, C4, C5, C6
520     DATA  0,  0,  0,  0,  0,  0
580  RETURN
590  '
600  'SUB ONE ROLL
610     LET R = INT(6 * RND) + 1
620  '  CASE
630        IF R = 1 THEN LET C1 = C1 + 1
640        IF R = 2 THEN LET C2 = C2 + 1
650        IF R = 3 THEN LET C3 = C3 + 1
660        IF R = 4 THEN LET C4 = C4 + 1
670        IF R = 5 THEN LET C5 = C5 + 1
680        IF R = 6 THEN LET C6 = C6 + 1
690  '  END CASE
780  RETURN
790  '
800  'SUB OUTPUT
810     PRINT
820     PRINT "ONES   ="; C1
830     PRINT "TWOS   ="; C2
840     PRINT "THREES ="; C3
850     PRINT "FOURS  ="; C4
860     PRINT "FIVES  ="; C5
870     PRINT "SIXES  ="; C6
980  RETURN
```

What parts of program DICE would you need to change if the die had 12 sides instead of 6? The answer is simple: You would have to change all the subroutines that use counter variables C1, C2, and so on. Those are subroutines INITIALIZATION, ONE ROLL, and OUTPUT. What changes would you have to make? The answer is again simple: First, you would need 12 counter variables. Second, you would need random numbers from 1 to 12. Third, the body of the last two subroutines would become twice as long.

There ought to be a simpler way to do this. Fortunately, there is. *As a rule, whenever you see a long list of similar statements in a program, there is a simpler way to write the program.* Program DICE has several such lists.

Notice that the counter variables appear in each of these repeated statements. That is the clue to the change you need to make. Instead of having a separate statement for each counter, it would be simpler to have *one* statement that did the same job for all counters. You already know how to do that: Use an array variable for the counters.

Let's call the array C. Then C(1) will take the place of C1, the counter for the number of times that a 1 was rolled. C(2) will replace C2. C(3) will replace C3, and so on. Let's make these changes now in subroutine INITIALIZATION. The new version should look like this:

```
500  'SUB INITIALIZATION
510     DIM C(50)
520     LET NUM = 6
530     FOR J = 1 TO NUM
540        LET C(J) = 0
550     NEXT J
580  RETURN
```

Line 510 sets aside space in memory for up to 50 counters. Line 520 defines the number of counters actually needed for the problem of a single die. Later, it will be easy to change that number to something else. The loop in lines 530 through 550 tells the computer to set all counters, from C(1) through C(NUM), equal to zero.

Enter the new subroutine body shown above. Debug it by entering GOSUB 500 in the immediate mode.

Now let's make the changes we need in subroutine ONE ROLL. **List this subroutine on your screen. Think about what needs to be done.** How can the new array variable be used here?

The first thing you might think of is to just substitute C(1) for C1, C(2) for C2, and so on. If you did that, the case block would look like this:

```
620  '   CASE
630        IF R = 1 THEN LET C(1) = C(1) + 1
640        IF R = 2 THEN LET C(2) = C(2) + 1
650        IF R = 3 THEN LET C(3) = C(3) + 1
660        IF R = 4 THEN LET C(4) = C(4) + 1
670        IF R = 5 THEN LET C(5) = C(5) + 1
680        IF R = 6 THEN LET C(6) = C(6) + 1
690  '   END CASE
```

That would work, but it would not solve our problem. We would still need a separate statement for each counter. Suppose we wanted to add counters for another problem. In that case, we would have to enter extra statements.

Look at the case block closely. There is a wonderful way to simplify it. The whole block can be replaced by a single statement! Stop for a minute and think about how you might do that.

Notice that the variable R tells the computer which of the six assignment statements to perform. If R is 1, the first is performed. If R is 2, the second is performed, and so on. Notice also that in every one of the six statements, the value of R is the same as the subscript of C. What if we simply wrote the single statement

```
620     LET C(R) = C(R) + 1
```

instead of the whole case block? Would that do the job?

The answer is yes. Let's look more closely. Suppose the value of R is 4. Then this statement says to add 1 to C(4). But that is exactly what the case block said to do. The same is true for any value of R. Moreover, we do not have to add any extra statements if we later decide to add more counters: Even if R is bigger than 6, the new statement continues to work.

Replace your case block with the new statement, as shown below:

```
600   'SUB ONE ROLL
610      LET R = INT(NUM * RND) + 1
620      LET C(R) = C(R) + 1
780   RETURN
```

Now line 610 generates random numbers from 1 to NUM. Notice that you have used an array *variable* to replace a whole block of *statements*. Remember that we said at the beginning of this session that arrays and branches are connected. Now you can see how. You can often simplify the structure of a program by choosing variables carefully. Using array variables is especially helpful whenever you have lists of things. In the present example, you have a list of counters.

The last change needed is in subroutine OUTPUT. **List subroutine OUTPUT, which begins at line 800. Think about how to change it so that it uses the new array.**

As with the INITIALIZATION subroutine, you will need a loop to tell the computer to print the values of each of the counters. The loop will replace the six PRINT statements. At the top of the next page you can see one way to make the changes.

```
800  'SUB OUTPUT
810     PRINT
820     FOR J = 1 TO NUM
830        PRINT J; "'S ="; C(J)
840     NEXT J
980  RETURN
```

The loop in lines 820 through 840 tells the computer to repeat the PRINT statement for values of J from 1 through NUM. Remember that NUM was defined in subroutine INITIALIZATION. When J is 1, the PRINT statement tells the computer to print the label 1 'S = followed on the same line by the value of counter C(1). When J is 2, the computer prints 2 'S = followed by the value of counter C(2), and so on.

Run the program. Fix any errors. Run it a few more times.

After you have made all these changes, your program should be working properly again. It is shorter and simpler now. However, it should be doing the same job as before: It should be simulating the roll of a single die. The big difference between the old version and the new is that the new version is very, very easy to change. You will see this now.

Suppose you are using a 12-sided die, such as you find in some fantasy games. You need to change only one line of your program to handle this problem. You need to change the number of counters from 6 to 12. In your program, the variable NUM tells the computer how many counters to use. NUM is defined in line 520. **Change this line as shown below. Run the new version of DICE a few times.**

```
520     LET NUM = 12
```

That was easy. Now let's do something else that is easy and a lot more interesting. Suppose you want to simulate the roll of two dice at once, as in most board games. In this case, the roll is the sum of the numbers on the top faces of the dice. So the total can go from 2 up through 12.

What changes need to be made this time? The value of NUM is OK for this problem. But we do not yet have a way to tell the computer to roll two dice and add the results. What subroutine do we need to change? If you guessed ONE ROLL, you are right. At the top of the next page is the new version of this subroutine.

```
600 'SUB ONE ROLL
610    LET R = INT(6 * RND) + 1
615    LET R = R + INT(6 * RND) + 1
620    LET C(R) = C(R) + 1
780  RETURN
```

Line 610 is the "roll" of one "die." Line 615 tells the computer to add that number to the "roll" of the second "die." After the computer performs both lines, the value of R is the sum of the two "rolls."

Make the changes in lines 610 and 615 in subroutine ONE ROLL. Run the program a few times. Notice that there are a lot more 7s than 2s.

This simulation is much more interesting than the others. It gives you a way of experimenting with complex chance events. That way, you can learn how they work. The program can be used for a two-sided die (a coin). It can also be used for several many-sided dice. The reason the program is very flexible is that you wrote the final version using array variables. Here is what your program should look like now:

```
100 'PROGRAM DICE
105    RANDOMIZE 128*INP(64) + INP(64)
110    GOSUB 200   'HOW MANY
120    GOSUB 400   'ROLL DICE
125    GOSUB 800   'OUTPUT
130  END
190  '
200 'SUB HOW MANY
210    CLS
220    PRINT "HOW MANY ROLLS"
230    INPUT N
240    CLS
380  RETURN
390  '
400 'SUB ROLL DICE
405    GOSUB 500   'INITIALIZATION
410    FOR COUNT = 1 TO N
420      GOSUB 600   'ONE ROLL
430    NEXT COUNT
480  RETURN
490  '
```

```
500 'SUB INITIALIZATION
510    DIM C(50)
520    LET NUM = 12
530    FOR J = 1 TO NUM
540      LET C(J) = 0
550    NEXT J
580  RETURN
590  '
600 'SUB ONE ROLL
610    LET R = INT(6 * RND) + 1
615    LET R = R + INT(6 * RND) + 1
620    LET C(R) = C(R) + 1
780  RETURN
790  '
800 'SUB OUTPUT
810    PRINT
820    FOR J = 1 TO NUM
830      PRINT J; "'S ="; C(J)
840    NEXT J
980  RETURN
```

6. What kind of program block is the body of subroutine ONE ROLL?
7. What kind of program blocks are in the body of subroutine OUTPUT?

PROJECTS

● You can make the program tell the computer to print a bar graph of the results. The first step is to define a string filled with whatever symbol you want to use for the bars. Then use the MID$ function to return a substring. The length of the substring should be equal to the value of the counter that you want to graph. Here is such a version of the OUTPUT subroutine:

```
800 'SUB OUTPUT
805    LET BAR$ = "*********I*********I*********I***?"
810    PRINT
820    FOR J = 1 TO NUM
830       PRINT J; MID$(BAR$, 1, C(J))
840    NEXT J
980 RETURN
```

Make these changes and run the program again. Notice that the bars cannot be any longer than BAR$ itself. If the counters are bigger than that, MID$ simply returns BAR$ as the result. The question mark at the end of the string warns that the count may be bigger than shown.

There is a slight problem with your bar graph: The bars for 0 through 9 start to the left of the later bars. To fix that problem, you need to know about the TAB feature of the PRINT statement. Change line 830 to this:

```
830 PRINT J; TAB(5); MID$(BAR$, 1, C(J))
```

Then rerun the program. TAB(5) tells the computer that the next output should begin in position 5 on the screen. Position 1 is the left side of the screen, and position 40 is the right side. In PC*jr* BASIC, you may not type a space after the word TAB.

● Use program DICE to experiment with three dice. Don't forget to change the value of NUM. Now try with five dice. You may want to use a FOR/NEXT loop to sum the rolls on all the separate dice. That way, you can make the number of dice another variable.

SUMMARY

In this session, you have seen that by choosing the right variables, you can simplify the structure of a program. By using an array variable, you were able to replace an entire case block and many repetitive statements.

Where Do You Go from Here?

A Backward Look

If you have come this far, you have come a long way. Your reading and hands-on explorations have introduced you to the main ideas of computing. You have used the BASIC language on the PC*jr*, but the things you have learned apply to any programming language on any computer.

In Part One, you learned the "survival skills" anyone needs for work with computers. You learned how to turn on the computer, operate the keyboard, enter a program, edit it, save it, and load it back into memory. Along the way, you began to get a picture of what goes on inside the computer when you are doing these things. At the end of Part One, you explored graphics and music on the PC*jr*.

Part Two introduced you to the "top-down" method of solving problems on the computer. You learned how to put the big ideas in the main routine of your program. You wrote the main routine in a mixture of English and BASIC. Then you translated the English phrases into BASIC. To avoid getting bogged down in details, you often used GOSUB statements. Then you used the same method to write each subroutine. The result was a program that was easy to read, easy to get right, and easy to change.

In Part Three, you learned about the most important idea in programming languages: the variable. By using names to stand for the actual data, you could write a new kind of program. It told the computer to accept data as input from the user, to process the data, and to give the results as output. The same program, without any change, worked successfully with different data each time you ran it.

Parts Four and Five introduced you to "structured programming." You learned a standard way to write action blocks, loop blocks, and branch blocks in BASIC. You saw that one block could be nested inside another to solve complicated problems. Finally, you applied loop and branch blocks in several fairly long programs.

In Part Six, you learned about array variables. These are also called subscripted variables. They allow you to simplify programs that deal with lists of similar data, such as the names of students in a class, or their grades. Arrays are the only practical solution when the lists are long or when the length of the list can vary.

These six parts have introduced all the essential programming tools you will need to solve problems on the computer. You are now well equipped to begin tackling problems on your own. You know how to tell the computer to do what *you* want it to do.

What's Left?

The next step is to apply what you have learned. Think of a problem you would like to solve. Think of a program you would like to write. Think of a graphics or musical effect you would like to create. Then go to work. Use the tools you have learned.

Before long, you will discover a need to know more than you know now. You may want to explore other features of the PC*jr*, such as the rich variety of text and graphics modes. You may have a problem that cries out for a BASIC function you haven't learned about in this book. You may want to put the output from one program into a diskette file so another program can use the data as input. You may need to know a particular programming technique, such as how to sort a list of names in alphabetic order, or how to shuffle a list of numbers.

As these needs arise, you must look in other places for help and guidance. The paragraphs below offer a few suggestions about places to look.

Special PC*jr* features. Chapters 3 and 4 of the *BASIC* reference book are your main source of information. To explore graphics further, begin by reading about the DRAW statement. Then read about CIRCLE and PAINT. To explore other text and graphics modes, read (and reread) the description of the SCREEN statement. Then read (and reread) the description of the COLOR statement. If you want to write programs for use with a joystick, read about the STICK and STRIG functions. If you need to work with numbers with more than seven-digit precision, read in Chapter 3 about double-precision numbers. If you want to write programs to draw graphs of data, read about WINDOW and VIEW. If you want output to go to a printer, read about LPRINT.

More functions. You have used only seven of the five dozen functions in PC*jr* BASIC. Your best approach is to browse through the list of functions at the end of this book. If you see one that looks useful, go to Chapter 4 of the *BASIC* reference book and read more about it. Here are a few functions you will probably need soon: CHR$ and ASC, STR$ and VAL, INSTR$, TIMER, and CINT.

Using data files. If you write applications that use large amounts of data, you will want to learn about data files. Begin by reading in Chapter 4 of the *BASIC* reference book about the WRITE and INPUT# statements. You will also have to use the OPEN and CLOSE statements in the first form shown. There are more advanced file statements (FIELD, PUT, and GET), but you should master these simple ones first.

Programming techniques. People who do a lot of programming learn standard ways of solving problems that come up again and again. These ways are called *algorithms*. There are algorithms for sorting lists of data, shuffling lists, searching lists for one item, and doing many other tasks. Programmers also learn standard ways to organize data so that the programming job is easy. These are called *data structures*. The best place to learn about algorithms and data structures is from an advanced programming textbook. Go to a bookstore that has many computer books. Pick out one or two BASIC books that stress applications, not just the grammar of BASIC. Such books will contain long programs for solving serious problems. Read carefully and apply what you read.

Last Words

There is much to be learned from books about computers. In the end, however, a computer is like the world around us: It *is* what it *does*, not necessarily what we or others *say* about it. You can learn a lot by exploring, observing carefully, and coming up with your own ideas and programs. Like an English composition, a computer program is a personal expression of a thought or a feeling. We hope you will enjoy having this new way to think about things and to express your own ideas.

ANSWERS

PART ONE

Session 1

1. If the second line of the sign-on message begins with Version C, you are using Cassette BASIC. If the line begins with Version J, you are using Cartridge BASIC.
2. With the (Alt│Ctrl│→) keys.
3. If the second line of the sign-on message begins with Version C, you are using Cassette BASIC. If the line begins with Version J, you are using Cartridge BASIC.
4. With the (Alt│Ctrl│→) keys.
5. With the (Backspace) key.
6. With the (Esc) key.
7. Press the (Enter ←) key.

Session 2

1. To clear the screen.
2. The (Enter ←) key.
3. The computer erases the line you are typing.
4. The cursor is on the screen.
5. Press the (Backspace) key until all errors have been removed. Then retype the rest of the line.
6. To sound a short tone.
7. Tells the computer the frequency (pitch) of the sound.
8. Tells the computer the duration (length) of the sound.
9. In text mode, the cursor is a flashing underline. In medium-resolution graphics mode, the cursor is a solid square. In high-resolution graphics, the cursor is tall and narrow.
10. Switch to the medium-resolution graphics display mode.
11. Set the background color to red.
12. Print the word HELLO on the screen.
13. To divide the number on the left by the number on the right.

Session 3

1. The line number and the statement.
2. Print on the screen the lines of the program in the computer.
3. Perform the statements in the program, beginning with the first statement.
4. CLS
5. Erase the program from the computer.

6. Use a line number of 130, for example.
7. Type the number 50 and press the (Enter ⏎) key.
8. The new line takes the place of the old line.
9. Renumber the lines in a program. The first line will be numbered 500. The rest will be spaced 10 apart.

Session 4

1. To get information into the computer.
2. To receive information from the computer.
3. To store information inside the computer.
4. Type a line number and then the statement.
5. The line numbers.
6. It tells the computer which line to perform next.
7. It is waiting for input if the cursor is on.
8. Type LIST and look at the screen.
9. They are alike because they both tell the computer to erase information. NEW tells the computer to erase the program in memory. CLS tells the computer to erase the letters on the screen.

Session 5

1. The black plug is connected to the EAR socket. The red plug is connected to the AUX socket.
2. Leave it disconnected.
3. The RECORD and PLAY keys.
4. The SAVE command.
5. The LOAD command.
6. The PLAY key.
7. Anything from 1 to 8 characters long. It is a good idea to use only letters and numbers in file names.
8. Rewind the tape. Then ask the computer to load a file you know is not on the tape. Watch the screen and read the name of each file as it appears.

Session 6

1. To put special magnetic marks on a diskette so the computer can both store information on it and read information from it.
2. At the system level, the computer displays A> on the screen. In BASIC, the computer displays OK on the screen.
3. Write on the screen the names of all the files on the diskette in the diskette drive.
4. Type SAVE "RECORD".
5. Type LOAD "RECORD".
6. Type KILL "RECORD.BAS".

Session 7

1. To plot a point on the screen.
2. Type PSET (319, 0).
3. (160, 100)
4. PRESET
5. To draw a line on the screen from one point to another.
6. Tells what two lines to draw a line between.
7. Type EDIT 340.
8. To move the cursor to the end of the line.
9. Press and release the (Fn) key first. Then press and release the (↓) key.
10. Press the (Enter ←) key.
11. Cyan, magenta, and white.
12. Use the EDIT command to call up the line. Move the cursor to the place you want to insert. Press the (Ins) key. Then type the new characters. Press an arrow key or (Enter ←) to leave insert mode.
13. Use the EDIT command to call up the line. Move the cursor to the character you want to delete. Press the (Del) key.
14. Type EDIT 50. The cursor is at the 5 in 50. Type 6 and then press the (Enter ←) key.
15. You get an Illegal function call message.

Session 8

1. F+
2. There is no note named H.
3. Octave 4
4. 04 or >
5. P8
6. In octave 3, play a whole note C, a half note D, a quarter note E, and an eighth note F.
7. PLAY "O2 C16 D16 E16 F16 G16 A16 B16 > C16"
8. PLAY "ML T80"
9. Play staccato in octave 2 with a tempo of 180 quarter-note beats per minute.

PART TWO

Session 9

1. A RETURN statement.
2. With either the RUN command or the GOSUB statement.
3. A remark statement.
4. REM
5. With either the CLS statement or the (Ctrl|Home) function.

6. The (End) function moves the cursor to the end of the line. The (Ctrl | End) function deletes characters to the end of the line.
7. The friend probably forgot to press the (Enter ←) key after editing the line.

Session 10

1. PLAY "MF"
2. You will get a Syntax error message because the PLAY statement does not exist in Cassette BASIC.
3. Lines 1105, 1110, 1120, and 1130.
4. To make it clear that it *is* the body of the subroutine.
5. To make it easier to see the subroutines as separate program blocks.
6. LIST -375
7. LIST 440-
8. LIST 240-425
9. The statements (mainly GOSUB) between the opening remark statement and the END statement.
10. A remark statement.
11. An END statement.

Session 11

1. A subroutine.
2. A GOSUB statement.
3. The order of the GOSUB statements to the two subroutines.
4. A remark statement.
5. An END statement.
6. Because the subroutines will not be performed unless there are GOSUB statements in the main routine.
7. It tells the computer to return to the statement after the GOSUB that sent the computer to that subroutine.
8. To make it easy to see where the body begins and ends.
9. To separate routines from one another.
10. Breaking down complicated problems into simpler parts. Thinking about the main ideas first, and putting off the details until later.
11. It makes you think about what the whole program is supposed to do. It keeps you from getting bogged down in details.

Session 12

1. To conclude the main routine and tell the computer to stop performing statements.
2. The computer will "fall into" a subroutine without being sent there by a GOSUB statement. The computer will perform the body of the subroutine, but at the RETURN statement it will print the message RETURN without GOSUB.

3. It tells the computer to return to the statement after the GOSUB that sent the computer to that subroutine.
4. It "falls into" the next subroutine, if there is one in the program. Otherwise, the computer stops performing the program. Either way, there is no error message.
5. No.
6. Nothing. The computer will never see the second RETURN.
7. It tells the computer to go to a subroutine from the main routine (or possibly from another subroutine).
8. The action described in the subroutine is not performed when the program is run.
9. No.
10. It is a subroutine that is performed by a GOSUB statement in another subroutine.
11. The computer would never reach the main routine. Instead, it would perform the first subroutine without being sent there by a GOSUB statement. The result would be a RETURN without GOSUB error message.
12. Yes.
13. The computer reports an Out of memory error message.

Session 13

1. The Marine Hymn: "From the Halls of Montezuma." "Old MacDonald Had a Farm."
2. A-B-A-C. "The Battle Hymn of the Republic" has this form too.
3. Because both phrases in the B-part of "Twinkle, Twinkle" are exactly the same.
4. No. Only those in which both phrases of the B-part are the same. If the two phrases are different, you would have to add a PHRASE B2 subroutine.
5. By using a GOSUB statement in the immediate mode.
6. Because you can limit the errors you find to the few lines in the body of the subroutine.

PART THREE

Session 14

1. Because the LET statements changed what YEAR stood for each time you used the PRINT YEAR statement.
2. Zero.
3. Let the name DAY$ stand for the word BIRTHDAY.
4. The empty string.

5. When you tried to assign a string value to a numeric variable or the other way around.
6. String-variable names end with $.
7. Numeric constants are numbers. String constants are characters inside quotation marks.
8. A letter of the alphabet.
9. 2X does not begin with a letter. X* has a character that is neither a letter nor a number. NEW is a reserved word in PCjr BASIC.
10. 0
11. The two LET statements in lines 20 and 40.

Session 15

1. String and numeric.
2. *a.* The name is X, the type is numeric, and the value is the number 5.
   b. The name is A$, the type is string, and the value is the word DOG.
   c. The name is Z$, the type is string, and the value is the character 2.
   d. The name is P, the type is numeric, and the value is the number −3.
3. *a.* FRED is legal.
   b. A3 is legal.
   c. 3A is illegal because the name does not begin with a letter.
   d. BEEP is illegal because it is a reserved word.
   e. $C is illegal because the name does not begin with a letter.
   f. 27 is illegal because the name does not begin with a letter.
4. LET A = "PUPPY" and LET N$ = 3.14.
5. All string variables are assigned the empty string. All numeric variables are assigned 0.
6. The number 2010 would be printed on the screen, since that is the number in the YEAR box in memory when the program ends.
7. Zero, since that is the number in the YEAR box in memory when line 10 is performed. After that, line 20 tells the computer to put 2000 there.
8. COW. Line 20 tells the computer to erase HORSE from the X$ box in memory and to write COW in the box. Then line 30 tells the computer to print *whatever* is in the X$ box, which is COW.
9. HORSE. Line 10 says to put HORSE in the X$ box. Line 20 says to make a copy of HORSE and put the copy in the Y$ box. Line 30 says to print whatever is in the Y$ box, which is HORSE.
10. Because when you enter RUN, the computer writes 0 in all the boxes that hold numeric variables.
11. After line 10, P contains 7, Q contains 0. After line 20, P contains 7, Q contains 11. After line 30, P contains 11, Q contains 11. After line 40, P contains 11, Q contains 11.

Session 16

1. The computer puts the data in standard print zones, 14 characters wide.
2. The computer prints the data with no extra spaces between items. (When numbers are printed, the computer puts one space or a minus sign before the number and one space after the number.)
3. The LET statements in lines 20 and 30.
4. It tells the computer to add the number on the left to the number on the right.
5. Get copies of the numbers stored in the locations named P and Q, add them together, and put the sum in the location named R, erasing whatever was in R before.
6. Stop the program, print a ? on the screen, and wait for data to be entered at the keyboard. When the data are entered, put them in memory in places with the same name as the variables in the INPUT statement.
7. Because the program will now work for *any* values of P and Q.
8. A message is printed on the screen telling the user what to to.
9. It prints the message ?Redo from start.
10. It prints the message ?Redo from start.

Session 17

1. To separate items to be printed and control the spacing of output.
2. +, -, *, and /
3. To join (or concatenate) the strings together.
4. An expression is anything that has a value. This includes constants, variables, and combinations of these with operators.
5. Anywhere it is legal to write a constant in a BASIC statement.
6. On the left side of the equal sign in LET statements and in INPUT statements. (Later, you will learn about the FOR and NEXT statements, which also need a variable name.)
7. For processing data.
8. Yes. The INPUT statement causes a ? to be printed on the screen.
9. The number is put into the memory location named X.
10. Line 20 has the effect of writing CAT in the A$ box in memory, erasing DOG from the box.

Session 18

1. Use 523 for the frequency of the note. Use 10 for the duration of the note.
2. Because the duration in all the note subroutines is a constant.
3. To have a silence with duration 1.
4. Because now, the length of the notes can be changed by changing the value of the variable DURATION.

5. Change line 1130 to print the value of a string variable rather than the string constant "RE".
6. The duration would be 20.
7. The value of DURATION would be zero, so they would not be played at all.
8. Line 115.
9. 117 LET NOTE8 = NOTE4 / 2
10. Each note will sound for a length of 14. The silence will have a length of 2.
11. No. The DURATION value controls the tempo. The HOLD value controls the fraction of a beat that the note is actually sounded.

PART FOUR

Session 19

1. To move the line pointer to some statement in the program.
2. The computer prints an Undefined line number error message.
3. If the first statement is in line 100, put a GOTO 100 statement at the end of the program.
4. Both the (Pause) function and the (Break) function stop a running program. After the (Pause) function, you can restart the program by pressing any of the symbol keys. After the (Break) function, you can restart the program with the CONT command or you can enter any other command or program lines you want.
5. Use the (Break) function.
6. If the program was stopped with the (Pause) function, press any key in the symbol group. If the program was stopped with the (Break) function, type CONT.
7. Use the PRINT statement in the immediate mode.
8. 50. This statement tells the computer to find the value of the right side and assign it to the variable on the left side of the equal sign. Since the A-box at first has 5 in it, the right side is equal to 50. This number then goes back into the A-box.
9. To make it easy to see the body of the loop. The statements there are the ones to be performed again and again.
10. Documentation is material written about a program. A remark in a program is an example of documentation. Its purpose is to make the program easier to read and understand.
11. That the number after the word GOTO must be the same as the line number of the remark statement at the end of the jump arrow.

Session 20

1. The empty string.
2. One assignment and two outputs.
3. Get the value of A$ from the A$-box. Join the string ‑ ‑ ‑ ‑ > to the value of A$. Put the new value back in the A$-box.
4. 1
5. An output and an assignment.
6. Get the value of P from the P-box. Multiply the value by 1 0. Then put the new value back in the P-box.
7. 1 0 0 0 0 0 0 0
8. A 1 followed by seven 0s, or 1 0 0 0 0 0 0 0.
9. That the decimal point should be moved 37 places to the right.
10. 1 . 3 E + 0 9
11. About 1 . 7 E + 3 8.
12. 0 . 0 0 0 1
13. 2 . 9 3 8 7 3 6 E - 3 9
14. Left to right.
15. Multiplication.
16. Division.
17. Put the operation inside parentheses.
18. 1 E + 0 9
19. 1 2 3 . 4 5 6
20. Because it would require an infinite number of digits. There is a maximum number of digits that can be stored in a memory box.
21. 1 4

Session 21

1. A remark statement should be both at the beginning and the end of a loop block.
2. The I F statement.
3. The first "do something" *always* gets done at least once. The second "do something" may or may not get done, depending on the exit condition.
4. Here is the BASIC version of the instructions:

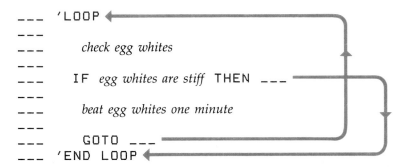

5. Here is another example:

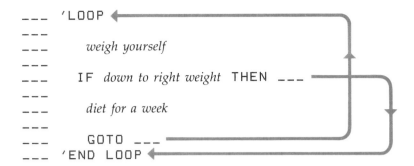

```
___   'LOOP
___
___       weigh yourself
___
___       IF  down to right weight  THEN ___
___
___       diet for a week
___
___           GOTO ___
___   'END LOOP
```

Session 22

1. Find the length of P$ measured in characters.
2. 10
3. It takes a piece out of a string.
4. The letter O.
5. PART
6. It drops everything after the decimal point.
7. The answer to question 6 is not quite right. If X is not already a whole number, INT(X) tells the computer to find the first whole number less than the value of X.
8. 153
9. -154
10. Takes the square root of a number.
11. 6
12. It prints an Illegal function call error message.
13. If the number ABS works on is positive, the function does nothing. If the number is negative, ABS changes the sign so that the number is positive.
14. 76,23
15. 346,92
16. They are alike because both get input from the keyboard. They are different because INPUT stops the program for input while INKEY$ does not.
17. A one-character string. The character is the same as the key that is pressed.
18. A number just less than 1.
19. A number just greater than 0.
20. None that was obvious.
21. 39
22. 0
23. Whole numbers from 0 to 39 are generated at random and printed on the screen.

24. 6
25. -254
26. Both a function and a subroutine tell the computer to carry out the steps of a process. The difference is that a function returns a value, but a subroutine does not.
27. A variable is a place in memory. A function is a process that produces a result.

Session 23

1. The first line should read LET C = 0. The third line should read IF C > 1000 THEN.
2. The fifth line should read LET C = C + 2.
3. 101
4. F
5. The statement in line 130.
6. C > L
7. The statement in line 170.
8. The statements in lines 130, 140, and 150.
9. The statements in lines 170, 180, and 190.
10. It is the first value of C that is greater than L.
11. Because the program counts by 1, and 11 is the first value of C greater than 10.
12. How much to add to the loop variable each time around the loop.
13. Change the statement in line 170 to read LET C = C + 10.
14. To decrease the value of the loop variable each time around the loop.
15. It is the first value of C less than the value of L.
16. Before starting the loop.
17. No.

Session 24

1. The empty string.
2. The simple version allows you to check the major routines in your program and make sure they work correctly. If problems come up later, you will know that they come from the new changes you make.
3. All the dots would be in the upper left-hand corner, since X1 and Y1 would always be numbers less than 1.
4. That you may not use PSET on the text screen.
5. To draw a line from the previous point drawn to the point (0, 199). This is the lower left-hand corner of the screen.
6. Two numbers are needed for the coordinates of one end of the line. Two more are needed for the other end.
7. If this condition is true, the computer is sent back to the beginning of the loop.

8. Line 840. The condition KY$ = " " will be false, so the computer simply goes to the next statement after the IF statement.
9. B means to draw the outline of a box. BF means to draw a box filled with a solid color.
10. Line 426 tells the computer to set C to be a number in the set 0, 1, 2, and 3. Line 610 uses the value of C for the color of the box.
11. It tells whether to use the colors on palette 0 or on palette 1 for drawing points, lines, and solid colors.

PART FIVE

Session 25

1. In the case of strings, > means "is later in the dictionary than." In the case of numbers, > means "is greater than."
2. *a.* True *b.* False
   c. True *d.* True
3. A condition with more than one comparison.
4. *a.* True *b.* False
   c. True *d.* True
5. Because in a loop block, something gets done again and again. But in a branch block, the computer either does one thing or another.
6. In the branch block, the IF statement determines which of two "do somethings" to do. In the loop block, the IF statement tells when to exit from the loop.
7. In the branch block, the GOTO statement tells the computer to skip the ELSE "do something" if it has performed the THEN "do something." In the loop block, the GOTO statement at the end tells the computer to loop back to the beginning.
8. The three remark statements mark the beginning of the THEN "do something," the ELSE "do something," and the end of the branch block.
9. Here is the BASIC version:

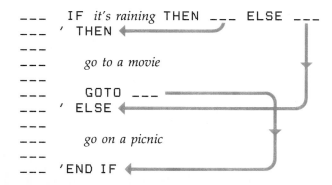

```
___    IF it's raining THEN ___ ELSE ___
___    ' THEN
___
___        go to a movie
___
___        GOTO ___
___    ' ELSE
___
___        go on a picnic
___
___    'END IF
```

10. Here is another example:

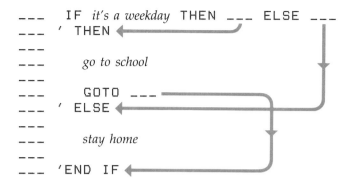

```
___    IF it's a weekday THEN ___ ELSE ___
___    ' THEN
___
___       go to school
___
___       GOTO ___
___    ' ELSE
___
___       stay home
___
___    'END IF
```

Session 26

1. To generate random numbers that will be used to simulate tossing a coin.
2. You would expect to get about 500 HEADS. If the coin is fair, you would expect about as many HEADS as TAILS.
3. An action block, a loop block, or a branch block; or a series of these blocks.
4. When a "do something" in a branch or loop block is itself a branch or loop block.
5. The statement should read
   425   IF HEADS = N OR COUNT = 1000 THEN 430
6. A branch block, since this is an either-or situation.
7. To cause a different set of random numbers to be generated each time the computer runs a program.

Session 27

1. It is not a new block. It is built by nesting one branch block inside another.
2. The three possible actions (PRINT statements) are all indented the same amount.
3. Line 430 will be performed if A$ = B$. Line 480 will be performed if A$ > B$. Line 510 will be performed if A$ < B$.
4.

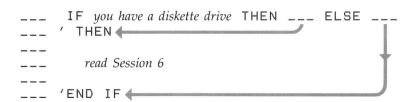

```
___    IF you have a diskette drive THEN ___ ELSE ___
___    ' THEN
___
___       read Session 6
___
___    'END IF
```

5. This is the one-line form:
   ___ IF *you have a diskette drive* THEN *read Session 6*
6. All of them.
7. Because you want only one of the cases to be performed.
8. It is a shortened form of a series of branch blocks.
9. The case block is usually easier to read and write than the series of branch blocks.
10. You must make sure that no two of the conditions in the case block overlap.
11. The cases must be defined by a variable that can take on the values 1, 2, 3, and so on.

Session 28

1. The computer still prints the letter on the screen. However, since all the case-block conditions are false, the program does not tally the letter as one of the vowels.
2. It will not print a $. The reason is that KY$ = "$" is the exit condition from the loop in subroutine PROCESS KEYS. The exit happens before the PRINT statement.
3. To set the vowel counter variables all equal to 0.
4. Expand the case block in subroutine PROCESS KEYS.

PART SIX

Session 29

1. Array variable names have two parts. The first part is an ordinary variable name. The second part is an expression written inside parentheses. As an example, W$ is the name of an ordinary string variable. W$(1) is the name of the first component of a string array variable.
2. Y$(14)
3. To store a collection of information under a single name.
4. "HARRY". The computer first finds the value of J + 1, which is 2. Then it uses 2 as the number that goes between parentheses in the array variable name.
5. It will round off the 1.4 to 1.
6. DIM tells the computer what the largest item number in a list can be.
7. If item numbers are going to be greater than 10.
8. Zero and all positive numbers.
9. BROWN   DOG

Session 30

1. Array variables are useful when the computer must deal with collections of data whose size is not known in advance.
2. Subscripted variable.
3. The terms *subscript* and *item number* have the same meaning.
4. The maximum value of the subscript for the array.
5. First, the computer converts $2*P$ to a number. Since the value of P is 5, $2*P$ is 10. Now the statement reads LET X(10) = 37. In the final step, the computer puts the number 37 into component number 10 of the array variable X.
6. The computer first evaluates the expression for the subscript of array X. Since the value of Q is 3, the value of Q – 1 is 2. So the statement becomes LET X(2) = Q + 1. Next, the computer evaluates the expression on the right. Since Q is still 3, Q + 1 is 4. So the statement becomes LET X(2) = 4. In the final step, the computer assigns the value 4 to the array variable X(2).

Session 31

1. The READ and INPUT statements are alike in that they both assign values to variables. They are different in that the data values come from different locations. The READ statement gets data values from DATA statements. The INPUT statement gets data values from the keyboard.
2. The computer pays no attention to the location of DATA statements. However, the computer does use the line-number order of the DATA statements to determine the order in which data items are read by READ statements.
3. The data pointer is set to the first data item in the DATA statement with the lowest line number.
4. The computer prints a Syntax error message. (A Type mismatch error message would be more informative, but it is not what you get.)
5. Subroutine INITIALIZE would need several changes. The dimension of the array variables would be changed from 4 to 8. The final value of the FOR loop would be changed from 4 to 8. Four more DATA statements containing four new sentences would be needed. Finally, subroutine SELECT PHRASES would be changed to generate random integers in the set 1 through 8.
6. So that a different series of sentences would be generated each time the program is run.
7. THE COW SWAM UNDER BANANAS

Session 32

1. A branch block.
2. To send the computer to a subroutine where the counting variables are initialized to zero.
3. An action block.
4. No two of the conditions in the IF statements overlap: Only one can be true at a time.
5. An action block.
6. Now it is an action block. Before, it contained a case block. The new line 620 replaced the entire case block.
7. An action block (the first PRINT statement) followed by a loop block.

A Guide to BASIC for the IBM PCjr

A Guide to BASIC for the IBM PCjr

The tables on the following pages contain the names and descriptions of all commands, statements, and functions available in PCjr BASIC. Names preceded by an asterisk are available only in Cartridge BASIC. Names printed in boldface are used in this book. In many cases, the description is incomplete. The note "See *BR*" means that you should look in the *BASIC* reference book for more information.

Commands

Command	Example	Description
AUTO	AUTO 1000	Generates line numbers automatically when entering statements. The line numbers begin at 1000 with steps of 10. Use the (Break) function to turn AUTO off.
	AUTO 500, 20	Generates line numbers beginning at 500 with steps of 20.
BLOAD	BLOAD "GRAPH", 0	Loads binary file GRAPH into memory with offset 0. See *BR*.
BSAVE	BSAVE "PICTURE", 0 &H4000	Saves binary file PICTURE on the diskette with offset 0 and length H4000. See *BR*.
*CHDIR	CHDIR "XYZ"	Changes the file directory to XYZ. See *BR*.
CLEAR	CLEAR	Sets all numeric variables to zero and all string variables to empty. See *BR*.
CONT	CONT	Restarts a program after the (Break) function or an error.
DELETE	DELETE 150-280	Deletes lines 150 through 280 from the program in memory.
	DELETE -500	Deletes program lines from the beginning through line 500.
	DELETE 475-	Deletes program lines from 475 to the end.
EDIT	EDIT 175	Displays line 175 for editing.
*FILES	FILES	Displays the names of files on a diskette. See *BR*.

400

Commands (continued)

Command	Example	Description
*KILL	KILL "TAXES.BAS"	Deletes a diskette file named TAXES.BAS. See *BR*.
LIST	LIST 230-780	Displays lines 230 through 780 of the program in memory.
	LIST -560	Displays program lines from the beginning through line 560.
	LIST 450-	Displays program lines from line 450 through the end.
LLIST	LLIST 230-780	The same as the LIST command except the lines are sent to the printer rather than to the screen.
LOAD	LOAD "TAXES"	Loads the file named TAXES.BAS from a diskette into memory. See *BR*.
MERGE	MERGE NUMBERS	Merges the diskette file NUMBERS with the program currently in memory.
*MKDIR	MKDIR "SALES"	From the root directory, creates a sub-directory called SALES. See *BR*.
*NAME	NAME "AB.BAS" AS "XY.BAS"	Changes the name of diskette file AB.BAS to XY.BAS.
NEW	NEW	Deletes the program currently in memory, sets all numeric variables to zero, and sets all string variables to empty.
RENUM	RENUM	Renumbers the entire program in memory. The first new line number is 10. Each line is 10 greater than the one before.
	RENUM 300, , 5	Renumbers the entire program in memory. The first new line number is 300. Each line is 5 greater than the one before.
	RENUM 1000, 900, 20	Renumbers the program in memory beginning with old line 900. The first new line number is 1000. Each line is 20 greater than the one before.

401

Commands (continued)

Command	Example	Description
*RESET	RESET	Closes all diskette files and clears the system buffer. See BR.
*RMDIR	RMDIR "SALES"	Removes the directory named SALES from a diskette. See BR.
RUN	RUN	Begins performing the program currently in memory.
	RUN 300	Performs the program currently in memory beginning at line 300. See BR.
SAVE	SAVE "MILEAGE"	Saves in diskette file MILEAGE.BAS the program currently in memory.
*SYSTEM	SYSTEM	Exits from BASIC and returns to DOS.
TROFF	TROFF	Turns line-number tracing off.
TRON	TRON	Turns line-number tracing on.

Statements

Statement	Example	Description
BEEP	BEEP	Causes the speaker to beep.
CALL	CALL 37	Calls the machine-language subroutine at location 37 in memory. See BR.
*CHAIN	CHAIN "BOXES"	Transfers control to a program named BOXES on the diskette in the drive. See BR.
*CIRCLE	CIRCLE (160, 100), 60	Draws a circle of radius 60 centered at screen coordinates (160, 100). See BR.
CLOSE	CLOSE #1	Closes the file and device associated with file channel 1. See BR.
CLS	CLS	Clears the screen.
COLOR	COLOR 14, 1	In text mode, sets yellow for characters on a blue background. In medium-resolution graphics, sets the background to yellow and the foreground to palette 1. See BR.

402

Statements (continued)

Statement	Example	Description
*COM(n)	COM(1)	Enables trapping of communications activity to communications adapter number 1. See ON COM(n) statement. See *BR*.
*COMMON	COMMON A$, X	Passes the variables A$ and X to a chained program. See CHAIN.
DATA	DATA 5, -3, "QUIT"	Stores the constants to be assigned to variables by a READ statement.
*DATE$	DATE$ "8/15/83"	Sets the date to August 15, 1983.
DEF FN	DEF FNA(R) 3.14*R*R	Defines the function FNA to be the area of a circle of radius R. See *BR*.
DEF SEG	DEF SEG	Sets the current segment of storage to the beginning of BASIC. See *BR*.
DEF *types*	DEFDBL L-P	Declares that all variables beginning with the letters L, M, N, O, or P are double-precision variables. See *BR*.
DEF USR	DEF USR 24000	Specifies the starting address of a machine-language subroutine that is later called by the USR function. See *BR*.
DIM	DIM X(12), A$(24)	Sets the maximum value of the subscript in arrays X and A$.
*DRAW	DRAW "U50 R50 D50 L50"	Draws a box on the graphic screen. See *BR*.
END	END	Stops performing the program. Closes all files and returns to the command level in BASIC.
ERASE	ERASE B, WORD$	Erases the arrays B and WORD$ from memory.
ERROR	ERROR 20	Simulates the occurrence of BASIC error number 20. See *BR*.
*FIELD	FIELD #1, 20, AS N$	Allocates the first 20 positions in the random file buffer to the string variable N$. See *BR*.

Statements (continued)

Statement	*Example*	*Description*
FOR	FOR X = 1 TO 10	Opens a counting loop with a loop variable X to take on the whole-number values from 1 to 10. See *BR*.
*GET	GET #2, 3	(Files) Loads record number 3 from file channel number 2 into the random file buffer. See *BR*.
*	GET (50,50)-(90,100), A	(Graphics) Moves into array A a copy of all the points on the screen inside the rectangle with diagonal corners (50,50) and (90,100). See PUT. See *BR*.
GOSUB	GOSUB 1200	Performs the subroutine beginning in line 1200.
GOTO	GOTO 450	Moves the line pointer to line 450 next.
IF	IF X > 3 THEN 525	If the condition X > 3 is true, moves the line pointer to line 525. Otherwise, performs the next line in the program. See *BR*.
INPUT	INPUT A, W$	Receives input from the keyboard and assigns values to the variables A and W$. See *BR*.
INPUT #	INPUT #2, X	Receives input over file channel number 2 for the variable X.
KEY	KEY OFF	Erases the soft key values displayed on the 25th line of the screen. See *BR*.
*KEY(n)	KEY(12) ON	Activates trapping of the (⟵) key on the keyboard. See ON KEY statement. See *BR*.
LET	LET A$ = "AARDVARK"	Assigns the string constant "AARDVARK" to the string variable A$.
LINE	LINE (40,50) - (100,200)	Draws a line on the graphics screen from screen coordinates (40,50) to (100,200). See *BR*.

Statements (continued)

Statement	Example	Description
LINE INPUT	LINE INPUT A$	Reads a line from the keyboard into the string variable A$. The computer ignores delimiters. See *BR*.
	LINE INPUT #1, A$	Same as LINE INPUT except that the string is read from file channel number 1.
LOCATE	LOCATE 25, 10	Places the cursor in row 25 at column 10.
LPRINT	LPRINT X, Y	Prints the values of X and Y on the printer. See *BR*.
	LPRINT USING F$, X, Y	Same as LPRINT except the values of the variables X and Y are formatted using the instructions in F$. See *BR*.
*LSET	LSET A$ = X$	Moves data into a random file buffer. A$ is the name of a variable defined in a FIELD statement. X$ is a variable containing the data. See *BR*.
MID$()=	MID$(A$, 11)= "OHIO"	Replaces four characters in the variable A$, beginning with character number 11, with the characters OHIO.
MOTOR	MOTOR	Turns on the cassette recorder motor if it is off. Turns off the motor if it is on. See *BR*.
NEXT	NEXT X	Marks the end of a loop begun by a FOR X statement.
*NOISE	NOISE 4, 10, 20	Generates white noise over the loudspeaker with a volume of 10 and a duration of 20 clock ticks. See *BR*.
*ON	ON COM(2) GOSUB 200	Performs the subroutine beginning in line 200 as soon as information comes into communications buffer 2.
	ON ERROR GOTO 450	Jumps to line 450 when an error is detected.
	ON N GOSUB 200, 300, 400	Performs the subroutine beginning in line 200 if N is 1. Performs the subroutine beginning in line 300 if N is 2, and so on.

Statements (continued)

Statement	Example	Description
	`ON N GOTO 200, 300, 400`	Jumps to line 200 next if N is 1. Jumps to line 300 next if N is 2, and so on.
*	`ON KEY(11) GOSUB 1500`	Performs the subroutine beginning in line 1500 whenever the ⬆ key is pressed. See *BR*.
*	`ON PEN GOSUB 1000`	Performs the subroutine beginning in line 1000 whenever the light pen is activated.
*	`ON PLAY(5) GOSUB 1000`	Performs the subroutine beginning in line 1000 whenever five or fewer notes are left in the background music buffer. See *BR*.
*	`ON STRIG(2) GOSUB 3200`	Performs the subroutine beginning in line 3200 whenever trigger B1 on the joysticks is pressed. See *BR*.
*	`ON TIMER (60) GOSUB 500`	Performs the subroutine beginning in line 500 60 seconds after the timer is turned on. See *BR*.
OPEN	`OPEN "O", #1, "DATA"`	Opens the file named DATA for sequential output on file channel 1. See *BR*.
*	`OPEN "COM1:" AS 1`	Opens file channel 1 for communication with all defaults. See *BR*.
OPTION BASE	`OPTION BASE 1`	Sets the minimum value for array subscripts to be 1. See *BR*.
OUT	`OUT 32, 100`	Sends the value 100 to output port 32.
*PAINT	`PAINT (40,50), 2`	Fills in the area enclosing the point (40,50) with color number 2. See *BR*.
*PALETTE	`PALETTE 1, 3`	Puts color 3 in position 1 on the palette. See *BR*.
*	`PALETTE USING A(1)`	Sets all palette locations to the color numbers in array A. See *BR*.

Statements (continued)

Statement	Example	Description
*PCOPY	PCOPY 2, 3	Copies from screen page 2 to screen page 3. See *BR*.
PEN	PEN ON	Turns the light pen on.
*PLAY	PLAY "C D E"	Plays the musical notes C, D, and E. See *BR*.
POKE	POKE 2400, 50	Puts 50 in memory location 2400.
PRINT	PRINT C, M$	Displays the values of C and M$ on the screen. See *BR*.
	PRINT USING A$; C, M$	Displays the values of C and M$ on the screen using the formatting information contained in the string A$. See *BR*.
	PRINT #1, A; B	Writes the values of A and B sequentially to file channel 1
	PRINT #1, USING X$; A; B	Writes the values of A and B sequentially to file channel 1 using the formatting information in string X$.
PRESET	PRESET (50, 75)	Erases the point at screen coordinates (50, 75). See *BR*.
PSET	PSET (50, 75)	Plots a point at screen coordinates (50, 75). See *BR*.
*PUT	PUT #5, 25	(Files) Transfers a record from the random file buffer to record 25 over file channel 5.
*	PUT (15,80), A	(Graphics) Draws the image stored in array A, putting the upper left-hand corner at screen coordinates (15,80) See *BR*.
RANDOMIZE	RANDOMIZE	Reseeds the random-number generator.
READ	READ X, B$	Reads data values from a DATA statement and assigns them to the variables X and B$.
REM	REM LOOP	Inserts the explanatory remark LOOP into a program.
RESTORE	RESTORE	Moves the data pointer to the beginning of the data values in the DATA statements.

Statements (continued)

Statement	Example	Description
RESUME	RESUME 200	Continues program perform-ance at line 200 after an error recovery.
RETURN	RETURN	Stops performing a subrou-tine and returns to the state-ment after the GOSUB state-ment that began performing the subroutine.
SCREEN	SCREEN 0	Sets text mode. See *BR*.
SOUND	SOUND 440, 15	Sounds a note with frequency 440 Hz and duration 15 clock ticks. See *BR*.
STOP	STOP	Stops performing the pro-gram. Prints a Break mes-sage.
STRIG	STRIG ON	Sets the buttons of the joy-sticks so they can be read by the computer.
*	STRIG(4) OFF	Disables interrupts from but-ton A2 on the joysticks. See *BR*.
SWAP	SWAP X, Y	Swaps the values of the varia-bles X and Y.
*TIME$ =	TIME$ = "12:00:00"	Sets the clock in the computer to twelve noon.
*VIEW	VIEW (50,50)-(100,100)	Defines a viewport on the screen with diagonal corners equal to the screen coordi-nates (50,50) and (100,100). See *BR*.
WAIT	WAIT 32, 2	Stops program performance until port 32 receives a 1 bit in the second bit position.
WEND	WEND	Marks the end of a WHILE loop in a BASIC program.
WHILE	WHILE N < 3	Opens a WHILE loop and performs the body of the loop as long as N < 3.
WIDTH	WIDTH 40	Sets the width of the output line to 40 characters.
*WINDOW	WINDOW (-1,-1)-(1,1)	Redefines the screen coordi-nates. The lower left coordi-nate becomes (-1,-1). The upper right coordinate becomes (1,1). See *BR*.

Statements (continued)

Statement	Example	Description
WRITE	WRITE A, B, C$	Writes the values of the variables A, B, and C$ on the screen. Puts commas between the values.
	WRITE #2, A, B, C$	Writes the values of the variables A, B, and C$ to a sequential file using file channel 2. Puts commas between the values.

Functions

Function	Value In	Value Out
ABS	Number	Absolute value of the number.
ASC	String	ASCII code (0 to 255) for the first character in the string.
ATN	Number	Arctangent (radians) of the number.
CDBL	Number	The same number converted to double-precision format.
CHR$	Number (0 to 255)	ASCII character equivalent of the number.
CINT	Number	The same number rounded to an integer and converted to integer format.
COS	Number (radians)	Cosine of the number.
CSNG	Number	The same number converted to single-precision format.
CSRLIN	None	Vertical coordinate of the cursor.
*CVD	String (8 byte)	Double-precision number equivalent to the number expressed by the string.
*CVI	String (2 byte)	Integer equivalent to the number expressed by the string.
*CVS	String (4 byte)	Single-precision number equivalent to the number expressed by the string.
*DATE$	None	Date expressed in the form mm-dd-yyyy.

Functions (continued)

Function	Value In	Value Out
EOF	Number (file channel)	"True" if the end of the file has been reached. "False" otherwise.
ERL	None	Line number in which the last error was detected.
ERR	None	Error code for the last error detected.
EXP	Number	The base of the natural logarithm (e) raised to the same number power.
FIX	Number	The same number, with all digits to the right of the decimal point removed.
FRE	Number (dummy)	Number of bytes in memory not being used by BASIC.
HEX$	Number	Hexadecimal string that represents the decimal value of the same number.
INKEY$	None	Single-character string. The key down on the keyboard determines the single character. If no key is down, the value out is the empty string.
INP	Number (0 to 65535)	A byte read from a port with the same number.
INPUT$	Number	The same number of characters read from the keyboard.
INSTR	String, string	The position of the second string in the first string.
INT	Number	Largest integer equal to or less than the same number.
LEFT$	String, number	The same number of the leftmost characters in the string.
LEN	String	Number of characters in the string.
*LOC	Number	Current position in the file with the same channel number.
*LOF	Number	Length of the file with the same channel number.
LOG	Number (positive)	Natural logarithm of the same number.

Functions (continued)

Function	Value In	Value Out
LPOS	Number	The current position of the print head within the printer buffer. The number indicates which printer is being tested.
MID$	String, number, number	The portion of the string beginning at the character position equal to the first number and with length equal to the second number.
*MKD$	Number (double-precision)	String representation of the number.
*MKI$	Number (integer)	String representation of the number.
*MXS$	Number (single-precision)	String representation of the number.
OCT$	Number	Octal string representation of the number.
PEEK	Number (0 to 65535)	The byte in the memory location defined by the number.
PEN	Number (0 to 9)	Status of the light pen. The number selects the type of information to be returned. See BR.
*PLAY(n)	Number (0 to 2)	The number of notes left in the music background buffer. The number selects the voice channel.
*PMAP	Number, number	Maps the coordinate represented by the first number using a process selected by the second number. See BR.
POINT	Number, number	The color of the point at the screen coordinates defined by the numbers.
POS	Number (dummy)	Current column position of the cursor.
RIGHT$	String, number	The same number of characters taken from the rightmost part of the string.
RND	Number	A random number between 0 and 1. The number used in the argument affects the returned value. See BR.

Functions (continued)

Function	Value In	Value Out
SCREEN	Number, number	The ASCII code (0 to 255) for the character on the screen at the coordinates defined by the two numbers.
SGN	Number	The sign of the number.
SIN	Number (radians)	The sine of the number.
SPACE$	Number	A string consisting of the same number of spaces.
SQR	Number (positive)	The square root of the number.
STICK	Number	The X or Y coordinate of the two joysticks. The number selects a coordinate on a joystick.
STR$	Number	A string representation of the number.
STRING$	Number, string	A string whose length is equal to the number, and whose characters are all equal to the first character in the string.
TAN	Number (radians)	The tangent of the number.
*TIME$	None	The time in the form hh:mm:ss.
*TIMER	None	The number of seconds that have elapsed since midnight or system reset.
USR	Number, number	The result of the machine-language subroutine identified by the first number. The second number is the argument of the subroutine.
VAL	String	Numerical value of the string.
*VARPTR	Variable name	Memory address of the variable.
*VARPTR$	Variable name	Character form of the memory address of the variable.

Reserved Words in IBM PCjr BASIC

The words in the table below are all the keywords used in PCjr BASIC. You may not use any of these words as names of variables or functions.

ABS	DIM	IOCTL	OPTION	SIN
AND	DRAW	IOCTL$	OR	SOUND
ASC	EDIT	KEY	OUT	SPACE$
ATN	ELSE	KILL	PAINT	SPC(
AUTO	END	LEFT$	PALETTE	SQR
BEEP	ENVIRON	LEN	PCOPY	STEP
BLOAD	ENVIRON$	LET	PEEK	STICK
BSAVE	EOF	LINE	PEN	STOP
CALL	EQV	LIST	PLAY	STR$
CDBL	ERASE	LLIST	PMAP	STRIG
CHAIN	ERDEV	LOAD	POINT	STRING$
CHDIR	ERDEV$	LOC	POKE	SWAP
CHR$	ERL	LOCATE	POS	SYSTEM
CINT	ERR	LOF	PRESET	TAB(
CIRCLE	ERROR	LOG	PRINT	TAN
CLEAR	EXP	LPOS	PRINT#	THEN
CLOSE	FIELD	LPRINT	PSET	TIME$
CLS	FILES	LSET	PUT	TIMER
COLOR	FIX	MERGE	RANDOMIZE	TO
COM	FNxxxxxxxx	MID$	READ	TROFF
COMMON	FOR	MKDIR	REM	TRON
CONT	FRE	MKD$	RENUM	USING
COS	GET	MKI$	RESET	USR
CSNG	GOSUB	MKS$	RESTORE	VAL
CSRLIN	GOTO	MOD	RESUME	VARPTR
CVD	HEX$	MOTOR	RETURN	VARPTR$
CVI	IF	NAME	RIGHT$	VIEW
CVS	IMP	NEW	RMDIR	WAIT
DATA	INKEY$	NEXT	RND	WEND
DATE$	INP	NOISE	RSET	WHILE
DEF	INPUT	NOT	RUN	WIDTH
DEFDBL	INPUT#	OCT$	SAVE	WINDOW
DEFINT	INPUT$	OFF	SCREEN	WRITE
DEFSNG	INSTR	ON	SGN	WRITE#
DEFSTR	INT	OPEN	SHELL	XOR
DELETE	INTER$			

Index

REFERENCE TABLES

MUSIC PITCHES AND DURATIONS

The numbers in the table below give the frequencies of the 12 notes in each of the seven octaves of the piano keyboard. These are the numbers to use as the first item in the SOUND statement. The second item in the SOUND statement is the duration. A duration of 18.2 is 1 second. The smallest allowed duration is .2.

Note	Oct. 0	Oct. 1	Oct. 2	Oct. 3	Oct. 4	Oct. 5	Oct. 6
C	65	131	262	523	1047	2093	4186
C♯	69	139	277	554	1109	2217	4435
D	73	147	294	587	1175	2349	4699
E♭	78	156	311	622	1245	2489	4987
E	82	165	330	659	1319	2637	5274
F	87	175	349	698	1397	2794	5588
F♯	92	185	370	740	1480	2960	5920
G	98	196	392	784	1586	3136	6274
A♭	104	208	415	831	1661	3322	6645
A	110	220	440	880	1760	3520	7040
B♭	117	233	466	932	1865	3729	7459
B	123	247	494	988	1976	3951	7902

MEDIUM-RESOLUTION COLORS SCREEN 1

		Foreground	
Background		**Palette 0**	**Palette 1**
0 Black	8 Dark Gray	0 Background	0 Background
1 Blue	9 Light Blue	1 Green	1 Cyan
2 Green	10 Light Green	2 Red	2 Magenta
3 Cyan	11 Light Cyan	3 Brown	3 White
4 Red	12 Light Red		
5 Magenta	13 Light Magenta		
6 Brown	14 Yellow		
7 Gray	15 White		

NOTE: On the text screen with color enabled (SCREEN Ø , 1), you may use the COLOR statement to select the color of the letters printed. The first number in the COLOR statement selects 1 of the 16 colors shown at the left above. By adding a second number to the COLOR statement, you may also select a background color from the first 8 colors in the table above.

SPECIAL KEYS

(Alt | Ctrl | Caps Lock) Turns on or off a clicking sound whenever you type a key on the keyboard.

(Alt | Ctrl | Del) Restarts the computer when power is on.

(Alt | Ctrl | →) Moves TV picture to right.

(Alt | Ctrl | ←) Moves TV picture to left.

(Backspace) Moves cursor left one space and erases what is there.

(Caps Lock) Makes letter keys type capital letters. Same key resets letter keys to lowercase.

(Del) Deletes the character at the current cursor position. Moves the rest of the line to the left, filling the gap.

(Enter ↵) Accepts as input whatever line the cursor is on when this key is pressed.

(Esc) Erases all characters from the line containing the cursor.

(Ins) Sets insert mode. Symbols typed in this mode are inserted into the line at the cursor position. (Enter ↵) or one of the arrow keys will end this mode.

(→) (←) (↑) (↓) Moves the cursor.

(Break) **function** Stops a running program and returns the cursor. Press the (Fn) key followed by the (B) key.

(End) **function** Moves the cursor to the end of the line.

(Ctrl | End) **function** Erases characters from the cursor position to the end of the line. While holding down the (Ctrl) key, press the (Fn) key followed by the (↓) key.

(Home) **function** Moves the cursor to the upper left-hand corner of the screen. Press the (Fn) key followed by the (↑) key.

(Ctrl | Home) **function** Clears the screen and moves the cursor to the upper left-hand corner of the screen. While holding down the (Ctrl) key, press the (Fn) key followed by the (↑) key.

(Pause) **function** Temporarily stops a running program. Press the (Fn) key followed by the (Q) key. Restart by pressing any symbol key.

How to Use the Quick Reference

The Quick Reference *that follows is intended to refresh your memory about the features of BASIC on the PCjr. Wherever possible, specific examples of commands and statements are shown. This will help you remember how to define parameters for each command or statement.*

You will be using different parameters in the programs you write. If you need more help, use the index to locate a fuller explanation of a given item.

QUICK REFERENCE

NOTE: For help in using this *Quick Reference*, see page 431 of this book.

COMMANDS

CONT Continue performing program in memory at the point it stopped after (Break) or error.

DELETE 150-370 Delete from memory all program lines with line numbers 150 through 370.

EDIT 520 Display program line 520 on the screen for editing.

FILES Display on the screen the names of all files on a diskette.

KILL "OLDPROG.BAS" Erase BASIC file OLDPROG from diskette.

LIST Display on the screen all lines of the program in memory.

LIST 350-565 Display program lines with line numbers 350 through 565.

LLIST Works like LIST, except that output goes to the printer.

LOAD "TOOLKIT" Move a copy of the file TOOLKIT from diskette or cassette to memory.

NEW Erase the current program and variables from memory.

RENUM 100 Make the first program line number equal to 100. Renumber all lines after that so each line number is 10 greater than the previous line number.

RENUM 1000, 100, 5 Renumber program lines, beginning at old line number 100. Change old line 100 to new line 1000. Renumber all lines after that so each line number is 5 greater than the previous line number.

RUN Perform program in memory.

SAVE "SONG" Move a copy of the program in memory to the diskette or cassette file named SONG.

SYSTEM Leave BASIC and go to the DOS or "system" level.

TRON Turn line-number tracing on. When the computer performs each line of a program, it prints the line number on the screen.

TROFF Turn line-number tracing off.

PROGRAM CONTROL STATEMENTS

END Stop performing program statements.

FOR J = 1 TO N STEP 2 Start a counting loop. Set J equal to 1. Set the exit condition so the loop will stop if J is greater than N. 2 is the amount to add to J each time around the loop. If STEP is omitted, a step size of 1 is used.

FOR C = 10 TO 5 STEP -1 Start a counting loop. Set C equal to 10. Set the exit condition so the loop will stop if C is less than 5. 1 is the amount to subtract from C each time around the loop.

GOSUB 1200 Perform the subroutine beginning at line 1200.

GOTO 1050 Move the program line pointer to line 1050.

IF N > 10 THEN 320 Move the program line pointer to line 320 if the condition is true. Otherwise, move the line pointer to the next line after IF statement. Used to exit from a loop block.

IF X < 0 THEN Perform the statement after THEN if the condition is true. Otherwise, skip the statement.

IF P = 0 THEN 20 ELSE 40 Move the program line pointer to line 20 if the condition is true. Otherwise, move the program line pointer to line 40. Used to make a branch block.

ON P GOSUB 100, 110, 120 If P is 1, perform the subroutine beginning at line 100. If P is 2, perform the subroutine beginning at line 110. And so on.

ON P GOTO 500, 650, 735 Works like ON/GOSUB, except that the program line pointer is moved to a line number in the list.

RETURN Stop performing a subroutine and return to the line after the GOSUB statement that began performing the subroutine.

STOP Stop performing statements. Print Break message on screen.

NEXT J Mark the end of a counting loop. See FOR.